# Select
## Hotels & Inns
### NORTH AMERICA

FEATURED ON FRONT COVER:
Newcastle Inn, Maine

Copyright © U.S. Welcome Limited

All rights reserved.
No part of this book may be reproduced in any manner whatsoever without the written permission of the publishers.

ISBN 0 9522508 7 X
First edition March 1998

Editor
Marilyn Messik

Editorial Team
Carole Bernholt, Andree Curtis, Estelle Hilsum, Denise Bridge, Keith Gissing

Whilst every possible care has been taken in the compilation of this guide, the publishers cannot accept responsibility for any inaccuracies or changes since going to press, or for consequential loss arising from such changes or inaccuracies, or for any other loss, direct or consequential arising in connection with information describing properties in this publication.

Published in the United Kingdom by:
U.S. Welcome Limited
33a High Street, Ruislip, Middx, England, HA4 7AU
Tel (0)1895 622233    Fax (0)1895 622244
mail@uswelcome.com    www.uswelcome.com
Freephone in the U.S. 888 INN VISIT

Printing and origination: Garden House Press, Perivale, England

*T*his book is dedicated to those hundreds of travellers who have given me invaluable feedback; to the hoteliers, innkeepers and professional associations who have shared their acquired wisdom so generously with me and to the saintly crew in my office. Grateful thanks also to my intrepid research team of inspectors who must, of necessity, remain anonymous, but who leave no stone unturned in their search for excellence.

MARILYN MESSIK

# Selected Hotels & Inns

## Entry Criteria

Hotels and inns in this guide are carefully selected and invited to join us on the basis of consumer feedback and our own inspection. Each property pays a membership fee to be a part of our group, without which we would be unable to produce a book of this quality, nor maintain the watching brief that we do.

We believe that every single choice we recommend, whether large or small, offers excellence in its own sphere. We confidently expect your stay at any of these properties to be completely enjoyable and invite you to write and tell us about your experiences. If your stay does not live up to your expectations, then we hope you would also notify us immediately.

## International Associations

U.S. Welcome is proud to be associated with those who share the same philosophy of hospitality in Great Britain, Ireland and South Africa

# Meeting your expectations

*We* believe that the definition of a good holiday or business trip is one where expectations are met (and hopefully exceeded!). When making your plans, it is important to consider the differences between full-service hotels or resorts, country inns and small bed & breakfasts. How you make your choices will depend entirely on your own personal preferences.

*Whilst* the charm of smaller establishments is their size and informality, bear in mind that some services and facilities are not automatically available. There may be no-one to help with luggage at check-in, rooms do not always have tv and phone and there isn't usually 24-hour room service. If you have a heavy case and a bad back, need to be in constant touch with the outside world and are subject to food cravings in the middle of the night, this will not be the right place for you! On the other hand, if you travel light, loathe tv, never want to hear from the office again, and can struggle through from a cordon bleu five-course candlelit dinner to a gourmet breakfast, without a midnight snack – you'll be in heaven!

*Small* inns often offer wonderful opportunities for guests to socialise; over breakfast or pre-dinner drinks, or perhaps dining family-style with everyone seated around one table. This can be a highlight of the holiday, a chance to meet and mix with interesting folk you might never normally come across and to forge friendships that may last long beyond the holiday. If, however, you are going away for peace and solitude and want to commune with nothing more than nature, each other and some excellent food, then you might prefer a slightly larger inn.

continued...

## *Meeting your expectations*

*If* you have special dietary requirements, do mention this when making a reservation so that you can be reassured you will have no problems when you arrive. The same applies to any pet hates or phobias - too late, when greeted enthusiastically by an inn's Great Dane, to point out that you can't stand dogs.

*Some* inns and resorts cater for children, some don't; do take note and not offence at this; telling you in advance is just as much for your benefit as the innkeeper's. Few parents amongst us can relax while a boisterous toddler wreaks havoc with the antiques and throws-up the gourmet cuisine!

*We* do strongly suggest that you book ahead at peak times such as foliage season in New England. Nothing spoils a holiday more than arriving at an inn or hotel after a long drive, only to be told that they are full. Even the most even-tempered of couples can be reduced to exchanging recriminations at this point!

*Although* we shouldn't generalise, hoteliers and innkeepers are a warm, professional, friendly and helpful bunch of people - if they weren't they wouldn't still be in business! They want you to enjoy your trip as much as you do. So, before booking, take the time to ask as many questions as you need - the sign of a good hotel or inn is their willingness to give you all the answers and information you require. Alternatively you can call our FREE Booking Service on 01895 622233 in the U.K. or 1-888-INN-VISIT in the U.S. we are always happy to offer you as much help as we can.

## Terms used in the Directory

We're not great believers in using symbols - in our experience they can lead to confusion and a migraine! You will find information about each property set out as follows:

✻ **ROOM RATES** are quoted per room, per night, for two people, unless stated otherwise.
Children are often welcome to stay free in a room with their parents, but there is usually an additional charge made for teenagers or another adult.

✻ **EUROPEAN PLAN (EP)** indicates that no meals are included in the rate.

✻ **BED & BREAKFAST (B&B)** can range from a simple coffee and Danish, to a cooked country breakfast that will set you up for the day and beyond!

✻ **MODIFIED AMERICAN PLAN (MAP)** means that breakfast and dinner are both included in the quoted rate.

✻ **AMERICAN PLAN (AP)** is still offered by a few of the traditional family resorts and this covers three meals a day.

✻ **PRICE RANGES** reflect the size, views or facilities of the room. At off-season periods, prices may be lower and it is always worth asking if there are any Special Rates available. For example, city hotels may offer a reduction on some week-ends, while resort hotels often have a special rate for longer stays, or to include sports facilities and tuition. Rates are quoted, in most cases, exclusive of tax, which varies from state to state.

✻ **SUITES, APARTMENTS, COTTAGES OR CONDOMINIUMS.** As a general rule anything that is defined as self-contained has its own entrance. A condominium is a property that is privately owned but rented out and managed by a hotel, inn or resort complex.
Cottages, apartments or houses usually have fully equipped kitchens, whereas this is not always the case with suites. If you are unsure, always check with US Welcome's Booking Service or with individual establishment.

✻ **SERVICE CHARGE.** Some properties include a service charge in their rate, others leave gratuities to the discretion of guests. N.B. tipping is more formalised in America and ranges between 15-20%.

DO MENTION **U.S. Welcome** when you make a booking directly with a hotel or inn - it often gets you a better deal!

# Contents

## EASTERN CANADA
Eastern Canada Map 10

### ONTARIO
| | |
|---|---|
| Briars | 12 |
| Little Inn of Bayfield | 13 |
| Millcroft Inn | 14 |

### QUEBEC
| | |
|---|---|
| Auberge des Sablons | 15 |
| Auberge Handfield | 16 |
| Auberge Saint-Antoine | 17 |
| Ripplecove Inn | 18 |
| Auberge des Gallant | 19 |

## MID ATLANTIC STATES
Mid Atlantic Map 20

### DELAWARE
Inn at Montchanin Village 22

### MARYLAND
| | |
|---|---|
| Antrim 1844 | 23 |
| Harbor Court Hotel | 24 |
| Inn at Perry Cabin | 25 |
| Historic Inns of Annapolis | 26 |
| Kent Manor Inn | 26 |
| Mr. Mole | 27 |
| Private Pleasure | 27 |
| Wades Point Inn on the Bay | 28 |

### NEW JERSEY
| | |
|---|---|
| Bernards Inn | 29 |
| Chimney Hill Farm | 30 |
| Inn at Millrace Pond | 30 |

### NEW YORK
| | |
|---|---|
| Copperfield Inn | 31 |
| Craftsman Inn | 32 |
| Geneva-on-the-Lake | 33 |
| Manhattan East Suites Hotels | 34 |
| Roycroft Inn | 35 |
| Sagamore on Lake George | 36 |
| Bird & Bottle | 37 |
| Chestnut Inn on Oquaga Lake | 37 |
| Halsey House | 38 |
| Rose Inn | 38 |
| Sedgwick Inn | 39 |

### PENNSYLVANIA
| | |
|---|---|
| Baladerry Inn | 40 |
| Barley Sheaf Farm | 40 |
| Boxwood Inn | 41 |
| Carnegie House | 41 |
| Evermay on the Delaware | 42 |
| French Manor | 42 |
| Historic Smithton Inn | 43 |
| Inns at Doneckers | 43 |
| King's Cottage | 44 |
| Mansion Inn | 44 |
| Pineapple Hill | 45 |
| Settlers Inn | 45 |
| Sterling Inn | 46 |
| Wedgwood Inn of New Hope | 46 |

### VIRGINIA
| | |
|---|---|
| Bailiwick Inn | 47 |
| Berkeley Hotel | 48 |
| Boar's Head Inn | 49 |
| High Meadows | 50 |
| Keswick Hall | 51 |
| L'Auberge Provencale | 52 |
| Morrison House | 53 |
| Staunton Hill Country Inn | 54 |
| Tides Inn | 55 |
| Chester House | 56 |
| Clifton - The Country Inn | 56 |
| Colonial Capital | 57 |
| Frederick House | 57 |
| Henry Clay Inn | 58 |
| Homestay | 58 |
| Hummingbird Inn | 59 |
| Inn at Gristmill Square | 59 |
| Inn at Narrow Passage | 60 |
| Llewellyn Lodge | 60 |
| The Oaks | 61 |
| Seven Hills Inn | 61 |
| Steeles Tavern Manor | 62 |
| Trillium House | 62 |

### WASHINGTON DC
| | |
|---|---|
| George Washington University Inn | 63 |
| Embassy Inn | 64 |
| Normandy Inn | 64 |
| Windsor Inn | 65 |

### WEST VIRGINIA
| | |
|---|---|
| Country Inn | 66 |
| Hillbrook Inn | 67 |

# Contents

## NEW ENGLAND
### CONNECTICUT

| | |
|---|---|
| Connecticut Map | 68 |
| Bee & Thistle Inn | 69 |
| Boulders | 70 |
| Homestead Inn (Greenwich) | 71 |
| Inn at National Hall | 72 |
| Norwich Inn & Spa | 73 |
| Brigadoon | 74 |
| Griswold Inn | 74 |
| Homestead Inn (New Milford) | 75 |
| Manor House | 75 |
| Old Mystic Inn | 76 |
| Riverwind Inn | 76 |
| White Hart Inn | 77 |

### MAINE

| | |
|---|---|
| Maine Map | 78 |
| Bar Harbor Hotel-Bluenose Inn | 79 |
| Bayview Hotel | 80 |
| Black Point Inn | 81 |
| Captain Daniel Stone Inn | 82 |
| Captain Lord Mansion | 83 |
| Gorges Grant Hotel | 84 |
| Harraseeket Inn | 85 |
| Inn By The Sea | 86 |
| Spruce Point Inn | 87 |
| Stage Neck Inn | 88 |
| Sugarloaf | 89 |
| Andrews Lodging | 90 |
| Bagley House | 90 |
| Blue Harbor House | 91 |
| Blue Hill Inn | 91 |
| Captain Lindsay House Inn | 92 |
| Dockside Guest Quarters | 92 |
| Greenville Inn | 93 |
| Kennebunkport Inn | 93 |
| Lawnmeer Inn | 94 |
| Lodge at Moosehead Lake | 94 |
| Maine Stay Inn | 95 |
| Maine Stay Inn & Cottages | 95 |
| Mira Monte Inn | 96 |
| Newcastle Inn | 96 |
| Ocean Gate | 97 |
| Ocean Point Inn | 97 |
| York Harbor Inn | 98 |

### MASSACHUSETTS

| | |
|---|---|
| Massachusetts Map | 100 |
| Blantyre | 102 |
| Boston Harbor Hotel | 103 |
| Captain's House Inn of Chatham | 104 |
| Charles Hotel | 105 |
| Chatham Bars Inn | 106 |
| Colonnade Hotel | 107 |
| Dan'l Webster Inn | 108 |
| Deerfield Inn | 109 |
| Harbor Light Inn | 110 |
| Jared Coffin House | 111 |
| Lenox Hotel | 112 |
| Ocean Edge Resort & Golf Club | 113 |
| Publick House Historic Inn | 114 |
| Red Lion Inn | 116 |
| Salem Inn | 117 |
| Thorncroft Inn | 118 |
| Whalewalk Inn | 119 |
| Yankee Clipper Inn | 120 |
| Addison Choate Inn | 122 |
| Bradford Inn | 122 |
| Cambridge House | 123 |
| Corner House Inn | 123 |
| Captain Nickerson Inn | 124 |
| Grafton Inn | 124 |
| Hawthorne Inn | 125 |
| Inn at Stockbridge | 125 |
| Isaiah Hall | 126 |
| Isaiah Jones Homestead | 126 |
| John Carver Inn | 127 |
| Liberty Hill Inn | 127 |
| Lighthouse Inn | 128 |
| Longfellow's Wayside Inn | 128 |
| Marlborough | 129 |
| Mary Prentiss | 129 |
| Mostly Hall | 130 |
| Onset Pointe Inn | 130 |
| Pheasant Hill | 131 |
| Pleasant Bay Village Resort | 131 |
| Queen Anne Inn | 132 |
| Rocky Shores Inn & Cottages | 132 |
| Sharon Inn | 133 |
| Village Green Inn | 133 |
| Weathervane Inn | 134 |
| Wedgewood Inn | 134 |
| Wildflower Inn | 135 |

### NEWHAMPHIRE

| | |
|---|---|
| New Hampshire Map | 136 |
| Chesterfield Inn | 137 |
| Inns at Mill Falls & Bay Point | 138 |
| Inn at Thorn Hill | 139 |
| Inn of Exeter | 140 |
| Manor on Golden Pond | 141 |

# Contents

| | |
|---|---|
| Sise Inn | 142 |
| Snowvillage Inn | 143 |
| Waterville Estates Resort | 144 |
| Adair | 145 |
| The Balsams | 145 |
| Buttonwood Inn | 146 |
| Colby Hill Inn | 146 |
| Dexter's Inn & Tennis Club | 147 |
| Ellis River House | 147 |
| Forest, A Country Inn | 148 |
| Foxglove | 148 |
| Franconia Inn | 149 |
| Hancock Inn | 149 |
| New London Inn | 150 |
| Notchland Inn | 150 |
| Olde Orchard Inn | 151 |
| Sugar Hill Inn | 151 |
| Village House | 152 |

## RHODE ISLAND

| | |
|---|---|
| Rhode Island Map | 154 |
| Block Island Resorts | 155 |
| Cliffside Inn | 156 |
| Vanderbilt Hall | 157 |
| Bed & Breakfast on the Point | 158 |
| Grandview Bed & Breakfast | 158 |
| Larchwood Inn | 159 |
| The Villa | 159 |

## VERMONT

| | |
|---|---|
| Vermont Map | 162 |
| Basin Harbor Club | 165 |
| Cornucopia of Dorset | 166 |
| Cortina Inn | 167 |
| Equinox | 168 |
| Four Columns Inn | 169 |
| Golden Eagle Resort | 170 |
| Hawk Inn & Mountain Resort | 171 |
| Inn at Essex | 172 |
| Inn at Ormsby Hill | 173 |
| Inn on the Common | 174 |
| Mountain Road Resort | 175 |
| Old Tavern at Grafton | 176 |
| Pitcher Inn | 177 |
| Rabbit Hill Inn | 178 |
| Red Clover Inn | 179 |
| Sugarbush Inn & Resort | 180 |
| Windham Hill Inn | 181 |
| Woodstock Inn & Resort | 182 |
| Ardmore Inn | 184 |

| | |
|---|---|
| Barrows House | 184 |
| Blueberry Hill Inn | 185 |
| Brandon Inn | 185 |
| The Castle | 186 |
| Chipman Inn | 186 |
| Churchill House Inn | 187 |
| Deerhill Inn | 187 |
| Gables Inn | 188 |
| Green Mountain Inn | 188 |
| Hamilton House | 189 |
| Inn at the Brass Lantern | 189 |
| Inn at the Round Barn Farm | 190 |
| Inn at West View Farm | 190 |
| Jackson House Inn | 191 |
| Landgrove Inn | 191 |
| Lareau Farm Country Inn | 192 |
| Maple Leaf Inn | 192 |
| Middlebury Inn | 193 |
| October Country Inn | 193 |
| Quechee Bed & Breakfast | 194 |
| Shield Inn | 194 |
| Shire Inn | 195 |
| The Siebeness | 195 |
| Smugglers' Notch Inn | 196 |
| Sugar Lodge at Sugarbush | 196 |
| Sugartree | 197 |
| Tucker Hill Lodge | 197 |
| Vermont Inn | 198 |
| Village Country Inn | 198 |
| West Hill House | 199 |
| West Mountain Inn | 199 |
| Whitford House Inn | 200 |
| Wiley Inn | 200 |
| Willoughvale Inn | 201 |
| The Woods | 201 |

## SOUTHEASTERN STATES

| | |
|---|---|
| Southeastern States Map | 202 |

## FLORIDA

| | |
|---|---|
| Amelia Island Plantation | 203 |
| Elizabeth Pointe Lodge | 204 |
| Heron House | 205 |
| Lakeside Inn | 206 |
| Blue Moon Hotel | 207 |
| Chalet Suzanne | 207 |
| Darst Victorian Manor | 208 |
| Hibiscus House | 208 |
| Verona House | 209 |

# Contents

## GEORGIA

| | |
|---|---|
| Little St. Simons Island | 210 |
| 1842 Inn | 211 |
| Glen-Ella Springs | 211 |

## NORTH CAROLINA

| | |
|---|---|
| First Colony Inn | 212 |
| Swag Country Inn | 213 |
| Lords Proprietors' Inn | 214 |

## SOUTH CAROLINA

| | |
|---|---|
| Fulton Lane Inn | 215 |
| Planters Inn | 216 |
| Ashley Inn | 217 |
| Cannonboro Inn | 217 |
| Red Horse Inn | 218 |

## SOUTHWESTERN STATES

| | |
|---|---|
| Southwestern Map | 220 |

## ARIZONA

| | |
|---|---|
| Casa Sedona | 221 |
| Merv Griffin's Wickenburg Inn | 221 |

## COLORADO

| | |
|---|---|
| Hearthstone Inn | 222 |
| Hotel Jerome | 222 |
| Queen Anne Bed & Breakfast | 223 |

## WEST COAST

| | |
|---|---|
| West Coast Map | 224 |

## CALIFORNIA

| | |
|---|---|
| Beazley House | 225 |
| La Playa Hotel | 226 |
| Martine Inn | 227 |
| Seal Beach Garden Inn | 228 |
| Blackthorne Inn | 229 |
| Carter House Victorians | 229 |
| Casa Cody | 230 |
| Goose & Turrets | 230 |
| Joshua Grindle Inn | 231 |
| Ollalieberry Inn | 231 |
| Willows Historic Inn | 232 |

## OREGON

| | |
|---|---|
| Campbell House, A City Inn | 233 |
| Hood River Hotel | 233 |

## WASHINGTON

| | |
|---|---|
| Haus Rohrbach Pension | 234 |
| Sun Mountain Lodge | 234 |
| Turtleback Farm | 235 |
| Willcox House Country Inn | 235 |

## HISTORIC HOTELS

| | |
|---|---|
| Hotel La Rose | 237 |
| Jekyll Island Club | 237 |
| Hotel St. Francis | 237 |
| John Rutledge House | 237 |

## TASTERS

| | |
|---|---|
| Tasters Map | 238 |
| Empress of Little Rock | 239 |
| Southwest Inn at Sedona | 239 |
| Laburnum Cottage | 239 |
| Camellia Inn | 239 |
| Campbell Ranch Inn | 239 |
| Cheshire Cat Inn | 239 |
| Inn at Union Square | 240 |
| Two Angels Inn | 240 |
| Abriendo Inn | 240 |
| Alpine Inn | 240 |
| Castle Marne | 240 |
| Woodland Inn | 240 |
| Chalet Kilauea | 241 |
| Shipman House | 241 |
| Bear Creek Lodge | 241 |
| Channel House | 241 |
| Columbia Gorge Hotel | 241 |
| Peacock Hill | 241 |
| Brown Pelican | 242 |
| Mariposa Ranch | 242 |
| Rosevine Inn | 242 |
| Shelburne Inn | 242 |
| Mansion Hill Inn | 242 |

# Eastern Canada

## ONTARIO
1. The Briars — 12
2. Little Inn of Bayfield — 13
3. Millcroft Inn — 14

## QUEBEC
4. Auberge des Gallant — 19
5. Auberge des Sablons — 15
6. Auberge Handfield — 16
7. Auberge Saint-Antoine — 17
8. Ripplecove Inn — 18

# DISCOVER

## ...some of the finest scenery in the world.

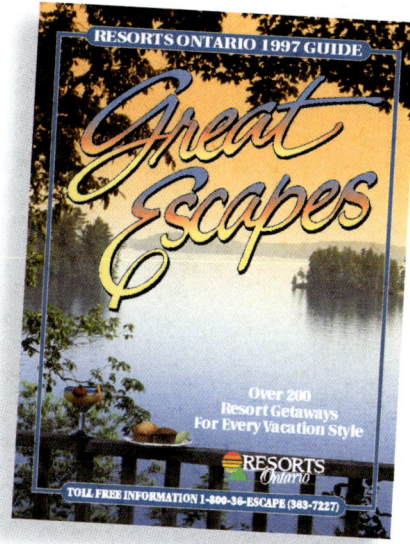

Unspoiled forests, lakes, rivers and sandy beaches are the backdrop for a wonderful resort escape to beautiful Ontario, Canada. Whether you're looking for your own rustic cabin and fireplace or the ultimate in luxury and amenities, you'll find the experience you were searching for.

The Great Escapes Guide is a colourful catalogue of over 220 Ontario resorts with photos, descriptions and pertinent contact information.

Just telephone, fax, write or e-mail and ask for your free copy.

Tel: 705-325-9115    Fax: 705-325-7999
E-mail: escapes@resorts-ontario.com
Internet: http://www.resorts-ontario.com
P.O. Box 2148, Orillia, Ontario, Canada L3V 6S1

# ONTARIO

## THE BRIARS
### JACKSON'S POINT

This magnificent 200-acre Lake Simcoe estate is less than an hour from Toronto and its many attractions, theatres and shopping, but provides so many recreation, sporting and entertainment diversions that guests simply don't want to leave. Here, guests return year after year to fifth generation Sibbald family hospitality.

This idyllic setting inspires romantic strolls among expansive gardens and towering trees, along sweeping shoreline reflecting fluffy clouds, or amid marked nature trails that provide sanctuary to you and over 140 species of birds.

Of course, The Briars experience also includes attentive service, fine country dining and charming accommodations in the Manor House, adjoining wings, lakeside and woodland cottages.

It's another world. You'll be glad you came.

55 Hedge Road, RR1
Jackson's Point,
Ontario L0E 1L0

•

Tel 905 722 3271
Fax 905 722 9698
Freephone in US & Canada
800 465 2376

•

Owner & Manager:
John D. Sibbald

•

80 rooms plus 12 one and
two bedroom cottages and
suites

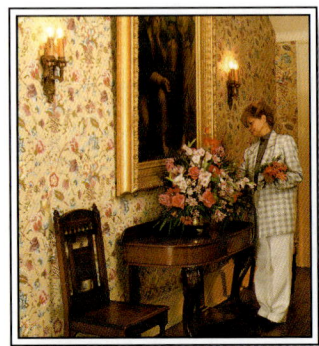

Doubles, suites and cottages
$290 - $390 (Can.$)  AP
Tax 12%  s.c. 15%

•

Indoor and outdoor pools,
whirlpool, sauna, tennis,
golf, sailing, cruises,
cycling, summer theatre,
fitness centre, childrens'
programmes, skiing,
skating, conference facilities

•

Children welcome

•

VS • MC • Amex

## ONTARIO

# LITTLE INN OF BAYFIELD
## BAYFIELD

This AAA Four Diamond Award winner has been welcoming guests to its two-storey gingerbread embellished porch, comfortably shaded by an old willow tree, since the 1830s. With the beaches of beautiful Lake Huron for boating and water sports nearby, the picturesque village of Bayfield is ideally located for Ontario explorations whilst in Fall and Winter the Little Inn is a popular destination for hikers, cross-country skiers and snowshoers.

Guest rooms are individually and thoughtfully decorated, many with double whirlpools and a few with fireplaces. Dining at the Little Inn, which has just achieved the accolade of the Wine Spectator Award of Excellence, is an experience not to be missed - an imaginative menu full of fresh local produce, beautifully presented and topped by one of the Inn's superb desserts for which they are justifiably famed.

Within comfortable driving distances are three theatre festivals, or drive a little further to the Mennonite communities around Elmira and hike through dramatic Elora Gorge.

Main Street,
P.O. Box 100,
Bayfield,
Ontario N0M 1G0
•
Tel 519 565 2611
Fax 519 565 5474
Freephone in US
800 565 1832
•
General Manager:
Richard Fitoussi
•
30 rooms & suites
•
Doubles $99 - $215
(Can $.)B&B

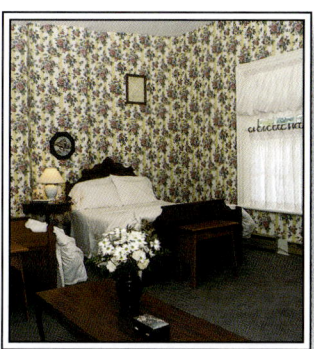

Tax 12%
•
Conference facilities, beach.
•
Nearby: Outdoor pool,
tennis, golf, riding,
cycling, sailing, water
skiing, cross-country
skiing, snowshoeing
•
Children welcome.
•
Non-smoking
•
VS • MC • Amex
Diners • En Route

## ONTARIO

# MILLCROFT INN
### ALTON

Nestled in the rolling Caledon Hills, only 40 minutes from Toronto, the Millcroft Inn's understated elegance and charm is a balm for the soul.

The award-winning, Four Diamond Millcroft Inn is a beautifully restored 19th century knitting mill, set serenely on the Credit River. Warm hospitality, luxurious accommodations decorated in period antiques and four diamond cuisine are just a few of the reasons for you to pay a visit. Savour delicious meals in the historic dining room, on the outdoor patio overlooking the peaceful millpond or in the glass dining area spectacularly suspended over the falls. For extra privacy you may choose to stay in one of the Crofts, two storey chalet type accommodations with outdoor hot tub.

The 100 acre woodland property offers wonderful hiking and cycling or simply drift over the countryside in a hot air balloon.

55 John Street, Alton,
Ontario LON 1AO
•
Tel 519 941 8111
Fax 519 941 9192
Freephone in Ontario
800 383 3976
•
Innkeeper
Wolfgang Stichnothe
•
52 rooms
•
Doubles $175 - $250
(Can.$) B&B

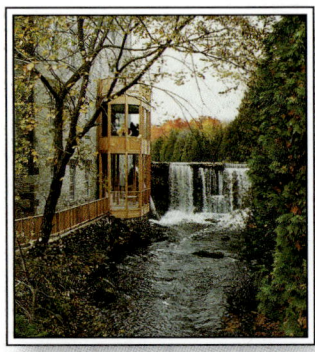

Tax 15%
•
Outdoor pool, sauna, tennis, hiking, biking, cross-country skiing, fly fishing.
•
Nearby downhill skiing, golf, horseriding, hot air ballooning
•
Children welcome
•
VS • MC
Amex • Diners

## QUEBEC

# AUBERGE DES SABLONS
## ST-IRÉNÉE

"Villa des Sablons" was built in 1902 by Joseph Lavergne, an Ottawa District Superior Court judge. As a lawyer, he was an associate and close friend of Sir Wilfrid Laurier, the first French Canadian to be elected Prime Minister.

In 1983, the house was renovated and became l'Auberge des Sablons. Each of its rooms is decorated artfully, inspired by the countryside, some rooms have fireplaces, others have a balcony from which guests can experience the unparalleled scenery of this breathtaking area. Your hosts and innkeepers, Marielle and Jean-Guy Alain, are known for their special way of welcoming guests as friends. Enjoy a peaceful retreat in an intimate setting, and a traditional fine cuisine considered to be among the best in the area.

Located in the magnificent Charlevoix region of Quebec, Auberge des Sablons is just 1½ hours of beautiful scenery Northeast of Quebec City.

223 Chemin les Bains,
St-Irénée,
Quebec, G0T 1V0
•
Tel 418 452 3594
Fax 418 452 3240
Freephone in US & Canada
800 267 3594
•
Owner/Innkeeper:
Jean-Guy Alain
•
15 rooms, 13 of which
have private baths.
1 one bedroom suite
4 apartments with fireplaces

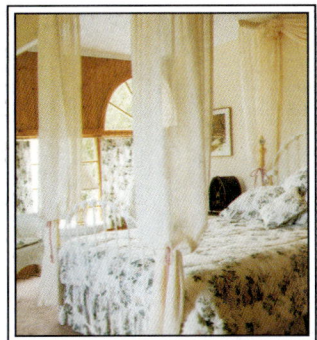

Doubles $158 - $268
(Can $) MAP
Suites and apartments
$198 - $248 EP
•
Tax 13.5%
•
Conference facilities.
Nearby: golf courses, riding,
sailing, water skiing, down-
hill & cross-country skiing
Children over 12 welcome.
•
Non-smoking
•
VS • MC
Amex • Diners

### QUEBEC

# AUBERGE HANDFIELD
## ST-MARC-SUR-RICHELIEU

In an historic French-Canadian village on the Richelieu River, 30 minutes north of Montreal, enjoy the atmosphere, rustic decor and country crafted furnishings of a venerable, 160 year old mansion.

The warm and cosy log cabin style dining room serves outstanding cuisine and opens to a sunny converted glassed-in porch. All rooms have colour cable tv, phones and private baths with the deluxe Laflamme Pavillon located right by the river and offering extra facilities such as balcony, fireplace and whirlpool bath.

A marina, and resort facilities including an extremely well equipped health club and spa and the attentions of professional staff to administer luxurious treatments, complete the pleasure of your stay at the Auberge Handfield.

555 Chemin du Prince,
St-Marc-Sur-Richelieu,
Quebec JOL 2EO

•

Tel 514 584 2226
Fax 514 584 3650
Freephone in US & Canada
800 667 1087

•

General Manager:
Pierre Handfield

•

Owner: Conrad Handfield

•

53 rooms

3 one-bedroom suites
1 two-bedroom suite

•

Doubles $65 - $110
(Can $) EP
Suites $145 - $160

•

Tax 13.96%

•

Outdoor pool,
fitness center, spa,
conference facilities

•

VS • MC

**QUEBEC**

# AUBERGE SAINT-ANTOINE
## QUEBEC

Auberge Saint-Antoine is unquestionably one of the most captivating inns within Quebec City. Every thought has been given to making our guests feel at home. The living room, has a quiet relaxing atmosphere with its stone walls, wooden beams, subdued lighting and furniture upholstered with warmly coloured fabrics. In the winter, sit by the windows and daydream while watching the drifting ice on the St. Lawrence River, in summer watch the cruising and sailing boats.

Guest rooms are unique and beautifully appointed, offering amenities usually reserved for the most luxurious hotels. For social and business functions, the personnel of the Auberge Saint-Antoine guarantees the success of each of your initiatives. In short, many say that the Auberge Saint-Antoine is a small paradise nestled in a heavenly city!

Museums, antiques, art galleries and boutiques are minutes away, and the area is rich with restaurants and cafes, from the charming to the very sophisticated.

10 rue Saint-Antoine,
Quebec City,
Quebec G1K 4C9
•
Tel 418 692 2211
Fax 418 692 1177
Freephone in US
888 692 2211
•
General Manager:
Julie Leclerc
•
31 rooms
including 5 one bedroom suites, 2 two bedroom suites

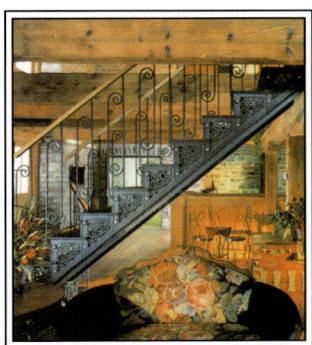

Doubles $169 - $439
(Can $) B&B
Suites $199 - $439
•
Tax 13.5%
•
Conference facilities
Nearby: swimming, tennis, golf, riding, sailing, skiing
•
Free parking available
•
Children welcome.
•
Non-smoking
•
VS • MC • Amex • Diners

## QUEBEC

# RIPPLECOVE INN
## AYER'S CLIFF

On a beautifully landscaped, 12 acre lakeside estate, 75 minutes east of Montreal and just three hours north of Boston, stands the Ripplecove Inn. Recipient of the coveted Four Diamond Award every year since 1987, this establishment has grown to be one of Canada's most prestigious and luxurious Country Inns.

In Winter enjoy 35 km of groomed and tracked ski trails, ice fishing and skating, or excellent downhill skiing at five nearby mountains. In Summer we offer a fully equipped waterfront facility, with private beaches, heated pool, lake cruises, sailing and waterskiing.

Rooms and suites are beautifully decorated, many with whirlpool baths, balconies and fireplaces to add to your comfort and enjoyment. Award-winning French cuisine is served in the Victorian style dining room and lakeside terrace and Pub. Our pristine rural setting, together with luxurious accommodations and friendly bilingual service, makes Ripplecove Inn a must when visiting the beautiful province of Quebec.

700 Ripplecove Road,
Ayer's Cliff, Quebec,
J0B 1C0
•
Tel 819 838 4296
Fax 819 838 5541
•
Innkeeper/Owners:
Jeff & Debra Stafford
•
25 rooms
5 one bedroom suites
3-bedroom log cabin
with private beach,
porch, fireplace

Doubles $184 - $350
(Can $) MAP
Suites/cottage $310 - $420
•
Tax 14%
•
Outdoor pool, sailing,
waterskiing, canoeing,
windsurfing, conference
facilities. Nearby: golf,
horseriding, spa
•
Best meets the needs of
children over age 4
•
VS • MC • Amex

## QUEBEC

# AUBERGE DES GALLANT
### RIGAUD

Situated on the southern side of Rigaud Mountain in the centre of a deer and bird sanctuary, surrounded by cedars and maples and just forty five minutes from Montreal, is the delightful cedar frame inn- Auberge des Gallant.

Linda and Gerry Gallant recently celebrated twenty-five years of making people feel special at this family run, twenty-five room inn where welcoming touches such as terry cloth bathrobes, fruit baskets and fireplaces in each room add to the warmth of your welcome from the members of the family and the friendly staff.

Memorable meals and excellent wines can be relished in the light airy dining room with forest and lake views and, if you're lucky, you may catch sight of the deer that visit daily. Additionally there are over two hundred and fifty different species of birds to be spotted.

| | | | | | | |
|---|---|---|---|---|---|---|
| 1171 St. Henri Road, Ste-Marthe, Rigaud, JOP IWO | Tel 514 459 4241 Fax 514 459 4667 Freephone in US & Canada 1-800 641 4241 | Owners: Linda & Gerry Gallant 25 rooms Doubles $199 - $250 | (Canadian) MAP Suites $250 - $290 Tax 15% s.c. 15% Outdoor pool, cross-country skiing | Nearby: horse riding, golf, down-hill skiing Children over 6 welcome | Smoking in designated areas VS•MC•Amex•Diners |

## COMPLIMENTARY BOOKING SERVICE

Don't forget we offer an advisory and booking service and you can make all your reservations with just one phone call to us. The service is completely free and prices are not loaded in any way.

Call for a chat on
# 01895 622233

# Mid-Atlantic

# Mid-Atlantic States

**DELAWARE**
1. Inn at Montachanin Village — 22
**MARYLAND**
2. Antrim 1844 — 23
3. Harbor Court Hotel — 24
4. Historic Inns of Annapolis — 26
5. Inn at Perry Cabin — 25
6. Kent Manor Inn — 26
7. Mr. Mole — 27
8. Private Pleasure — 27
9. Wades Point Inn on the Bay — 28
**NEW JERSEY**
10. Bernards Inn — 29
11. Chimney Hill Farm — 30
12. Inn at Millrace Pond — 30
**NEW YORK**
13. Bird & Bottle Inn — 37
14. Chestnut Inn on Oquaga Lake — 37
15. Copperfield Inn — 31
16. Craftsman Inn — 32
17. Geneva on the Lake — 33
18. Halsey House — 38
19. Manhattan East Suites — 34
20. Rose Inn — 38
21. Roycroft Inn — 35
22. Sagamore on Lake George — 36
23. Sedgwick Inn — 39
**PENNSYLVANIA**
24. Baladerry Inn — 40
25. Barleysheaf Farm — 40
26. Boxwood Inn — 41
27. Carnegie House — 41
28. Inns at Doneckers — 43
29. Evermay on the Delaware — 42
30. French Manor — 42
31. Historic Smithton Inn — 43
32. King's Cottage — 44
33. Mansion Inn — 44
34. Pineapple Hill — 45
35. Settlers Inn — 45
36. Sterling Inn — 46
37. Wedgwood Inn of New Hope — 46
**VIRGINIA**
38. Bailiwick Inn — 47
39. Berkeley Hotel — 48
40. Boar's Head Inn — 49
41. Chester House — 56
42. Clifton-The Country Inn — 56
43. Colonial Capital — 57
44. Frederick House — 57
45. Henry Clay Inn — 58
46. High Meadows — 50
47. Homestay — 58
48. Hummingbird Inn — 59
49. Inn at Gristmill Square — 59
50. Inn at Narrow Passage — 60
51. Keswick Hall — 51
52. L'Auberge Provencale — 52
53. Llewellyn Lodge — 60
54. Morrison House — 53
55. The Oaks — 61
56. Seven Hills Inn — 61
57. Staunton Hill Country Inn — 54
58. Steeles Tavern Manor — 62
59. Tides Inn — 55
60. Trillium House — 62
**WASHINGTON DC**
61. Embassy Inn — 64
62. George Washington Inn — 63
63. Normandy Inn — 64
64. Windsor Inn — 65
**WEST VIRGINIA**
65. Country Inn — 66
66. Hillbrook Inn — 67

# DELAWARE

## INN AT MONTCHANIN VILLAGE
### MONTCHANIN

In the heart of the beautiful Brandywine Valley and extremely conveniently located for the area's abundant attractions, the Inn at Montchanin Village exists in a world in which time has seemingly stood still. Eleven buildings comprise this historic village built in the late 1800's just miles outside of Wilmington.

Today, having been carefully restored, the village contains thirty-three guest units of various size, with no two alike. Perched on a gently sloping hillside, the accommodations are furnished with selected period and reproduction furniture. Outside, guests can delight in the stone walkways, terraces and garden enclaves which wreathe through the property.

Each luxurious room contains a spacious private bath, cable television, dual line telephones, refrigerator, ice maker, microwave and in-room gourmet coffee maker as well as imported Frette towels and linens and Anichini bedspreads. A full breakfast at the award-winning restaurant, Krazy Kat's, is included in your nightly rate.

Route 100 & Kirk Road,
Montchanin,
DE 19710
•
Tel 302 888 2133
Fax 302 888 0389
Freephone in US
800/COWBIRD
•
Owners:
Mr & Mrs Dan Lickle.
Innkeeper: Brooke J. White
•
33 rooms, including 11
one bedroom suites

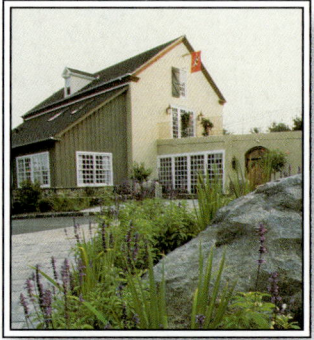

7 two bedroom suites
•
Doubles $150 - $180 B&B
Suites $190 - $325
•
Tax 8%
•
Nearby: tennis, horse
riding, golf, canoeing
•
Children over 12 welcome
•
Non-smoking
•
VS•MC•Amex•Diners

# MARYLAND

## ANTRIM 1844
### TANEYTOWN

Forty miles west of Baltimore, sixty miles north of Washington DC, on twenty three acres of gardens and orchards nestled in the rolling Catoctin Mountains, experience the grace, elegance and hospitality of 19th century America that is Antrim 1844.

Guest rooms at this beautifully restored country inn resort feature antiques, fireplaces, canopy feather beds and marble baths, or for a truly romantic stay choose one of the secluded suites. Located beside the formal gardens the "Ice House" has the atmosphere of a country cottage. "The Barn" has two rooms, each with its own private deck overlooking woods and a brook.

The Condé Nast Flagship Inn for Maryland, Antrim 1844 is acclaimed for superb cuisine and during the warmer months guests will find dinner served on the veranda overlooking the gardens. With the arrival of chillier weather, dinner is served in the "Smokehouse" with brick floor and walk-in fireplaces. The inn has proved to be an ideal environment for small business meetings and magnificent wedding receptions held in the Pavillion.

30 Trevanion Road,
Taneytown, MD 21787
•
Tel 410 756 6812
Fax 410 756 2744
Freephone in US
800 858 1844
•
Owners/Innkeepers:
Dorothy & Richard Mollett
General Manager:
Stewart Dearie
•
14 rooms including
5 one-bedroom suites

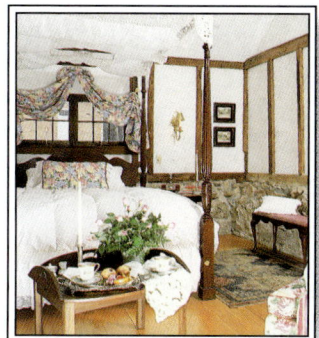

Doubles $150 - $175 B&B
Suites $200 - $300
5-course set-price dinner $50
•
Tax 5%
•
Outdoor pool, tennis, croquet, putting, conference facilities. Nearby: Indoor pool, golf, horseriding.
•
Children over 12 welcome
•
Restricted smoking
•
VS • MC • Amex

## MARYLAND

# HARBOR COURT HOTEL
### BALTIMORE

Located on Baltimore's revitalised Inner Harbor the Four Diamond, Four Star Harbor Court Hotel offers an elegant retreat with a sweeping view of the heart of the city.

Relax in the sumptuous library containing volumes from all over the world, or enjoy the Explorers Lounge with handpainted African scenes and exotic objets d'art. Savour a delicious dinner in Hamptons with its acclaimed American Cuisine and unique view of the harbour, or enjoy a more informal meal in Brightons. All of the Harbor Court's guest rooms, staterooms and suites offer elegant furnishings and decor designed for maximum comfort.

One of the special pleasures awaiting guests is the Fitness Center located on the beautifully landscaped rooftop complete with a croquet court. Just steps away from the hotel visit attractions such as the National Aquarium, The Maryland Science Center or simply enjoy the numerous shops and vital nightlife.

550 Light Street
Baltimore, MD 21202
•
Tel 410 234 0550
Fax 410 659 5925
Freephone in US
800 824 0076
•
Managing Director:
Werner Kunz
•
203 rooms including
10 one bedroom,
10 two bedroom suites
•
Doubles from $175 EP

Tax 12%
•
Parking available
at $15 per day
•
Indoor pool, tennis courts,
conference facilities,
full service fitness center.
•
Nearby: Outdoor pool,
golf, horseriding
•
Children welcome
•
VS • MC • Amex

**MARYLAND**

# INN AT PERRY CABIN
## ST. MICHAELS

Built in 1820, The Inn at Perry Cabin was restored, expanded and re-opened in 1990 by Sir Bernard Ashley. The Inn is under two hours from Washington DC on a twenty-five acre waterfront site. With forty-one rooms and suites, it is a perfect "Country House Hotel", in harmony with its natural surroundings on Maryland's Eastern Shore.

The charm and elegance of the Laura Ashley interiors are beautifully complemented with fine antiques and objets d'art throughout the Inn. The mood is one of peace and character. Luxury is achieved through attention to detail, complete comfort and courteous, unobtrusive service.

The Inn's award-winning Chef, Mark Salter, bases his specialities on the riches of the locality, fresh fish and produce mixed with fine international fare. Guests also enjoy the Inn's indoor pool and health facility with exercise room, sauna and steam room.

308 Watkins Lane
St. Michael's, MD 21663
•
Tel 410 745 2200
Fax 410 745 3348
Freephone in US
800 722 2949
•
General Manager:
Stephen Creese
•
41 rooms including
3 one-bedroom suites
•
Tax 8%

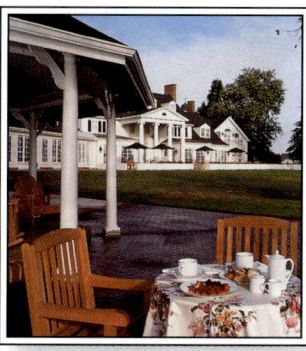

Doubles and suites
$195 - $575 EP
•
Sailing, indoor pool,
conference facilities, exercise
room, sauna and steam.
•
Nearby: horseriding,
water skiing.
•
Children over 10 welcome
•
No smoking in dining room
•
VS • MC • Amex • Diners

# MARYLAND

# HISTORIC INNS OF ANNAPOLIS
## ANNAPOLIS

A town as historic as Annapolis calls for accommodations as historic as ours. Four charming inns take you back in time; handsomely restored and tastefully furnished in original and reproduction antiques whilst at the same time offering all modern conveniences. Soak up more historic atmosphere in our elegant yet cosy Treaty of Paris Restaurant, our Drummer's Lot Pub or our King of France Tavern.

Whether you stay for a couple of nights or a week, Annapolis with its cobblestone streets, quaint shops, historic attractions and colourful waterfront has a great deal to offer – tour the U.S. Naval Academy or charter your own yacht. We're just 45 minutes from Washington DC, 40 minutes from Baltimore and a short drive from Baltimore Washington International Airport.

58 State Circle,
Annapolis,
MD 21401

Tel 410 263 2641
Fax 410 268 3813
Freephone in US
800 847 8882

General Manager:
Russ Finch
137 rooms

Doubles $110 - $165
B&B
Tax 12%
Parking available $10

Conference facilities
Nearby: swimming, tennis, golf, horseriding, sailing.

Children welcome
Non-smoking
VS • MC
Amex • Diners

# KENT MANOR INN & RESTAURANT
## STEVENSVILLE

Situated on 226 waterfront acres, Kent Manor Inn (circa 1820) has 24 individually decorated, waterview guest rooms. Most have porches or balconies and several boast working fireplaces. Kent Manor Inn's fine dining restaurant is open to the public every day for lunch, dinner and a sumptuous Sunday brunch. Executive Chef Dennis Shakan came to the inn last year from a five-star, five diamond resort in Colorado and we are proud of his outstanding New American seasonal menus and artful presentations.

On our working farm, guests enjoy the swimming pool, hiking paths, bicycles, paddleboats at our new eight-slip pier, volleyball, horse-shoes and croquet. Nearby is world-class golf, outlet shopping, the historic towns of Annapolis, Easton and St. Michael's, antiquing, boating fishing, hunting and the scenic beauty of Maryland's Eastern Shore.

500 Kent Manor
Drive,
Stevensville,
Kent Island,
MD 21666

Tel 410 643 5757
Fax 410 643 8315
Freephone in US
800 820 4511
Managing Director:
Alan J. Michaels

24 rooms
including 1 one
bedroom suite
Doubles $120 - $190
B&B

Suite $205 - $225
Tax 8%
Outdoor pool, sailing,
conference facilities,

boat lock, bicycles,
free paddle boats
Nearby: tennis, riding,
water skiing

Children welcome.
Non-smoking
VS • MC • Amex
Diners • Discover

## MARYLAND

# MR. MOLE
## BALTIMORE

Mr. Mole, Maryland's only Four Star B&B, is a large 1870 Baltimore house located in the quiet tree lined neighbourhood of historic Bolton Hill and close to the Inner Harbor with its numerous shops and restaurants. Within easy reach are Orioles Park, Antique Row, John Hopkins University, Meyerhoff Symphony Hall and other attractions.
Collin has decorated the house with great style and elegance, complete with 18th and 19th century antiques. The first floor living room, breakfast room and parlour feature 14-foot ceilings, bay windows and marble fireplaces. Of the five individually decorated suites, The London Suite and The Print Room include a private sitting room and two bedrooms.
Garage parking with an automatic garage door opener is included as is a large, Dutch-style continental breakfast.

| 1601 Bolton Street, Baltimore, MD 21217 Tel 410 728 1179 Fax 410 728 3379 | Innkeeper: Collin Clarke | 5 rooms including 3 one-bedroom suites 2 two-bedroom suites | Suites $97 - $155 B&B Tax 12% | Free parking Children over 10 welcome | Non-smoking VS • MC Amex • Diners |

# PRIVATE PLEASURE
## ANNAPOLIS

Enjoy a getaway with a difference in this elegant Boat and Breakfast - a 60 foot classic motor yacht built in 1947 by John Trumpy and Sons with the style and excellence of craftsmanship that is typical of all Annapolis built Trumpys. Private Pleasure's spacious layout accommodates two couples in complete luxury and privacy - rich, natural wood enhancing well-appointed staterooms with comfortable bed, private bath and air conditioning/heating, allowing you to relax and unwind in unique style.
The richly panelled main salon, spacious aft deck area and seating, forward of the pilot house, are available for breakfast, afternoon tea, evening cocktails or simply watching the sun set over the Annapolis waterfront. An evening aboard includes all the above, a one hour cruise, a restful night, lulled by the lapping of the water and a delicious continental breakfast. Longer packages can be arranged just to suit you, perhaps a two-night, three-day cruise to Baltimore, Rock Hall and St. Michael's a trip to make a special occasion even more memorable.

| P.O. Box 3057 Annapolis MD 21403 | Tel 410 267 7802 Fax 410 267 7802 | Freephone in US 800 877 9930 Owners: Peter & Vicky Giardini | 2 one bedroom staterooms Doubles $230 B&B For 2 couples booking together $400 B&B | Tax 10% Outdoor pool Children over 6 welcome | Smoking in designated areas VS•MC•Amex |

**MARYLAND**

# WADES POINT INN ON THE BAY
## ST. MICHAELS

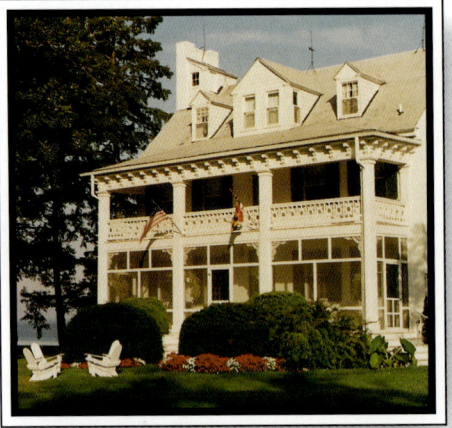

This country bed & breakfast inn overlooking Chesapeake Bay, is ideal for those seeking country serenity and the splendour of the bay. All rooms enjoy a waterview. The Inn's 120 acres of fields and woodland (with one-mile nature trail), a dock for fishing and crabbing, and the ever-changing view of boats, birds and water lapping the shoreline, provide a peaceful setting for relaxation and recreation.

Interesting shops and fine dining, the famed Chesapeake Bay Maritime Museum and abundant recreational opportunities are just a few miles away. Couples, families, executive retreats or seminars are welcome.

| | | | | | |
|---|---|---|---|---|---|
| PO Box 7, St. Michaels, MD 21663 Tel: 410 745 2500 Fax: 410 745 3443 | General Partners: John E. Feiler & Elizabeth M. Feiler | 26 rooms including 2 two bedroom suites | Doubles $110 - $180 B&B (rooms with shared bath $84 - $95) | Tax 8% Nearby: tennis, golf, sailing | Children over 1 welcome No smoking VS • MC |

## THE BEST INSPECTORS ARE OUR GUESTS!

Your feedback is the basis on which our business is built.

Were your expectations met?
Was the welcome warm?
Did you feel you received good value for the money you spent?

It is vital to maintain the excellent standard of U.S. Welcome's Selected Hotels and Inns and your input is of great value to us. If you have a moment, please write, call, fax or email and let us know what you think of the hotels and inns in which you stayed.

U.S. Welcome Limited
FREEPOST (HA 4595) Northwood, England, HA6 3BR
Tel (0)1895 622233  Fax (0)1895 622244
mail@uswelcome.com   www.uswelcome.com
Freephone in the U.S. 888 INN VISIT

## NEW JERSEY

# BERNARDS INN
### BERNARDSVILLE

The Bernards Inn is a tranquil retreat where history surrounds you, graceful architecture shelters you, privacy comforts you and gracious hospitality envelopes you. Situated in the quaint country town of Bernardsville, in New Jersey's picturesque Somerset Hills, the inn has been the delight of weary New Yorkers and others for nearly ninety years.

It continues its tradition of gracious hospitality, welcoming guests with all the service, style, intimacy and elegance of a small European luxury hotel while preserving the discreet charm of an historic American country inn.

Awaken to the luxury of world-class accommodations, impeccable service and residential comfort. Enjoy lavish terry bathrobes, orchids in bloom and services by appointment such as in-room personal training and massage therapy.

Chef Edward Stone's menu of progressive American cuisine masterfully reflects nature's seasonal charms and culinary innovations are wonderfully enhanced by an award-winning wine list.

27 Mine Brook Road
Bernardsville
NJ 07924
•
Tel 908 766 0002
Fax 908 766 4604
Freephone in US
888 766 0002
•
General Manager/Owner:
Alice Rochat

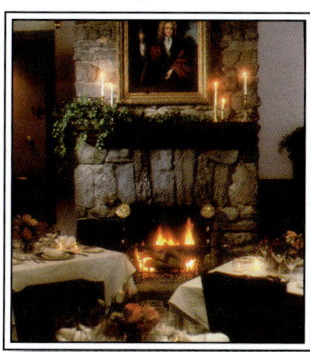

20 rooms
including 4 one bedroom suites
Doubles $150 - $200  EP
•
Tax  6%
•
Conference facilities
•
Nearby: indoor pool, golf, riding
•
VS • MC
Amex • Diners

**NEW JERSEY**

# CHIMNEY HILL FARM
## LAMBERTVILLE

High on a ridge, overlooking the charming city of Lambertville, sits Chimney Hill Farm, situated on eight acres of naturally landscaped grounds filled with gardens and wildlife - an "architectural treasure" and an ideal base for exploring the Delaware Valley.

Enjoy a choice of five designer decorated guest rooms, some with fireplaces. Spend a quiet Winter weekend sipping mulled cider in front of a blazing fire or a Summer stay, kayaking on the Delaware River. Take a historic mule barge ride, visit a local winery, shop at Lambertville, New Hope or Lahaska, or perhaps take in a show at the Bucks County Theatre.

We look forward to meeting you.

| 207 Goat Hill Road Lambertville NJ 08530 | Tel 609 397 1516 Fax 609 397 9353 Owner: Terry Anderson | 5 rooms Doubles $85 - $160 B&B | Tax 6% Small business meetings | Nearby: outdoor pool, tennis, golf, down hill skiing, riding, cross country skiing | Children over 12 welcome. Non-smoking VS • MC • Amex |

---

# INN AT MILLRACE POND
## HOPE

The Inn at Millrace Pond is a gracious country inn situated on 23 acres in historic Hope. The main building with its fine restaurant and tavern was an active gristmill until 1952.

Rooms are decorated with the simple elegance of a fine Colonial American home. Besides the main building with nine rooms, there are six in the original Miller's house and two more in the original stone Wheelwright's Cottage. The parlour has a fireplace and library. In warm weather Cordie and Charles offer rides in a 1921 Cadillac touring car. There is a tennis court, and golfers have a good selection of courses nearby.

Situated on the wooded western side of New Jersey, Hope is no more than 90 minutes (75 miles West) from New York City, a mile south off Interstate 80.

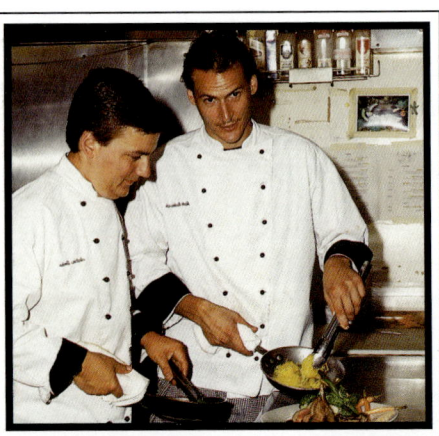

| PO. Box 359, Hope, NJ 07844 | Tel 908 459 4884 Fax 908 459 5276 Freephone in US 800 7 INNHOPE | Innkeepers: Charlie & Cordie Puttkammer | 17 rooms Doubles $85 - $165 B&B Tax 6% | Tennis Nearby: golf, horseriding. All children welcome | Non-smoking VS • MC Amex • Diners |

30

# NEW YORK STATE

## COPPERFIELD INN
### NORTH CREEK

In the heart of the spectacular Adirondacks rests the Copperfield Inn. In Winter, Gore Mountain Ski Area features a 2100 foot vertical drop, 9 lifts and 41 trails plus the state's only gondola.

When the snow melts it runs off into the Hudson, the water rises and races downriver to create Class IV white water rafting - spine chilling excitement for those who love the water. Summer tames the Hudson; float down the river in an inner tube or enjoy boating, fishing and swimming in numerous beautiful lakes. Hike, bike, rock climb and enjoy bird and wild-life watching in the mountains. When temperatures slowly descend, magical shades of autumn are created, as nature colours the majestic mountains in hues of red, orange and yellow. Soon the first snow begins to fall, the skiers return and the cycle of the seasons in the Adirondack Park begins anew.

Relax in comfort and style at the exquisite AAA Four Diamond Award winning Copperfield Inn.

P.O. Box 28,
North Creek,
NY 12853
•
Tel 518 251 2500
Fax 518 251 4143
Freephone in US
800 424 9910
•
General Manager:
Laura Hollenbeck
•
25 rooms
including 3 one bedroom suites.

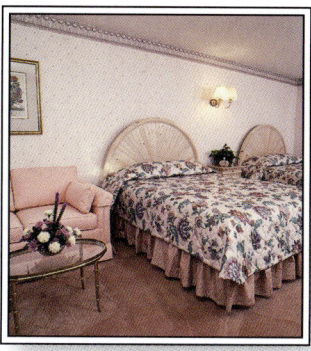

Doubles $120 - $190 B&B.
MAP available
Suites $150 - $200
•
Tax 7%  s.c. $1.00 per person
•
Outdoor pool, tennis, conference facilities, health club, shuttle to Gore Mountain
Nearby: golf, riding, water skiing, skiing
•
Children welcome.
VS • MC • Amex Diners • Discover

**NEW YORK STATE**

# CRAFTSMAN INN
## FAYETTEVILLE

*Comfortable and gracious, this elegant new country inn has been designed with all the modern amenities required by today's business and leisure travellers. Each room is individually decorated for your ultimate comfort, featuring tv, radio and large work areas. Complimentary light breakfast is served in the beautifully decorated breakfast room and, with the fire burning brightly, the lobby is an inviting place to relax and meet friends or colleagues. For your dining pleasure, our new restaurant will offer the same tasteful decor in which to enjoy a variety of delicious meals.*

The Craftsman Inn puts you in the heart of New York State's business centres and area attractions. Only 17 minutes from Carrier Circle, Syracuse University and downtown, the inn is located near shopping areas, numerous restaurants and golf courses.

The staff at the Craftsman Inn is dedicated to making your stay comfortable, enjoyable and memorable.

7300 E. Gowesee St
Fayetteville
NY 13066
•
Tel 315 637 8000
Fax 315 637 2440
Freephone in US
800 797 2469
•
General Manager:
David Garrett
•
70 rooms
including 3 one bedroom
suites, 2 two bedroom
suites

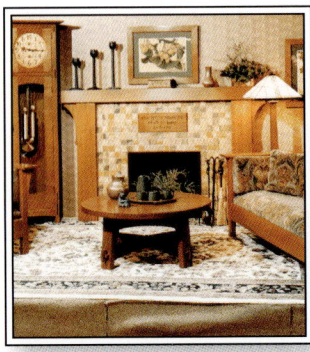

Doubles $69 - $84 B&B
Suites $82 - $125
•
Tax 12%
•
Conference facilities.
Nearby: outdoor &
indoor pools, tennis, golf,
riding, sailing.
•
Children welcome.
•
Non-smoking
•
VS • MC • Amex
Diners • Discover

## NEW YORK STATE

# GENEVA ON THE LAKE
## GENEVA

Set on ten acres in the heart of the beautiful wine-growing Finger Lakes region, is the elegant AAA Four Diamond, Italian Renaissance style Geneva-On-The-Lake. Formal gardens, outdoor sculpture, woodland walks to the lakeshore, natural landscaped paths, secluded nooks and a boathouse and dock with sailboats and canoe, are all designed with romance and relaxation in mind.

Enchanting architecture, marble fireplaces, antiques, 18th century panelled walls and heraldic tapestries in the public rooms set the tone for this small resort. Guest suites offer living rooms and fully equipped kitchens while thoughtful touches such as fresh coffee, flowers, fruit basket and wine add to the warmth of your welcome. Enjoy candlelight gourmet dining on Friday, Saturday and Sunday evenings with complimentary continental breakfast served daily.

Savour the elegance of this historical resort – the getaway for all seasons.

1001 Lochland Road,
Rt 14 South,
Geneva, NY 14456
•
Tel 315 789 7190
Fax 315 789 0322
Freephone in US
800 GENEVA
•
General Manager:
William J. Schickel
•
14 one bedroom, 10 two
bedroom suites

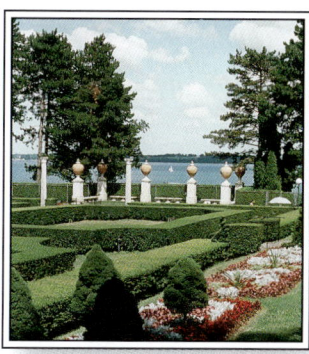

Suites $162 - $481 B&B
•
Tax 7%
•
Outdoor pool, sailing,
croquet, badminton,
cycling
•
Nearby: tennis, golf,
horseriding, wineries
•
Children welcome
•
VS • MC
Amex • Diners

**NEW YORK STATE**

# MANHATTAN EAST SUITE HOTELS
## NEW YORK CITY

A unique blend of convenient locations, spacious suites and outstanding service - staying at one of the Manhattan East Suite Hotels is like having your own apartment in New York. Kitchens so well equipped you can fix anything from simple snacks to full meals. A range of dining experiences from four star restaurants to the convenience of room service. The hotels are ideal for family travelling, impromptu meetings, entertaining or simply a great place to sit back and relax. At our family-owned, family run properties you're not a customer but our personal guest and we go out of our way to make your stay as special as possible.

Choices include the Surrey Hotel on the Upper East Side close to museums, art galleries and scenic Central Park, Plaza Fifty set in the dynamic centre of midtown Manhattan near Rockefeller Center, Park Avenue and Fifth Avenue or Lyden House, small, intimate and located in Sutton Place.

Nine locations in Manhattan's best neighbourhoods, from West 31st Street to Midtown and the Upper East Side.

Tel  212 465 3690
Fax  212 465 3663
Freephone 0800 89 6931

•

1,954 rooms & suites
Suites ranging from studio and junior to one and two bedrooms

•

Doubles $189 - $270  EP
Suites $224 - $545. Weekly & monthly rates available, also seasonal promotional packages.

•

Tax 13.25 %  s.c. $2 per room per night.

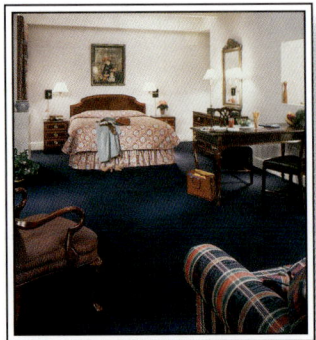

Conference facilities, most hotels have fitness centers, some with saunas

•

Parking available
$20.75 - $35.00 per day according to location.
Tax 19%

•

Children  welcome

•

Non-smoking suites available in all hotels

•

VS • MC • Amex
Diners

**NEW YORK STATE**

# ROYCROFT INN
## EAST AURORA

In 1895 the Roycroft Arts and Crafts Community, a self-contained group, based on the Medieval Guild system and supporting hundreds of craftspeople, was founded in East Aurora. In 1905, the Roycroft Inn opened to accommodate visitors to what had become a cultural Mecca. After the death of the movement's Founder, the writer-philosopher Elbert Hubbard, the Roycroft was operated by his son and then passed through several hands until being granted National Landmark Status in 1987. In June 1995 the Roycroft re-opened its doors to guests.

An exquisite collection of furniture and fixtures adorn the meticulously refurbished inn and the names of notable personalities remain carved into doors. Blending the historical significance of the Roycroft movement with completely modern amenities, the Inn provides the utmost in style, comfort and luxury. From unique guest suites to dining and function rooms, exceptional quality, service and hospitality abound. The Inn is located a convenient 30 minutes from downtown Buffalo.

40 South Grove Street,
East Aurora,
NY 14052
•
Tel 716 652 5552
Fax 716 655 5345
•
Innkeeper:
Martha Beardsley Augat
•
22 suites
•
Doubles $120 - $210 B&B
•
Tax 11%

Conference facilities
Nearby: outdoor pool,
tennis, golf, down-hill
skiing, cross-country
skiing
•
Parking available free
of charge
•
Children welcome
•
Non-smoking
•
VS • MC • Amex
Diners • Discover

## NEW YORK STATE

# SAGAMORE ON LAKE GEORGE
## BOLTON LANDING

The Sagamore Resort offers an unrivalled setting on a private island on scenic Lake George. The hotel's main house is a restored Victorian landmark surrounded by landscaped gardens, walking and jogging trails, and a white sand beach. Dining ranges from casual to gourmet in a choice of four restaurants. Guests savour the charm of an historic hotel with all the modern amenities of a Mobil Four Star and AAA Four Diamond resort.

Year-round the Sagamore's indoor facilities include a spa, health club, tennis and racquetball. Outdoor activities include extensive water sports, golf or a leisurely cruise on the hotel's own deluxe yacht. In the winter enjoy cross-country skiing and ice skating. Value and holiday packages, and supervised childrens' programmes are available.

A 4 hour drive from New York City and Boston, and an easy driving distance from many cities in the mid-Atlantic, Quebec and Ontario regions the Sagamore is also accessible by train or plane to Albany, from where the resort provides transportation.

110 Sagamore Road,
Bolton Landing,
NY 12814

•

Tel 518 644 9400
Fax 518 644 3033
Freephone in US
800 358 3585

•

Managing Director:
Robert McIntosh

•

174 rooms
176 suites

Doubles $159 - $310 EP
Suites $255 - $390

•

Tax 7%
s.c. $4 per person per day

•

Indoor pool, lake swimming, tennis, golf, horseriding, sailing, fitness center, spa
Complete conference centre for groups up to 800

VS • MC • Amex

## NEW YORK STATE

# BIRD & BOTTLE INN
### GARRISON

*From 1761 when it began life as Warren's Tavern, the inn has had a colourful and romantic history. Restored with great care to its original 18th century appearance the re-named Bird & Bottle is dedicated to preserving the Central Hudson Valley's traditions of fine dining and hospitality and has attained an international reputation for its food, with the guest book full of compliments from satisfied patrons.*

*Recently the second floor rooms and a cozy cottage were beautifully refurbished, so now, after a 40-year lapse, overnight accommodations are once again available. Each of the guest rooms has a fireplace, as has the cottage and all are meticulously furnished with period furniture and either a four-poster or canopied bed.*

| | | | | | | |
|---|---|---|---|---|---|---|
| Route 9, Old Albany Post Road, Garrison, NY 10524 | Tel 914 424 3300 Fax 914 424 3283 Freephone in US 800 782 6837 | Innkeeper: Ira Boyar 4 rooms including 1 one bedroom suite 1 cottage | Doubles $210 - $240 MAP Suite or cottage $240 Tax 7.25% | Small meeting facilities Nearby: outdoor pool, tennis, golf, riding, sailing, cross-country skiing | Children over 12 welcome. Non-smoking VS • MC Amex • Diners |

# CHESTNUT INN AT OQUAGA LAKE
### DEPOSIT

*Built in 1928 and almost totally constructed of the now extinct North American chestnut wood, the Chestnut Inn is an example of architecture and building construction at its very best with lumber casings, trim, panelling and basic construction all milled on the premises by skilled craftsmen.*

*For many years Deposit has been a popular holiday destination, with many people staying at the beautifully constructed lodge which, until renamed Chestnut Lodge in 1947, was known as Monaquaga. In 1992, the inn was purchased by two local businessmen who embarked on an ambitious project to restore its original lustre and transform the lodge into the first class inn it is today.*

*At this lakeside resort guests can relish fine dining in relaxed elegance in the main dining room, casual dining in the Sunroom or take a ride on Pickles, a replica of the inns original launch that once moved gracefully over the waters of lovely Oquaga Lake.*

| | | | | | | |
|---|---|---|---|---|---|---|
| 498 Oquaga Lake Road, Deposit, NY 13754 Tel 607 467 2500 Fax 607 467 5911 | Freephone in US 0800 467 7676 Innkeeper: Tom Spaulding 30 rooms | including 3 one bedroom suites Doubles $69 - $149 EP Suites $99 - $209 | Cottages $1000 - $1250 (weekly only) Tax 11% s.c. 10% Water skiing, cross-country skiing | Nearby: tennis, horse riding, golf, down-hill skiing, bicycling, hiking, lake swimming | Children welcome Smoking in designated areas VS•MC•Amex Diners•Discover |

## NEW YORK STATE

# HALSEY HOUSE
## LONG ISLAND

*Located halfway between Southampton and Bridgehampton, Halsey House in Water Mill offers a relaxed and reflective pace, great white sand beaches, vast skies and a porch on which to gaze over acres of wildflowers rioting across the road, geese grazing cornfields in the distance, or Mecox Bay, shimmering a half mile to the south.*

*The Halseys have been in these parts for centuries - Thomas Halsey settled in Southampton in 1640 - and in 1994 Jane Halsey and her mother Gwen, lovingly restored the two-storey brown shingle farmhouse her grandparents built in 1910.*

*You'll enjoy the festive Waverly wallpapers, lustrous fir floors and fresh flowers in the bedrooms, the pretty common sitting room with comfortable overstuffed couches, the big country kitchen and Jane's blueberry pancakes.*

| | | | | | |
|---|---|---|---|---|---|
| 258 Halsey Lane, Water Mill, Long Island, NY 11976 Tel 516 726 6527 | Innkeeper: Jane E. Halsey 3 rooms including 1 one bedroom suite, | 2 two bedroom suites (2 rooms share 1 bath, 1 room has private bath) | Doubles $100 - $190 B&B Tax 9 % | 5 minutes to beaches. Nearby: tennis, golf, riding, sailing, water skiing | Children over 12 welcome. Non-smoking VS • MC |

# ROSE INN
## ITHACA

*Rose Inn's magnificent setting with twenty landscaped acres of lawns and gardens is at the heart of New York's glorious wine-growing area, the Finger Lakes, half way between New York City and Niagara Falls, minutes from Cornell Univerity. This AAA Four Diamond and Mobil Four Star Award winning inn is a masterpiece of the woodcrafters art, with a unique and stunning circular mahogany staircase rising gracefully through the two storeys of the house to a cupola on the roof. Fifteen guest rooms with period furniture and imaginative and luxurious use of fabrics, reflect a mood of elegance from days gone by. The formal parlour is a delightful gathering place for guests to enjoy a fine library and good company whilst dinner, served Tuesdays to Saturdays, is a very special experience for which advance reservations are recommended.*

| | | | | | |
|---|---|---|---|---|---|
| Route 34 North, P.O. Box 6576, Ithaca, NY 14851-6576 | Tel 607 533 7905 Fax 607 533 7908 Innkeepers: Charles & Sherry Rosemann | 15 rooms including 5 one bedroom suites. Doubles $125 - $475 B&B | Tax 11%. s.c. 15% Conference facilities | Nearby: Outdoor & indoor pool, tennis, golf, riding, sailing, down-hill skiing, cross-country skiing | Children over 10 welcome. Non-smoking VS • MC |

38

**NEW YORK STATE**

# SEDGWICK INN
## BERLIN

In the beautiful Taconic Valley on the New York side of the Berkshires, this 1791 historic colonial, described as the "Quintessential country inn" is a place of casual elegance and old world charm with well-stocked library and inviting fireplaced parlour.

There are five antique-filled bedrooms in the main house and six, with colonial style furnishings in the annexe. An old carriage barn houses unusual gift and craft items.

The Inn is renowned for its fine food and breakfast is included in the rates. The Inn is a member of the Independent Innkeepers Association and ideally located for all attractions in the Berkshires and Southern Vermont.

| | | | | | |
|---|---|---|---|---|---|
| Rt 22, Box 150, Berlin, NY 12022 | Tel 518 658 2334<br>Fax 518 658 3998<br>Freephone in US<br>800 845 4886 | Owner/Innkeeper:<br>Edith Evans<br>10 rooms<br>including 1 one<br>bedroom suite | Doubles $75 – $125<br>B&B<br>Tax 11% | Nearby: tennis,<br>golf, hiking,<br>swimming, skiing | Annexe rooms best suited to families with children<br>VS • MC |

## COMPLIMENTARY BOOKING SERVICE

Don't forget we offer an advisory and booking service and you can make all your reservations with just one phone call to us. The service is completely free and prices are not loaded in any way.

Call for a chat on

# 01895 622233

# PENNSYLVANIA

## BALADERRY INN AT GETTYSBURG
### GETTYSBURG

*Baladerry Inn is located at the edge of the Gettysburg Battlefield near Little Round Top. This circa 1812 brick Federal-style home served as a hospital during the War between the states. A large two-storied great room dominated by a massive brick fireplace is both a dining and gathering area. A brick terrace, off the great room, provides an outdoor area for socialising. Four guest rooms in the Carriage House, newly renovated in 1994, feature fireplaces or private patios plus a common area with fireplace, sunroom, and brick patio. Private and spacious, the Inn is an excellent choice for history buffs, leisure travellers, small business meetings and reunions. A full country breakfast is served each morning.*

| | | | | | |
|---|---|---|---|---|---|
| 40 Hospital Road, Gettysburg, PA 17325 Tel 717 337 1342 | Owner/Innkeeper: Tom and Caryl O'Gara 8 rooms | Doubles $85 - $99 B&B Tax 6% | Tennis, conference facilities Nearby: outdoor & indoor pools, golf, horseriding | Children over 14 welcome. Non-smoking | VS • MC Amex • Diners |

## BARLEY SHEAF FARM
### HOLICONG

*In an exquisite country setting, choose between the gracious accommodation at the Farm or escape to a truly pastoral retreat in our two distincitve barn suites, with long-distance, tranquil views of horse farms and meadows. All guest rooms are air-conditioned. Three fireplaced common rooms offer a peaceful ambience for relaxation, leisurely reading or socialising.*

*That all-important first meal of the day may include fresh seasonal fruit with yoghurt and granola, stuffed baked apples, fresh farm eggs, scrambled and served with salmon, or a sweet pepper and onion frittata, ham or sausage, complemented with a variety of fragrant, home-baked Swiss breads, home-made jams and genuine farm honey. Served in the Farm's rustic brick-floored dining room and sun porch overlooking the lawns, pool and pond.*

| | | | | | |
|---|---|---|---|---|---|
| 5281 York Rd (Rte 202), PO Box 10, Holicong, PA 18928-0010 | Tel 215 794 5104 Fax 215 794 5332 Owners: Peter & Veronika Suess | 12 rooms including 2 one bedroom suites, 2 two bedroom suites | Doubles $105 - $175 B&B Suites $155 - $255 Tax 8% | Outdoor pool, conference facilities, cross-country skiing Nearby: indoor pool, tennis, golf, riding, sailing, skiing | Children over 8 welcome. Non-smoking VS • MC • Amex |

## PENNSYLVANIA

# BOXWOOD INN
## LANCASTER COUNTY

The AAA Three Diamond inn is set in four acres adjacent to well-kept Amish and Mennonite farms. Guests receive an extraordinary introduction into the simplistic lifestyle of the "Pennsylvania Dutch".

The 1768 stone farmhouse was fully renovated with guests in mind – classic simplicity with country elegance. Enjoy a full breakfast in our formal dining room followed by an activity-filled day exploring covered bridges and visiting farmers' markets, passing horse-drawn buggies en route.

Return to a relaxing cup of tea served in the Garden Room overlooking the patio and stream.

Plan your evening meal at a fine local restaurant. Your elegantly appointed room with private bath and cosy handmade Amish quilts awaits you.

| PO Box 203, 12 Tobacco Road, Akron, PA 17501 | Tel 717 859 3466 Fax 717 859 4507 Freephone in US 800 238 3466 | Owners/Innkeepers: June & Dick Klemm | 5 rooms Carriage house good for families | Doubles $85 - $145 B&B Tax 6% | Children welcome Non-smoking VS • MC |

# CARNEGIE HOUSE
## STATE COLLEGE

A luxurious 22 room country inn nestled in woods near Penn State University, Carnegie House offers all the comforts of a European Country House Hotel. The oak panelled library, with its glowing fire; the comfortable dining room offering evening table d'hôte and a la carte menus, full Scottish breakfast on Sundays, leisurely luncheons and daily complimentary buffet breakfasts. Sunny sitting rooms and guest bedrooms with individually controlled heat and air conditioning, tv and telephones with computer outlets.

This Four Diamond AAA award winner is the first United States Outpost of The Carnegie Club of Skibo Castle in Scotland. Yours hosts are German born Peter and Helga Schmid who have created a relaxed, welcoming atmosphere for guests to enjoy.

| 100 Cricklewood Drive, State College, PA 16801 | Tel 814 234 2424 Fax 814 231 1299 Freephone in US 800 229 3505 | Hosts/Owner: Peter & Helga Schmid 20 rooms including 2 one bedroom suites. | Doubles $125 - $175 B&B Suites $195 - $275 Tax 6% | Conference facilities, Courtesy Van for airport service. Nearby: tennis, golf, skiing. | Children over 12 welcome. Non-smoking VS • MC • Amex |

## PENNSYLVANIA

# EVERMAY ON THE DELAWARE
### ERWINNA

Located on 25 woodland acres, Evermay offers country elegance in a rural setting, with formal gardens overlooking the historic Delaware River to the east and bordering Delaware Canal to the west. Deer come to drink at dusk, lambs frolic on green fields and colourful peacocks strut and display their plumage.

All guest rooms are air conditioned with private baths, individually controlled heat, telephones, laptop computer capability, and Victorian antiques and collectibles. Continental plus breakfast is served in the garden room and afternoon tea in the parlour. There is a wonderfully conducive atmosphere for small conference meetings. The Evermay and its staff offer a relaxing environment that can inspire creativity, along with the opportunity to sit back and unwind.

| Headquarters River Rds, PO Box 60 Erwinna PA 18920 | Tel 610 294 9100 Fax 610 294 8349 Owner/Innkeeper: William & Danielle Moffly | 16 rooms including 1 two bedroom suite Doubles $85 - $220 B&B | Prix Fixe dinner Fri, Sat and Sun only Tax 8% Conference facilities | Nearby: outdoor pool, golf, riding, sailing, down-hill skiing, cross-country skiing | Children over 12 welcome. Non-smoking VS • MC |

# FRENCH MANOR
### SOUTH STERLING

An elegant storybook stone chateau, secluded and private and surveyor of the 45 acres it rests upon – miles of leafy treetops and a brilliant sunlit sky. Spacious, uncompromising accommodations, together with fine cuisine and service, make the French Manor perfect for a long or short-term stay.
From our spacious stone veranda, enjoy the beautiful crests and ridges of the northern Pocono Mountains. Within our own grounds are miles of trails for hiking, biking and cross-country skiing. Alternatively, spend time in our cosy lounge where you can read, watch tv or relax with good company and your favourite liqueur.
The French Manor's guest rooms are designed and decorated to emphasise luxury, whilst maintaining the intimate atmosphere of a country inn. Dinner is a celebration of authentic French cuisine.
We invite you to join us.

| Box 39, Huckleberry Road, South Sterling, PA 18460 | Tel 717 676 3344 Fax 717 676 9786 Freephone in US 800 523 8200 | Owner/Innkeepers: Ron & Mary Kay Logan 9 rooms including 2 one-bedroom suites, 1 two-bedroom | Doubles $120 - $180 B&B Suites $175 - $225 Tax 6% s.c.10% | Hiking, fishing, guests are welcome to use facilities at the Sterling Inn (1½ miles). Nearby: sailing, water-skiing. | No facilities for children Non-smoking VS • MC • Amex |

**PENNSYLVANIA**

# HISTORIC SMITHTON INN
## EPHRATA

*Smithton with its large, square, sunny rooms is picturesque and historic. Each room has its own working fireplace and sitting area with comfortable chairs, reading lamps and writing desk; chamber music is provided as are good books and private refrigerators. Most beds have canopies, soft goose down pillows and bright, hand-made Pennsylvania Dutch quilts. Feather beds are available on request. Long leisurely evenings can be enjoyed in the library and adjacent great room with a crackling fire in the cooler months. A delicious full country breakfast is served daily.*

*For extra privacy our suite offers a snack room, parlour with working fireplace, bedroom with queen canopy bed and bathroom with whirlpool tub and separate shower. At Smithton you will encounter matchless hospitality, provided by people who really care.*

| | | | | | |
|---|---|---|---|---|---|
| 900 West Main Street, Ephrata, PA 17522 | Tel 717 733 6094 Innkeeper: Dorothy Graybill | 8 rooms including 1 one bedroom suite. | Doubles $75 - $150 B&B Suite $140 - $170 Tax 6% | Nearby: outdoor & indoor pools, tennis, golf | Children welcome Non-smoking VS • MC • Amex |

# INNS AT DONECKERS
## EPHRATA

*Experience Doneckers' warm hospitality in the picturesque setting of historic Lancaster County. Described as "an oasis of sophistication in Pennsylvania Dutch Country", the Doneckers Community includes four distinctive, handsomely preserved inns of 40 rooms and suites dating from 1777 to the Victorian era.*

*Appointed in fine antiques and hand-stencilled walls, the inns surround the award-winning restaurant, the Farmers Market and the Artworks, a complex of 30 artisans' studios and galleries featuring fine art, quilts and crafts.*

*Minutes from Amish farmlands and famous antique markets, Doneckers is conveniently located midway between Philadelphia and Gettysburg, ideally situated for a couple of nights stopover or a central point from which to explore the whole area.*

| | | | | | |
|---|---|---|---|---|---|
| 318-324 N. State Street, Ephrata, PA 17522 Innkeeper: Jan Grobengieser | Tel 717 738 9502 Fax 717 738 9554 Freephone in US 800 377 2289 | 40 rooms 13 one bedroom suites 2 cottage suites, 1 with kitchenette | Doubles $59 - $185 B&B Suites and cottages $149 - $185 | Tax 6% Nearby: swimming, tennis, golf | Children welcome VS • MC • Amex |

## PENNSYLVANIA

# KING'S COTTAGE
## LANCASTER

The King's Cottage, recently listed in the American Historic Inns "Top Ten List", is snuggled in the midst of historic Lancaster County, the heart of the Amish country. It combines beautiful antiques with designer decorating, modern luxury with old fashioned hospitality. From polished oak floors to original crystal chandeliers, the inn envelopes guests in a warm elegant atmosphere.

Begin your day with a full breakfast including specialities such as Peaches 'n' Cream French toast and Lancaster County sausage. Your innkeepers will arrange tours, reserve you places at an Amish dinner and provide maps and information for exploring the beautiful Pennsylvania Dutch countryside.

After a days outing, relax in the library with hot cider or fresh lemonade. Located within easy reach of Washington DC, New York City, Philadelphia and Baltimore with airport and train terminals nearby.

1049 E. King Street,
Lancaster, PA 17602
Owner/Innkeepers:
Karen & Jim Owens

Tel 717 397 1017
Fax 717 397 3447
Freephone in US
800 747 8787

9 rooms
Carriage House,
honeymoon cottage

Doubles $69 - $145
B&B
Cottage $139 - $180

Tax 6%
Nearby: swimming,
tennis, golf,
horseriding

Children over
12 welcome
Non-smoking
VS • MC

---

# MANSION INN
## NEW HOPE

The 1865 Mansion sits in the heart of historic New Hope, Bucks County, and the sunny yellow manor home with breathtaking gardens is a magnificent example of Victorian Architecture of the Second French Empire. All rooms have private baths, some with whirlpool tubs and fireplaces. Feather beds have the finest linens, down comforters and a luxurious abundance of pillows. Excellent lamps for reading, tv and telephones are provided. Awake to an early morning coffee tray and newspaper at your door and prepare for a gourmet breakfast including a buffet of just-baked breads, fruit and home made granola. Hot entrees are served at individual tables with coffee or a " proper pot of tea."

Enjoy our collection of antique clocks, elegant antique glass and first editions; ride the mule barge, explore nearby museums, see a play at the historic Bucks County Playhouse or take a scenic drive along the Delaware River. Help is always on hand for sightseeing and dinner arrangements.

9 South Main Street,
New Hope,
PA 18938

Tel 215 862 1331
Fax 215 862 0277
Owner: Keith David

9 rooms
Doubles from $160
B&B
Tax 8%

Outdoor pool
Nearby: horse riding,
golf

Children over 16
welcome

Non-smoking
VS•MC•Amex

## PENNSYLVANIA

# PINEAPPLE HILL
### NEW HOPE

*This beautifully restored, 16 room, 1790 colonial farmhouse, set on five acres, offers a charming blend of comfort and convenience. Eighteen inch walls and original woodwork exemplify a craftsmanship long forgotten.*
*In the grounds, the ruins of a stone barn enclose a beautifully hand tiled pool. Spacious guest rooms, three of which are accompanied by a separate living room with cable tv, offer comfortable furnishings and are thoughtfully stocked with books and magazines. Full gourmet breakfasts served in the common room each morning are always a treat.*
*In the 1700's it was customary to place a pineapple on your front porch as a way of letting friends and neighbours know that you were welcoming guests. We continue this tradition by offering the same hospitality to our guests - we hope you'll always feel welcome at Pineapple Hill.*

1324 River Road,
New Hope,
PA 18938,
Tel 215 862 1790

Owners:
Charles & Kathryn Triolo

8 rooms including 3 one bedroom suites.
Doubles $95 - $165 B&B
Suites $145 - $165

Tax 8%
Outdoor pool,
conference facilities

Nearby: tennis, riding, sailing, water skiing, cross-country skiing
Children welcome.

Non-smoking
VS • MC
Amex

---

# SETTLERS INN
### HAWLEY

*Stone patios, flowers and herb gardens greet visitors to this restored Tudor Manor, whilst chestnut wood beams, enormous native bluestone fireplace and large comfortable chairs offer a continuing tradition of fine innkeeping and hospitality.*
*Eighteen rooms and suites are cheerfully decorated with white wicker furniture, antiques, flowered wallpaper and quilted bedcovers and have air-conditioning and phones. Some rooms have tv, all are non-smoking. Included in the rate is a hearty country breakfast with fresh home-baked goods. The dining room is widely known for its creative regional cuisine featuring locally grown produce, with seasonally changing menu to take advantage of the freshest fruits, vegetables and herbs. Delicious Amish farm cheeses, local maple syrup and Pennsylvania wines and beers are always available.*

4 Main Avenue,
Hawley,
PA 18428
Tel 717 226 2993
Fax 717 226 1874

Freephone in US
800 833 8527
Innkeepers:
Jeanne & Grant Genzlinger

18 rooms including 3 two bedroom suites.
Doubles $85 - $120 B&B

Suites $110 - $150
Tax 6%
Conference facilities,
gardens & gift shop

Nearby: indoor pool, tennis, golf, riding, sailing, water skiing, down-hill skiing, cross-country skiing

Children welcome.
VS • MC
Amex • Discover

45

## PENNSYLVANIA

# STERLING INN
## SOUTH STERLING

High in the beautiful Pocono mountains of north-east Pennsylvania, the Sterling Inn recaptures the charm and relaxed graciousness of times gone by, with personal attention from the Logan Family and their staff.

Enjoy boating, fishing, scenic hiking trails, nature programmes, swimming in our lake or indoor pool, tennis, volleyball, 9 hole putting course, shuffleboard, skiing, skating, tobogganing, horse drawn sleigh rides and weekend entertainment.

Choose from a variety of accommodations, charming rooms in the Main Inn, Lodge and Guest House, as well as individual cottages and suites. Enjoy hearty country breakfasts and candlelight dining in our Hearthstone Dining Room. Special diets always accommodated with advance notice.

| | | | | | |
|---|---|---|---|---|---|
| Rt 191, South Sterling, PA 18460 | Tel 717 676 3311 Fax 717 676 9786 Freephone in US 800 523 8200 | Innkeepers: The Logan Family 36 rooms including 12 one-bedroom suites | Doubles $126 - $160 MAP Suites $153 - $220 Tax 6% s.c. 15% | Outdoor/indoor pool, tennis, cross-county skiing, sledding, ice-skating, hiking, fishing, boating. | Nearby: golf, horseriding Children very welcome Non-smoking VS • MC • Amex |

# WEDGWOOD INN OF NEW HOPE
## BUCKS COUNTY

Located between New York City and Philadelphia, the Wedgwood is made up of three buildings offering guest rooms distinctive in style and decor. Each house has its own parlour with fireplace, good books, board games, menus from local restaurants and friendly conversation.

Steps from the centre of New Hope, an artists colony and antiques centre, the inn combines period charm of lofty windows, hardwood floors, brass ceiling fans and handmade quilts with modern essentials such as private baths and air-conditioning.

Begin the day with a delicious breakfast including home-baked muffins, and hot croissants. Spend the evening relaxing in the gazebo or in front of a roaring fire. At bedtime find a mint on your pillow and a tiny glass of Carl's secret recipe almond liqueur.

| | | | | | |
|---|---|---|---|---|---|
| 111 West Bridge Street (Rt. 179), New Hope, Bucks County, PA 18938-1401 | Tel 215 862 2520 Fax 215 862 2570 Owner/Innkeepers: Nadine & Carl Glassman | 12 rooms including 4 one-bedroom suites, 2 two-bedroom | Doubles $80 - $149 B&B Suites $150 - $200 Tax 8% s.c. 10% | Croquet, badminton. Nearby: swimming, tennis, golf, horseriding, sailing, waterskiing. | Children over 5 welcome Non-smoking VS • MC • Amex |

# VIRGINIA

## BAILIWICK INN
### FAIRFAX

As you walk through the door of this unique award winning inn and restaurant you'll step into the history and romance of days gone by, back to the early 1800's when this majestic house and the neighbouring Fairfax Courthouse were the centre of Northern Virginia's community life.

Enjoy the warm hospitality and fine details of our superbly restored and lovingly decorated Federal style inn – fourteen meticulously appointed guest rooms, with antiques and featherbeds, some with fireplaces or Jacuzzis. Revel in the exquisite cuisine of our gourmet chef. From polished balustrade and fresh cut flowers in the foyer, to cheery fires burning in book-lined parlours we invite you to discover Northern Virginia's hidden treasure.

Located midway between Dulles International Airport and Washington DC, the Bailiwick is an ideal base for the first or last few nights of your trip, with DC's museums, galleries and monuments only a short metro or auto trip away. Quaint shops and restaurants of Old Town Fairfax are steps from our door. Welcome to our past!

4023 Chain Bridge Road,
Fairfax,
VA 22030
•
Tel 703 691 2266
Fax 703 934 2112
Freephone in US
800 366 7666
•
Proprietors:
Bob & Annette Bradley
•
General Manager:
Stewart Schroeder

13 rooms including
1 one-bedroom suite
•
Doubles $130 - $195
B&B
Suite $295
•
Tax 8.5%
•
Parking available, no charge
•
Non-smoking
•
VS • MC • Amex

**VIRGINIA**

# BERKELEY HOTEL
## RICHMOND

The Berkeley Hotel is a small, elegant European-style hotel offering four diamond service and accommodations. The warm decor complemented by original maps hung throughout the hotel, the excellent restaurant and the lavish traditional furnishings of the guest rooms take one back to when innkeeping was an art.

Amenities for overnight guests include in-room Krup coffee-makers as well as complimentary valet parking and use of an exclusive health club. Located in historic Shockoe Slip, the city's oldest business district, and carefully designed to fit in with the surrounding cobblestoned streets and charming shops, The Berkeley is a short walk from many Richmond attractions and entertainment as well as a convenient headquarters for those wishing to explore the entire state of Virginia.

Guests looking for the personalised attention and hospitality of an elegant hotel will be delighted to find The Berkeley waiting to greet them in the Capital of the Confederacy.

1200 East Cary Street,
Richmond, VA 23219
•
Tel 804 780 1300
Fax 804 648 4728
•
General Manager:
Neal Rogers
•
55 rooms including
1 one bedroom suite
•
Doubles $118 - $395 EP

Tax 9.5%
•
Free parking available
•
Conference facilities
•
Nearby: indoor pool,
tennis, golf.
•
Children welcome
•
VS • MC
Amex • Diners

**VIRGINIA**

# BOAR'S HEAD INN, A COUNTRY RESORT
## CHARLOTTESVILLE

The Boar's Head Inn with the ambience of a Virginia gentleman's country estate, sprawls on 53 acres of genteel Virginia countryside. In this pristine setting, surrounded by manicured horse farms and in the burgeoning Monticello wine district, the Four Diamond Boar's Head continues to charm and relax guests as it has done for over three decades.

World class tennis, full service sports club and adjacent 18 hole championship Birdwood Golf Course offer unrivalled sports facilities while The Old Mill Room restaurant is one of only a handful in Virginia to hold the AAA coveted Four Diamond award. The wine list has won the Wine Spectator's Award of Excellence four years running.

Against the spectacular backdrop of the Blue Ridge Mountains, a stone's throw from Thomas Jefferson's Monticello and more than a century and a half later, at the Boar's Head Inn, one can still experience the warmth of hospitality for which Virginia is renowned.

PO Box 5307,
Charlottesville, VA 22905
•
Tel 804 296 2181
Fax 804 972 6024
Freephone in US
800 476 1988
•
General Manager:
Ms Sandie Greenwood
•
162 rooms including
11 one bedroom suites
•
Doubles $125 - $185 EP

Suites from $250
•
Tax 6.5%
•
Outdoor pool, tennis, conference facility, hot-air ballooning, massage, fitness center. Childrens' programme during Summer (nominal charge). Nearby: indoor pool, golf, horseriding.

Children Welcome
•
VS • MC • Amex • Diners

## VIRGINIA

# HIGH MEADOWS VINEYARD & MOUNTAIN SUNSET INN
### SCOTTSVILLE

A classic old world auberge in a new world setting, only a gentle drive to the Presidential homes Monticello and Ashlawn and local wineries. Nestled in countryside just south of Charlottesville, this Virginia landmark boasts a vineyard of Pinot Noir grape and spectacular mountain views, as well as a warmth and hospitality unusual in most National Historic Register sites. Fourteen painstakingly restored and renovated guestrooms make up the inn which is set on fifty rolling acres offering accommodation and diversions as individual as each traveller.

Follow a healthy, hearty country breakfast with a game of horseshoes, a nature trail walk or a visit to the pony corral and duck pond. Relish delicious candelight dinners; beautifully prepared weekday supper baskets and twilight wine tasting. Take seasonal strolls in award-winning gardens; enjoy water sports on the James River; drive along the unforgettable Blue Ridge Parkway or read by the warmth of a winter fire before retiring to your distinctive room to plan your next day's excursions. Come and see why Thomas Jefferson chose this beautiful part of Virginia for his retirement.

High Meadows Lane
Scottsville,
VA 24590
•
Tel 804 286 2218
Fax 804 286 2124
Freephone in US
800 232 1832
•
Owners: Peter Sushka &
Mary Jae Abbitt
•
14 rooms
•
Doubles $84 -$185 B&B

Tax 9.5% s.c. 15%
•
Nearby: tennis, horse riding, golf, sailing, hot tub spas, nature hiking trails, vineyard, cross-country and down-hill skiing.
•
Children over 8 welcome
•
Smoking in designated areas
•
VS•MC•Amex•Discover Novus

## VIRGINIA

# KESWICK HALL
### CHARLOTTESVILLE

When Sir Bernard Ashley first saw Keswick, he knew that his long-cherished ambition of creating a fine estate in the tradition of English country life would be fulfilled. The former Villa Crawford, built in 1912 has been transformed into a very special Country House Hotel with forty-eight outstanding bedrooms and exquisite country areas.

Residents may also enjoy the private Keswick Club which offers an eighteen hole Arnold Palmer signature golf course and other exceptional leisure facilities. As with all Ashley House properties Keswick Hall provides unobtrusive service from staff who genuinely delight in making guests feel at home.

Great dishes are created by our Chefs from a combination of European classic recipes and the best of modern cooking using fresh produce of the highest quality. A fascinating collection of wines from both the old and new worlds enhances the menus.

701 Club Drive,
Keswick, VA 22947
•
Tel 804 979 3440
Fax 804 977 4171
Freephone in US
800 Ashley 1
•
General Manager:
Stephen Beaumont
•
48 rooms including
4 one-bedroom suites
•
Tax 6.5%

Doubles and suites
$195 - $645
B&B
•
Outdoor and indoor pools, tennis, golf, conference facilities, full spa facilities including saunas, steam, exercise room, massage and facials.
Nearby: horseriding.
•
Children over 8 welcome
•
VS • MC • Amex • Diners

**VIRGINIA**

# L'AUBERGE PROVENCALE
## WHITE POST

Set on 10 acres in the heart of Virginia Hunt country is the culinary treasure L'Auberge Provencale. With extensive flower, herb, vegetable gardens and orchard, this premier country inn offers both charm and sophistication. Award winning Chef/Owner Alain Borel has been nationally and internationally acclaimed for his food. Dining in our intimate and romantic Four Diamond restaurant decorated with antiques, original art and Provencale ambience is an experience not to be missed.

Rooms are individually decorated with french charm and gracious timelessness, some with fireplaces, and included in your rate is a full gourmet breakfast. Relax on our spacious terrace with a glass of wine or enjoy one of our wonderful picnics as you tour the beautiful Blue Ridge countryside. Go horseback riding, canoeing, hiking or wine tasting at local vineyards.

L'Auberge Provencale is the inn where great expectations are quietly met.

P.O. Box 190,
White Post,
VA 22663
•
Tel 540 837 1375
Fax 540 837 2004
Freephone in US
800 638 1702
•
Owners:
Alain & Celeste Borel
•
10 rooms including
1 one bedroom,
1 two bedroom suite

Doubles $145 - $195
B&B
Suites $195 - $220
•
Tax 4.5%
•
Conference facilities.
Nearby: swimming, tennis,
golf, riding.
•
Children over 10 welcome
•
Non-smoking
•
VS • MC • Amex • Diners

VIRGINIA

# MORRISON HOUSE
## OLD TOWN ALEXANDRIA

The award-winning, Four Star, Four Diamond rated Morrison House resembles an 18th-century manor house combining the personalised service and warm atmosphere of an inn with the amenities of a larger hotel. Classic Federal-style architecture is complemented by interior design featuring mahogany four poster beds and Italian marble baths. Thoughtful touches such as robes, welcoming cookies and turndown service with chocolate, contribute to your welcome with a selection of things you might have forgotten to pack, kept in stock by the housekeeping department. Secretarial services and baby-sitting are also available. Enjoy the Elysium Dining Room for fine dining or the Elysium Grill for a club atmosphere, both featuring delicious Mediterranean-inspired cuisine.

Located in historic Old Town Alexandria, Morrison House is an easy walk to many historic landmarks, quaint shops and a wide range of restaurants. Ten minutes away, just across the river, are all the attractions of Washington DC, with National and Dulles Airports within easy reach.

116 South Alfred Street,
Alexandria,
VA 22314
•
Tel 703 838 8000
Fax 703 684 6283
Freephone in US
800 367 0800
•
Hotel Manager:
Wanda McKeon
•
45 rooms including
3 one-bedroom suites

Doubles $150 - $295 EP
Suites $295
•
Tax 9.5%
•
Conference, meeting
space for up to 45 people
•
Children welcome
•
Parking $6 per day
•
VS • MC
Amex • Diners

## VIRGINIA

# STAUNTON HILL COUNTRY INN
## BROOKNEAL

*The history of the Staunton Hill Plantation is tied to the accomplishments and personalities of the Bruce family. Under the ownership of Charles Bruce, State Senator, philanthropist and intellectual, one of the most valuable libraries in North America was founded and in 1861 he organised, equipped and financed a Confederate artillery which drilled on a cleared field called "Waterloo at Staunton Hill". In 1933, William Adams Delano was commissioned to build the last portico and landscape the gardens.*

*Today, several cottages with guest rooms; tennis and racquetball courts, pool, open air hot tub and exercise room, have been added to the Plantation House as has an up to date Conference Centre and an adjacent Bistro restaurant.*

*David S. Bruce, the latest generation of the family, returned from the Far East to Staunton Hill to develop a magnificent gathering place which visitors and guests leave with regret and with memories of a unique blend of history, landscape and graciousness.*

Rt 2, Box 244-B
Brookneal
VA 24528
•
Tel 804 376 4048
Fax 804 376 5929
•
Innkeeper:
Janet Bruce
•
20 rooms, 10 with private bath
including 10 one bedroom suites
3 cottages

Doubles $95 - $125 B&B
Suites & Cottages
$95 - $400
•
Tax 4.5% s.c. 15%
•
Outdoor pool., tennis, conference facilities
Nearby: golf
•
Children over 16 welcome.
•
Non-smoking
•
VS • MC • Amex

**VIRGINIA**

# TIDES INN
## IRVINGTON

Mr & Mrs E.A. Stephens opened The Tides Inn in 1947 with forty six rooms, a dining room, a bottle club and a dream. Locals by birth, entrepreneurs by spirit, they built the inn as something of a hobby after the war - "two amateurs with much enthusiasm and probably too much energy!". Energy which eventually yielded one of the world's finest resorts - a tranquil haven with a grand family tradition, an unrivalled quality of warmth and a loyal, long-serving staff, dedicated to ensuring your enjoyment.

Arrive by boat and you will find the soft beaches of the Tides Inn on the Chesapeake Bay's western shore, eight miles up the Rappahannock on Carter's Creek. By car, it is a splendidly scenic drive of just over an hour from Williamsburg or Richmond - and a million miles from your everyday worries. Join us for a moonlight cruise aboard our exquisite private yacht, indulge in 45 holes of championship golf, enjoy award-winning cuisine, partake of the many activities available at the inn or simply sit back in a chair and contemplate the serenity of your surroundings.

Box 480, King Carter Drive,
Irvington, VA 22480
•
Tel 804 438 5000
Fax 804 438 5222
Freephone in US
800 843 3746
•
President & General
Manager:
G. Michael Thomas CHA
•
111 rooms & suites
•
Doubles $250 - $408 MAP
Suites $388 - $744

Tax 4.5% s.c. $15 per person per day
•
Outdoor, saltwater heated pool, tennis, golf, yachting, small boat rentals, bicycles, games room, beach, conference facilities.
•
Children welcome, childrens' programmes available, free of charge June - August
•
VS • MC
Amex • Diners

**VIRGINIA**

# CHESTER HOUSE
## FRONT ROYAL

This stately, Georgian style mansion on two acres, now part of Front Royal's Historic District, features architectural details seldom seen today outside of museum houses. Crystal chandeliers, oriental rugs, artwork and family antiques blend the old with the new for a touch of comfortable elegance. Spacious bedrooms with private baths overlook the secluded, century old English gardens.

Special touches include homemade cookies, beverages and snacks, fresh flowers, turn-down service, bedside mints, robes, fine hand ironed linens and outstanding hospitality. Walk to antique and craft shops, historic attractions, wineries and excellent restaurants. Enjoy hiking, horseriding and canoeing and fishing on the Shenandoah River. A short drive to Skyline Drive (one mile) and only

| 43 Chester Street, Front Royal, VA 22630 | Tel 540 635 3937 Fax as above Freephone in US 800 621 0341 | Innkeepers: Ann & Bill Wilson 6 rooms, 4 with private bath, including 1 one-bedroom suite | Doubles $65 - $110 B&B Suite $135 Tax 10.5% | Free parking Nearby: outdoor pool, tennis, golf. | Children over 12 welcome Restricted smoking VS • MC • Amex |

# CLIFTON – THE COUNTRY INN
## CHARLOTTESVILLE

Clifton – The Country Inn offers guests a gracious escape: a chance to slip away to a less hurried Jeffersonian life. Every room has its own wood-burning fireplace, with firewood freshly laid, ready for the strike of a match. Guests are also warmed by down comforters on each of the antique beds. Each private bathroom is as individual and unique as the rooms themselves.

Warmer weather calls for use of the clay tennis court, swimming pool with waterfall, and heated spa. A short walk through the woods brings you to a private lake where oversized innertubes are perfect for a lazy float.

A highlight of your visit will be chef Craig Hartman's dinner. A graduate of the Culinary Institute of America, chef Hartman has been honored by the James Beard Foundation and the Wine Spectator.

| 1296 Clifton Drive, Charlottesville, VA 22901 | Tel 804 971 1800 Fax 804 971 7098 Innkeepers: Craig & Donna Hartman | 14 rooms including 7 one bedroom suites | Doubles $165 - $205 B&B Suites $215 - $225 | Tax 6.5% Outdoor pool, tennis, croquet, volleyball. | Well behaved children always welcome Non-smoking VS • MC |

**VIRGINIA**

# COLONIAL CAPITAL
## WILLIAMSBURG

*Warm hospitality awaits you in our AAA Three Diamond Bed & Breakfast just three blocks from the Colonial Williamsburg historic area.*

*Antiques, oriental rugs, cosy canopied beds and en suite baths blend charm, and elegance throughout this Colonial Revival (c. 1926) with modern comforts, gourmet breakfasts and afternoon tea and wine. Plantation parlour, screened porch, patio and deck await your enjoyment with friends old and new.*

*We're here to spoil you!*

501 Richmond Road,
Williamsburg,
VA 23185

Tel 757 229 0333
Fax 757 253 7667
Freephone in US
800 776 0570

Owners/Hosts:
Barbara & Phil Craig
5 rooms including
1 two-bedroom suite

Doubles $95 - $125, B&B
Suite $135 - $145
Additional person $20

Tax 8.5%
Lower tariffs Jan 1 - Mar 15
Children over 8 welcome

Free parking
No smoking indoors
VS • MC
Amex • Discover

---

# FREDERICK HOUSE
## STAUNTON

Made up of several connected buildings and ideally located for shops and restaurants, the Frederick House consists of several connected townhouses, originally built between 1810 and 1910. The warm and hospitable atmosphere at the inn is fostered by Joe and Evy and their staff who are always willing to offer assistance to travellers, with knowledgeable recommendations on places to eat, walking tours or mountain hiking or biking tours.

Rooms are comfortably furnished with period antiques and offer tv, phone, air-conditioning, ceiling fans and robes. There is a delightful flower-filled backyard. Breakfast is served in the inn's Chumley's Tea-room and includes fresh fruit, home-made breads, apple raisin quiche, waffles and syrup. For a small extra charge, exercise facilities and indoor swimming are available at an adjacent athletic club.

28 North New Street,
Staunton, VA 24401
Tel 540 885 4220
Freephone in US
800 334 5575

Owners:
Joe & Evy Harman
14 rooms including
5 one-bedroom suites,
2 two-bedroom suites.

5 bedroom, 3 bath cottage, 6 apartments with kitchens.

Doubles $65 - $105
B&B
Cottages & apartments $700 - $1800 per week EP

Tax 8.5%
Indoor pool
Children welcome

Non-smoking
VS • MC
Amex • Diners

57

**VIRGINIA**

# HENRY CLAY INN
## ASHLAND

Rebuilt in 1992 after fire destroyed its predecessor, the Henry Clay Inn combines the splendour of the original Georgian Revival building with modern comforts, fifteen spacious guest rooms decorated with floral and striped fabrics and a level of personal service that is exceptional. Early risers enjoy coffee in the upstairs parlour while downstairs a spacious Victorian style parlour/lobby and an oak-bannistered staircase welcomes guests. Homemade continental breakfast is included in the rates and a delightful extra touch is the art gallery featuring the work of local talents.

For the travelling businessman all rooms are fully equipped with phones and computer modem connections. For leisure travellers, the Inn is conveniently located 15 miles north of Richmond and 85 miles south of DC, making it an ideal base location for sightseeing in the area.

| | | | | | | |
|---|---|---|---|---|---|---|
| 114 North Railroad Avenue<br>Ashland, VA 23005<br>Tel 804 798 3100<br>Fax 804 752 7555 | Freephone in US<br>800 343 4565<br>General Manager/Innkeeper:<br>Carol Martin | 15 rooms including 1 one bedroom suite<br>Doubles $80 - $145 B&B | Suite $145<br>Tax 8.5%<br>Nearby: outdoor pool, tennis, golf, historic sites, amusement parks | Children welcome, does not meet the needs of babies. | Non-smoking<br>VS • MC • Amex |

# HOMESTAY
## WILLIAMSBURG

Cosy and convenient is this Colonial Revival home, furnished with turn-of-the-century family antiques and full of country charm whilst within easy reach of all the historic attractions.

A Noah's Ark collection enchants guests as they discover pieces in unusual locations all over the house. Relax with a lemonade on the porch or take a leisurely browse through the gardens.

Breakfast may include orange pecan pancakes, Virginia spoonbread or a pineapple soufflé.

| | | | | | |
|---|---|---|---|---|---|
| 517 Richmond Road, Williamsburg, VA 23185 | Tel 757 229 7468<br>Fax as above (call first)<br>Freephone in US<br>800 836 7468 | Innkeepers:<br>Barbara & Jim Thomassen<br>3 rooms | Doubles $75 - $90 B&B<br>Tax 8.5%<br>Free parking | Children over 10 welcome<br>Non-smoking<br>VS • MC |

58

**VIRGINIA**

# HUMMINGBIRD INN
## GOSHEN

From first view of white picket fence, unique Carpenter gothic facade, wrap-around two-storey verandas, and rose gardens, the Hummingbird Inn will be a case of love at first sight.

The original main room is now a welcoming rustic den, complete with open fireplace, and original pine flooring... a warm place to cosy up with a good book. In contrast, the rest of the Inn reflects the early Victorian era. The 1853 solarium, white wicker chairs bathed in sunlight, provides a tranquil area for morning coffee or afternoon tea. Spacious air-conditioned rooms with sitting areas combine old-fashioned ambience with modern convenience.

From "skip-lunch" full country breakfasts to romantic four-course continental candlelight dinners (complimentary wine), dining is a special experience. Goshen Pass, a spectacular rocky gorge, nearby historic Lexington and the beautiful Shenandoah Valley are among many area attractions.

| | | | | | |
|---|---|---|---|---|---|
| P.O. Box 147, Goshen, VA 24439 - 0147 | Tel 540 997 9065 Fax 540 997 0289 Freephone in US 800 397 3214 | Innkeepers: Diana & Jeremy Robinson | 5 rooms Doubles $70 - $95 B&B, $130 - $155 MAP (weekends only) | Tax 6.5% Children over 12 welcome | Non-smoking VS • MC Amex • Discover |

# INN AT GRISTMILL SQUARE
## WARM SPRINGS

In the picturesque village of Warm Springs on a babbling brook is a restored gristmill, the centrepiece of the five carefully restored 19th century buildings that make up the romantic and welcoming Inn at Gristmill Square.

What was once the mill is now the Waterwheel Restaurant offering delectable dinners each evening and a small pub for a relaxing drink and chat. The old blacksmith's shop houses the inn office and two guest rooms together with a small gift shop while the hardware store houses seven rooms and the Steel House once a private home, four more.

On the premises are three tennis courts and an outdoor pool. The historic Warm Springs pools for relaxing and rejuvenating thermal mineral bathing are just a mile away. The McWilliams family are always happy to advise you on all the local activities.

| | | | | | |
|---|---|---|---|---|---|
| Box 359, Warm Springs, VA 24484 Tel 540 839 2131 Fax 540 839 5770 | Innkeepers: The McWilliams Family | 17 rooms including 1 two bedroom suite 1 apartment | Doubles $80 - $100 B&B $150 - $170 MAP. Suite/apartment $140 EP. | Outdoor pool, tennis, conference facility for 40. Nearby: golf, horseriding, fishing, hunting, hiking. | Tax 4.5% Children welcome VS • MC • Discover |

**VIRGINIA**

# INN AT NARROW PASSAGE
## WOODSTOCK

This historic inn has welcomed travellers since the 1740's. The large common room features gleaming pine floors, wing chairs and massive limestone fireplace with hearty, fireside breakfasts served in the panelled dining room. Many nearby fine restaurants offer choices for other meals.

Older guest rooms have wood floors, stencilling and colonial atmosphere, more recent additions are decorated in similar style, but open onto porches, with views of the Shenandoah River and the Mountains. Fully air-conditioned, many of the rooms also have working fireplaces.

Enjoy hiking, riding, canoeing and fishing, wineries, antique shops, battlefields, caverns and traditional festivals. Relax and stroll along the country road from the inn, crossing the river to the foot of the mountain with the swinging footbridge adding a little excitement!

| PO Box 608, Woodstock, VA 22664 Tel 540 459 8000 Fax 540 459 8001 | Freephone in US 800 459 8002 Innkeepers: Ellen & Ed Markel | 12 rooms Doubles $85 - $110 B&B Tax 6.5% | Excellent fishing, small conference facilities | Nearby: outdoor pool, tennis, golf, riding, skiing. | Children welcome. Non-smoking VS • MC |

# LLEWELLYN LODGE AT LEXINGTON
## LEXINGTON

This charming brick colonial, is just a short walk to the historic district and many fine restaurants. Ellen and John Roberts offer comfort and a warm friendly atmosphere with country charm and a touch of class. Each morning while Ellen whips up a fabulous breakfast, John, a native Lexingtonian, will share his knowledge of the surrounding areas and particularly his secret fishing "holes".

After a day of touring – the Shenandoah Valley, historic Lexington home of Stonewall Jackson, Robert E. Lee Chapel and Museum – you'll be ready to relax in the Lodge's comfortable living room or in the tv room. Snuggle down with a book or enjoy good conversation in front of the roaring fire in winter. Relax outside on the deck and sip some iced tea in the summer months.

| 603 South Main Street, Lexington, VA 24450 | Tel 540 463 3235 Fax 540 464 3122 Freephone in US 800 882 1145 | Innkeepers: John & Ellen Roberts | 6 rooms Doubles $65 - $95 B&B Tax 7.5% | Nearby: outdoor pool, tennis, golf, horseriding, flyfishing, hiking and cycling – computerised routes and maps provided. | Children over 10 welcome Non-smoking VS • MC Amex • Diners |

**VIRGINIA**

# THE OAKS
## CHRISTIANSBURG

The warm hospitality and charm of Margaret and Tom Ray, comfortable elegance, romantic atmosphere and memorable breakfasts are the hallmark of this Four Diamond Victorian Inn.

Set on Christiansburg's highest hill in the beautiful mountain highlands of Southwest Virginia, the Oaks delights and welcomes leisure and business travellers from around the world. Surrounded by lawn, perennial gardens and 300 year old oak trees, the inn faces Main Street, once part of the Wilderness Trail blazed by American legends Daniel Boone and Davey Crockett.

A five hour drive from Washington, two miles from I-81 and only 26 miles from the Blue Ridge Parkway, perhaps America's most beautiful scenic highway, makes the Oaks a perfect stopover or destination. Relish the hospitality of small-town America.

| | | | | | |
|---|---|---|---|---|---|
| 311 East Main Street, Christiansburg, VA 24073 | Tel 540 381 1500<br>Fax 540 382 1728<br>Freephone in US<br>800 336 6257 | Owner/Innkeepers:<br>Margaret & Tom Ray<br>5 rooms | Doubles $115 - $150<br>B&B<br>Tax 8.5% s/c 10%<br>Meeting facilities for 12 | Nearby: swimming, tennis, golf, biking and hiking, fishing and boating.<br>Non-smoking | Children over 12 welcome<br>VS • MC<br>Amex • Discover |

# SEVEN HILLS INN
## LEXINGTON

A classic white-columned, brick Southern-style colonial mansion in historic Lexington at the heart of the Shenandoah Valley, surrounded and framed by the magnificent Blue Ridge and Allegheny mountains. Each of the seven comfortably furnished rooms is evocatively named after one of Rockbridge County's lovely 18th and 19th Century homesteads and farms - respectively, Fruit, Hickory, Rose, Clover, Holly, Cherry and Liberty Hill. Several of these were built by Captain John Grigsby, a forbear of the current owners.

Guests can relax in the large living room with fireplace, adjoining family library or on the large front porch overlooking landscaped grounds. The downtown location of Seven Hills makes the attractions of Lexington such as the Washington and Lee University, Virginia Military Institute, the Virginia Horse Center and the many civil war landmarks easily reachable, as are fine restaurants and charming shops.

| | | | | | |
|---|---|---|---|---|---|
| 408 South Main St, Lexington, Virginia<br>Tel 540 463 4715<br>Fax 540 463 6126 | Freephone in US<br>888 845 3801<br>Executive Innkeeper:<br>Jane Grigsby Daniel | 7 rooms<br>including 1 one bedroom suite, 1 two bedroom suite<br>Doubles $75 - $125 | B&B<br>Suites $160 - $180<br>Tax 7.5% | Nearby: outdoor pool, horse riding<br>Children welcome. | Smoking in designated areas<br>VS•MC•Amex |

## VIRGINIA

# STEELES TAVERN MANOR
### STEELES TAVERN

*Seeking the serenity of the country and the splendour of the mountains? We invite you to spend a few nights. Each bedroom offers a queen or king sized bed along with antique furniture, comfortable sitting areas and modern conveniences such as televisions, video recorders and a video library. View the majestic Blue Ridge Mountains and our scenic pond from your private haven in the Dahlia room, turn back the hands of time in the Buttercup Room.*

*Breakfast is a special time at Steeles Tavern Manor with fine china, classical music excellent food and friendly conversation and what's a B&B without afternoon tea! Refreshments are served each day between 4 and 5 p.m. after a day spent golfing, birdwatching, hiking along our creek or fishing in our stocked pond (worms & rods provided). Plan a visit to Steeles Tavern Manor, take a step back to a quieter time.*

| | | | | |
|---|---|---|---|---|
| Hwy 11, P.O. Box 39, Steeles Tavern, VA 24476 | Tel 540 377 6444<br>Fax 540 377 5937<br>Owners/Innkeepers:<br>Eileen & Bill Hoernlein | 5 rooms including 2 one-bedroom suites | Doubles, Suites<br>$95 - $140<br>B&B<br>Tax 6.5% | Dinner available Friday and Saturday<br>Children over 14 welcome | Non-smoking<br>VS • MC |

---

# TRILLIUM HOUSE
### NELLYSFORD

A country inn in the Devils Knob Village of Wintergreen (11,000 acres high in the Blue Ridge Mountains). Trillium House was designed and built in '83 as a small self-contained 12 room country hotel. Space and light have been cleverly combined to create in Trillium House a uniquely welcoming atmosphere year-round. All guest rooms have private baths with individually controlled heating and cooling. Relax alone or with other guests in the great room, garden room, tv room or the outstanding library.

The dining room looks out to professional bird feeding and the 17th hole of the Devils Knob golf course. Available to guests at preferred rates are two golf courses, four swimming pools, thirty tennis courts, 25 miles of mapped hiking trails, and downhill skiing in season. The entry gate to the Wintergreen Mountain Village is one mile from the Blue Ridge Parkway.

| | | | | | |
|---|---|---|---|---|---|
| PO Box 280A, Nellysford, VA 22958 | Tel 804 325 9169<br>Fax 804 325 1099<br>Freephone in US<br>800 325 9126 | Innkeepers:<br>Ed & Betty Dinwiddie<br>12 rooms including 2 one-bedroom suites | Doubles $90 - $105<br>B&B<br>Suites $120 - $150<br>Tax 6.5%. Food and beverage tax 4% | Small conference facilities. Nearby: indoor and outdoor pools, tennis, golf, riding, fishing, hiking. | Well-behaved children always welcome<br>Non-smoking<br>VS • MC |

# WASHINGTON DC

# GEORGE WASHINGTON UNIVERSITY INN

The George Washington University Inn (formerly The Inn at Foggy Bottom) is a newly renovated and upgraded boutique style hotel. We offer a charming and intimate atmosphere suitable for both the corporate and leisure traveller.

With the personalised and courteous service found only in smaller properties, we are ideally located on a quaint residential street of historic homes close to Georgetown, The Kennedy Center, The George Washington University and a mere two blocks from the Foggy Bottom Metro Rail Station.

Guest rooms are spacious and elegantly furnished. King size beds or two full size beds are available. Each guest room has a mini refrigerator, microwave, coffee maker, iron and ironing board. Fully equipped kitchenettes are also available. Guests will enjoy morning delivery of the Washington Post and evening turndown service with chocolates.

In addition there is a conference room available for meetings up to 35 people. A restaurant is located on the premises for guest convenience.

824 New Hampshire
Avenue NW,
Washington DC 20037

•

Tel 202 337 6620
Fax 202 337 2540
Freephone in US
800 426 4255

•

General Manager:
Steve Seeger

•

95 rooms including
31 one-bedroom suites
16 studios with kitchenettes

Doubles $105 - $155 EP
Suites and Studios
$125 - $195

•

Tax 13% + $1.50 occupancy
tax per room per night

•

Conference facilities

•

Children welcome

•

Non-smoking
rooms available

VS • MC • Amex • Diners

## WASHINGTON DC

# EMBASSY INN
### WASHINGTON DC

The Embassy Inn is a unique and charming alternative to the larger DC hotels. Our guests enjoy the convenience and great location of a hotel with the atmosphere of a bed and breakfast inn. Rooms offer direct dial phones, cable tv, all private bathrooms and radio alarm clocks. Close to metro, White House, sights and restaurants, the Embassy Inn offers complimentary continental breakfast, newspaper, evening sherry and snacks to guests.

Built in 1910 as an apartment house, converted into a tourist hotel in 1919 and renovated in 1987, the Embassy Inn tries to maintain the intimate atmosphere of days gone by. At the same time we like to offer the conveniences of fax and copier service, valet dry cleaning and a 24 hour desk.

| 1627 16th St. NW, Washington DC 20009 | Tel 202 234 7700 Fax 202 234 3309 Freephone in US 800 423 9111 | General Manager: Susan Stiles | 38 rooms Doubles $79 - $110 B&B Tax 13% | s/c $1.50 per night On-street parking available Children welcome | Non smoking rooms available VS • MC Amex • Diners |
|---|---|---|---|---|---|

# NORMANDY INN
### WASHINGTON DC

The Normandy Inn welcomes business travellers or sightseers with gracious old-world charm. This intimate 75-room hotel, in a cosmopolitan embassy neighbourhood, lies at the threshold of Washington's business and government districts. The Capital's famous sites, finest dining and fashionable shopping are within easy reach. Guest rooms, designed to create a comfortable retreat, are appointed with direct dial phone, cable tv, refrigerator, beverage maker and generous supply of bath amenities. The lounge is an inviting spot to rendezvous or relax, select a book from our library and settle by the fireplace with coffee and complimentary cookies. Each Tuesday, guests are invited to a complimentary wine and cheese reception. Continental breakfast is available. Whether business or pleasure brings you to Washington, you will find the Normandy Inn a delightful refuge.

| 2118 Wyoming Avenue, Washington DC | Tel 202 483 1350 Fax 202 387 8241 Freephone in US 800 424 3729 | General Manager: Peter Hilary | 75 rooms Doubles $79 - $113 EP Tax 13% Occupancy tax $1.50 | Parking available at $10 per day Children welcome | Non-smoking rooms available VS • MC • Amex Diners • Discover |
|---|---|---|---|---|---|

### WASHINGTON DC

# WINDSOR INN
### WASHINGTON DC

The Windsor Inn offers a variety of room options from suites to economical twin bed accommodations. We are located in the heart of Washington, close to metro, sights, the White House, and a variety of restaurants and unique shops. Our goal is to provide a comfortable, relaxed and homey atmosphere as well as great service and information on the many attractions of DC.

An expanded continental breakfast, newspapers and evening sherry are included in the rates. Rooms are equipped with private bathrooms, cable tv, movies and direct dial phones. Since we are small, we can give guests personalised attention and a secure environment in which to enjoy their stay.

If you enjoy the convenience of a hotel but the friendly charm of a bed and breakfast, then the Windsor Inn is ideal.

| | | | | | |
|---|---|---|---|---|---|
| 1842 16th St. NW, Washington DC 20009 | Tel 202 667 0300<br>Fax 202 667 4503<br>Freephone in US<br>800 423 9111 | General Manager:<br>Susan Stiles | 46 rooms<br>1 one-bedroom suite<br>Doubles $69 - $150<br>B&B | Tax 13%<br>s/c $1.50 per night<br>Children welcome | No smoking rooms available<br>VS • MC<br>Amex • Diners |

## The Welcome Privilege Card
## A SELECTION OF PROMISES

**EASTERN CANADA**
**ONTARIO**
*LITTLE INN OF BAYFIELD,
Bayfield, Ontario
*Stay 2nights on an MAP package and receive 3rd third night, accommodation only, free.

**QUEBEC**
*RIPPLECOVE INN,
North Hatley, Quebec
*Free room upgrade valid all year excl Holidays.

**MID ATLANTIC STATES**
**NEW JERSEY**
*CHIMNEY HILL BED & BREAKFAST
Lambertville, New Jersey
*Stay 2 nights and receive the 3rd night free, available any season but excludes Holiday Weekends.

**PENNSYLVANIA**
*EVERMAY ON THE DELAWARE
Erwinna, Pennsylvania
*Stay 2 nights, get 3rd night at a special privilege rate. Excluding weekends and Holidays
*Special celebration recognition for a birthday, anniversary or honeymoon.
**FRENCH MANOR**
South Sterling, Pennsylvania
*Special seasonal arrival gift
**WEDGWOOD HISTORIC INNS,**
New Hope, Pennsylvania
*Stay 4 nights get 5th night at 50%.
*Discount vouchers at Bucks Country Playhouse and other area attractions

*Welcome Privilege Cards are valid for one year from date of issue. One Card entitles a family or group of up to four people travelling together to relevant benefits. The Privilege Card is available for separate purchase at a cost of £10.00/$17.00 per card. All offers are subject to availability.

# WEST VIRGINIA

## COUNTRY INN
### BERKELEY SPRINGS

Nestled in the centre of the small historic town of Berkeley Springs, the 1832 Country Inn has continuously served the travelling public in a style befitting colonial days. Our motto "Retaining the Best of the Past", is practised each day.

A large lobby surrounded by antiques and fine art welcomes guests while the porches, rocking chairs and delightful gardens beckon them to spend some time relaxing and taking in the view. Dining is in two large and lovely dining rooms which feature live music at the weekends.

The Renaissance Spa sits high on the hill. Take advantage of the pure healthful spring water for which the town is named and enjoy whirlpool baths, massage, facials, manicure, pedicure and various other beauty treatments. Antique shops, park and theatre are only a short walk from the inn.

207 S. Washington Street,
Berkeley Springs, WV 25411
•
Tel 304 258 2210
Fax 304 258 3986
Freephone in US
800 822 6630
•
Innkeepers:
Jack & Alice Barker
•
70 rooms
(14 without bath en suite)
including 1 one bedroom,
1 two bedroom suite

Doubles $40 - $90 EP
Suites $105 - $145
•
Tax 6%
•
Spa facilities
Nearby: swimming,
golf, horseriding.
•
Children over
8 welcome
•
Non-smoking
•
VS • MC • Amex • Diners

## WEST VIRGINIA

# HILLBROOK INN
## CHARLES TOWN

*Gardens bursting with colour, a meandering stream, ducks on the pond, a hammock in the sun, the golden colours of autumn or the beauty of a winter storm when you are warm inside - Hillbrook is an inn for all seasons.*

*Built on a series of limestone ridges this small luxurious inn flows and blends into the landscape with cunningly contrived, imaginatively designed and decorated, cosy rooms all with delightful views, sitting areas and air-conditioning, some with working fireplaces.*

*Serving exceptional seven course dinners by candlelight, a delicious three course prix-fixe lunch or a splendid high tea from November through April, Hillbrook offers guests a chance to delight both the palate and the eye.*

Rt 2, Box 152,
Charles Town, WV 25414

•

Tel 304 725 4223
Fax 304 725 4455
Freephone in US
800 304 4223

•

Owner/Innkeeper:
Gretchen Carroll
Manager: Nadia Hill

•

6 rooms & suites

•

Doubles & suites
$198 - $400 MAP

Tax 3% room, 6% sales.
s.c. 15%

•

17 acres of gardens and
walking paths
Nearby: Harpers Ferry
National Park, golf,
riding.

•

Children over 12 welcome.

•

Non-smoking

•

VS • MC
Diners • Discover

# Connecticut

1. Bee & Thistle — 69
2. The Boulders — 70
3. Brigadoon — 74
4. Griswold Inn — 74
5. Homestead Inn (Greenwich) — 71
6. Homestead Inn (New Milford) — 75
7. Inn at National Hall — 72
8. Manor House — 75
9. Norwich Inn & Spa — 73
10. Old Mystic Inn — 76
11. Riverwind Inn — 76
12. White Hart Inn — 77

## CONNECTICUT

# BEE & THISTLE INN
## OLD LYME

The Bee & Thistle Inn, built in 1756, and described as the "Quintessential American Inn" by the London Financial Times sits on five tree shaded acres along the Lieutenant River in the charming historic district of Old Lyme. It is bordered by stone walls, containing a sunken English perennial garden and is next to the Florence Griswold Museum, the home of American Impressionist art.

Eleven antique filled guest rooms and parlors offer a warm and comfortable place to pause for a moment from today's hectic pace of living. Its three star restaurant has been voted the "Most Romantic" place to dine in Connecticut for eight straight years by the readers of Connecticut Magazine.

An easy two hour drive from New York or Boston, will bring you to the inn. Let us share with you the hospitality and warmth of our home. Truly experience a return to early American gracious living.

100 Lyme Street,
Old Lyme, CT 06371
•
Tel 860 434 1667
Fax 860 434 3402
Freephone in US
800 622 4946
•
Innkeepers:
Bob, Penny,
Lori & Jeff Nelson
•
11 rooms
including
1 one bedroom cottage

Doubles $69 - $140 EP
Cottage $195
•
Tax 12%
•
Nearby: tennis, golf, horseriding, sailing, fitness center, hiking
•
Children over
12 welcome
•
VS • MC
Amex • Diners

**CONNECTICUT**

# THE BOULDERS
## NEW PRESTON

Nestled in the Litchfield Hills, the Boulders Inn was built in 1895 as a private residence. This architecturally striking Victorian home combines mansion-like elegance with the warmth of the country. In the 40-plus years of its existence as an inn, it has established an outstanding reputation, receiving countless kudos from respected national publications such as the New York Times, The Wine Spectator, Travel and Leisure Magazine, Country Inns and B&B Magazine etc.

Set at the foot of Pinnacle Mountain, guests can view breathtaking sunsets over Lake Waramaug, while enjoying the renowned cuisine in the glass-enclosed Lake Room, the outdoor terraces or relaxing by a fire. Beach, boats, tennis court and bicycles are available to guests. A hike up Pinnacle Mountain is rewarded with a spectacular vista of the Lake and surrounding mountains.

Dutch born Kees Adema & his German wife Ulla run the inn with relaxed European flair. In 1991 the Boulders received the much coveted "10 Best Country Inns of the Year" award.

East Shore Road,
(Rt 45)
New Preston,
CT 06777
•
Tel 860 868 0541
Fax 860 868 1925
Freephone in US
800 55 Boulders
•
Innkeepers:
Kees & Ulla Adema

15 rooms/guesthouses
including
2 one bedroom suites
•
Doubles $250 – $350
MAP
Suites $285 - $350
•
Tax 9.6%. s.c. 15%
•
Tennis, sailing, hiking
•
VS • MC • Amex

**CONNECTICUT**

# HOMESTEAD INN
## GREENWICH

*Set among graceful trees and sweeping lawns in exclusive Belle Haven, just 45 minutes from New York City, the Homestead Inn's elegant facade invites the traveller to pause and savour the joys of a simpler time and place.*

*Each of the bedrooms in our three historic buildings reflects the romance and style of another era, many have canopy beds, and all are decorated in a simple yet elegant manner. Blending in with the many antiques are such civilised amenities as electric blankets, good reading lights, colour tv and clock radios.*

*A lovely old hydrangea bush drapes the front porch of the Main House, providing a shady nook for a cosy tête-à-tête on blue cushioned, white wicker settees. Fresh lemonade on warm, sunny afternoons encourages relaxation and renewal or enjoy the little Backgammon Room with its softly glowing fireplace in winter and The Chocolate Bar, an exceptionally pleasant spot for a quiet drink.*

420 Field Point Road
Greenwich
CT 06830
•
Tel: 203 869 7500
Fax: 203 869 7500
•
Co-owners
Lessie Davison &
Nancy Smith
•
23 rooms
including 6 one
bedroom suites.

Doubles: $127 - $185
B&B
Suites: $160 - $185
•
Tax 12%. s.c. 6%
•
Conference facilities
•
Children welcome.
•
VS • MC
Amex • Diners

**CONNECTICUT**

# INN AT NATIONAL HALL
## WESTPORT

Fashioned after Europe's elite Manor Houses, the deluxe Inn at National Hall invites you to journey into the rich heritage of yesteryear. Built in 1873, it displays a delightful mix of whimsy, privacy, and history blended together to create the perfect setting for your Westport visit. The inn is comprised of fifteen individually decorated rooms and suites, a large first class restaurant, awarded a Four Star rating by the New York Times, and a resident's drawing room. The hotel is a member of Relais and Chateaux.

Selected chambers feature soaring two-storey ceilings with loft bedrooms enhanced by expansive windows and sweeping river views.

Westport, an easy drive from New York, offers visitors an abundance of stimulating cultural and recreational activities. Art and antique galleries attract collectors from far and wide, theatre flourishes, and the area's lively calendar bursts with exciting events year round.

Two Post Road West,
Westport,
CT 06880

•

Tel 203 221 1351
Fax 203 221 0276
Freephone in US
800 NAT HALL

•

General Manager:
Nick Carter M.V.O.

•

Non-smoking

•

8 rooms
7 one bedroom suites

Doubles $195 - $395
B&B
Suites $325 - $475

•

Tax 12%

•

Conference facility for
up to 16 people.

•

Nearby: fitness center
and pool

•

VS • MC
Amex • Diners

**CONNECTICUT**

# NORWICH INN & SPA
## NORWICH

Set amidst forty acres of lush gardens and woodlands with spring fed ponds, this historic Georgian style inn reflects an era of quiet refinement. From charming inn rooms to private villas accented with Ralph Lauren fabrics and prints, the Norwich Inn & Spa is the perfect New England country retreat.

Superb dining, delicious and satisfying Spa cuisine and a professional and attentive staff devoted to the guests' ultimate pleasure are all part of the experience. Relax and revitalize, set your own pace and indulge body and mind in a selection of fitness classes and pampering spa treatments that will leave you with a fresh outlook on life.

Within easy driving distance from New York City, Boston and Newport and convenient to trains and airline services. Minutes from Old Mystic Seaport, many historic sites, shops, antiques, and gambling at nearby Foxwoods and Mohican Sun Casinos.

607 West Thames St,
Norwich,
CT 06360
•
Tel 860 886 2401
Fax 860 886 9299
Freephone in US
800 275 4772
•
Vice President of
Operations:
Mark Vinchesi
•
30 inn rooms, 70 villas

Doubles $85 - $220 EP
Villas $220 - $245
•
Tax 12%
•
Outdoor & indoor pools,
tennis, golf, conference
facilities
•
Does not meet the
needs of children.
•
Non-smoking
•
VS • MC
Amex • Diners

**CONNECTICUT**

# BRIGADOON
## MYSTIC

Experience the relaxed, friendly atmosphere of a 250-year-old Victorian farmhouse just 1.3 miles from town. Enjoy our famous country breakfasts and afternoon tea, served by a roaring fire in winter or in the shade of an old dogwood tree in summer. Relax in our eight air-conditioned bedrooms, all with private baths and king or queen beds. Visit with other guests in our keeping room where complimentary wine is served nightly, or enjoy the large colour tv and vcr, books, games, magazines and movies provided for your pleasure.

Both Kay and Ted are avid travellers and love to compare notes with their guests, who come to Brigadoon from all over the world. They are dedicated to providing comfortable rooms, good food and genuine hospitality.

| 180 Cow Hill Road, Mystic, CT 06355 Tel 860 536 3033 Fax 860 536 1628 | Owners/Innkeepers: Kay & Ted Lucas 8 rooms | Doubles $75 - $140 B&B including afternoon tea and evening beverage | Tax 12% Nearby: outdoor & indoor pools, tennis, golf, riding, sailing, | conference facilities, down-hill skiing, cross-country skiing Children over 5 welcome. | Non-smoking VS • MC • Amex |

# GRISWOLD INN
## ESSEX

The Griswold Inn. More than a country hotel, more than a comfortable bed, an extraordinary meal, or a superb drink, the "Gris" is what Essex is all about. It embodies a spirit understood perhaps only as one warms up to its potbelly stove, or is hypnotized by the magic of a crackling log in one of its many fireplaces. It is a kaleidoscope of nostalgic images: a lovely country place. A myriad of Currier and Ives steamboat prints. A taproom described as the most handsome bar-room in America. A library of fire-arms dating from the 15th century. A group of charming dining rooms from which marvellous aromas and smiling faces flow. An historic collection of Antonio Jacobsen marine art. A gentle smile and a helping hand from a waitress. An affable bartender. A cuisine unmatched for its authenticity and purity.

| 36 Main Street, Essex, CT 06426 | Tel 860 767 1776 Fax 860 767 0381 | Innkeepers: Gregory, Douglas & Geoffrey Paul | 27 rooms including 14 suites Doubles $95 EP Suites $105 - $185 | Tax 12% Conference facilities. Nearby: tennis, golf, sailing, horseriding | Children welcome VS • MC • Amex |

**CONNECTICUT**

# HOMESTEAD INN
## NEW MILFORD

Located just off the Village Green in the centre of New Milford, in a restored Victorian home, the Homestead Bed & Breakfast Inn offers comfortable rooms with phones, tv, desks, air conditioning and a warm welcome.

There is a hearty continental buffet breakfast served in the living room, tea and coffee are available on request any time during the day or evening.

Rolf, Peggy and their staff are dedicated to making your stay special. The atmosphere here is friendly, relaxed and homelike with the opportunity to mix with other guests if you choose, but plenty of space to allow privacy if you prefer. The inn holds the AAA Three Diamond rating.

| 5 Elm Street, New Milford, CT 06776 | Tel 860 354 4080 Fax 860 354 7046 | Owner/Innkeepers: Rolf & Peggy Hammer | 14 rooms, in main inn and annexe | Doubles $76 – $99 B&B Tax 12% | Children welcome VS • MC • Amex |

# MANOR HOUSE
## NORFOLK

Set on a quiet country road, with five acres of flower-filled gardens and a gazebo, the Manor House is within walking distance of the village and within easy reach of sporting activities and cultural events. Individually decorated rooms are special retreats and romantic getaways, amenities include fireplaces, canopy beds and private balconies.

The interior of the Manor has a traditional look with extensive cherry panelling, while the living room with its six foot fireplace and stunning Tiffany windows is the perfect spot to relax with a book from the extensive library or CD collection. Refreshments are available throughout the day. Delights at breakfast include homemade bread, poached egg with lemon-butter-chive sauce, bacon, banana pancakes and honey from the inn's own hives.

| 69 Maple Avenue, PO Box 447, Norfolk, CT 06058 | Tel /Fax 860 542 5290 | Innkeepers: Henry & Diane Tremblay 8 rooms | Doubles $95 – $175 B&B Tax 12% | Nearby: tennis, golf, horseriding, skiing, private lake for swimming | Non-smoking Children over 8 welcome. VS • MC • Amex |

**CONNECTICUT**

# OLD MYSTIC INN
## OLD MYSTIC

The warmth of a cosy fire and the aroma of freshly baked cookies welcome guests arriving at this 1784 Inn, built when Mystic was noted for whaling, fishing and ship-building.

Eight guest rooms with queen size beds and private baths, each named after a New England author, all have special touches to make you feel at home. Three rooms have working fireplaces and two have whirlpool tubs. Most rooms are hand-stencilled and many have canopy beds.

A complimentary full country breakfast served each morning in our cheery dining room will be the highlight of your day. Saturday evenings bring good cheer and conversation with complimentary wine and cheese. A wealth of attractions, including Mystic Seaport and Marinelife Aquarium, are minutes from the Inn.

52 Main Street, Old Mystic, CT 06372-0633
Tel 860 572 9422

Innkeepers: Mary & Peter Knight
8 rooms

Doubles $115 - $145
B&B
Tax 12%

Nearby: tennis, golf, riding, sailing, conference facilities

Children over 8 welcome.

Non-smoking
VS • MC • Amex

# RIVERWIND INN
## DEEP RIVER

Relax, step back in time and enjoy a stay amid an enchanting collection of New England and Southern country antiques. With eight delightful guest rooms and numerous common rooms there is ample opportunity for mingling or privacy. Four of these rooms boast fireplaces, including a breathtaking twelve-foot stone cooking fireplace in the 18th century keeping room.

Opt for a glass of sherry in the front parlour with its piano, choose a game from the trophy room where George, the Inn's resident deer, keeps stately watch over the antique checkerboard, or simply select a book from the library and curl up before the fire in the spacious upstairs study. Wonderfully appointed guest rooms, rambling common areas and informal country atmosphere, mean that Riverwind is more than just a place to stay – it's a destination!

209 Main Street, Deep River, CT 06417

Tel 860 526 2014
Innkeeper/Owners: Barbara Barlow, Bob Bucknall

8 rooms
1 two bedroom cottage with fully equipped kitchen

Doubles $90 - $155
B&B
Cottage $200 - $300
EP

Tax 12%
Nearby tennis and golf.

Children welcome in cottage suites
VS • MC • Amex

**CONNECTICUT**

# WHITE HART INN
## SALISBURY

*Welcome to the White Hart, in a picture perfect New England town at the foothills of the Berkshires. All of the Inn's rooms have been completely redecorated and feature private baths, cable tv, telephones and air-conditioning. We are proud that we have frequently been recognised for our dedication to fine food and wine, including an "excellent" rating from the New York Times. Breakfast, lunch and a light dinner are served in the Garden Room and in the historic tavern. Julie's New American Sea Grill is our showcase restaurant for dinner and Sunday brunch.*

*A short walk from local shops, with nearby swimming, boating, golf, skiing and hiking. Northwestern Connecticut and the adjacent Berkshires offer a wealth of festivals, Summer theatre and antiquing, as well as Tanglewood and the Jacob's Pillow Dance Festival. Please join us!*

| | | | | | | |
|---|---|---|---|---|---|---|
| The Village Green, (Rt 44) Salisbury, CT 06068, | Tel 860 435 0030 Fax 860 435 0040 Freephone in US 800 832 0041 | Innkeepers: Terry & Juliet Moore 26 rooms including 3 one bedroom suites. | Doubles $90 - $165 EP Suites $175 - $190 | Tax 12% Nearby: tennis, golf, horseriding, sailing, fitness center, hiking | Conference, function and wedding facilities VS • MC Amex • Diners |

---

# THE BEST INSPECTORS ARE OUR GUESTS!

**Your feedback is the basis on which our business is built.**

**Were your expectations met?
Was the welcome warm?
Did you feel you received good value for the money you spent?**

It is vital to maintain the excellent standard of U.S. Welcome's Selected Hotels and Inns and your input is of great value to us. If you have a moment, please write, call, fax or email and let us know what you think of the hotels and inns in which you stayed.

U.S. Welcome Limited
FREEPOST (HA 4595) Northwood, England, HA6 3BR
Tel (0)1895 622233   Fax (0)1895 622244
mail@uswelcome.com    www.uswelcome.com
Freephone in the U.S. 888 INN VISIT

# Maine

| | | | |
|---|---|---|---|
| 1 | Andrews Lodging | | 90 |
| 2 | Bagley House | | 90 |
| 3 | Bar Harbor Hotel-Bluenose Inn | | 79 |
| 4 | Bayview Hotel | | 80 |
| 5 | Black Point Inn | | 81 |
| 6 | Blue Harbor House | | 91 |
| 7 | Blue Hill Inn | | 91 |
| 8 | Captain Daniel Stone Inn | | 82 |
| 9 | Captain Lindsey House Inn | | 92 |
| 10 | Captain Lord Mansion | | 83 |
| 11 | Dockside Guest Quarters | | 92 |
| 12 | Gorges Grant Hotel | | 84 |
| 13 | Greenville Inn | | 93 |
| 14 | Harraseeket Inn | | 85 |
| 15 | Inn By The Sea | | 86 |
| 16 | Kennebunkport Inn | | 93 |
| 17 | Lawnmeer Inn | | 94 |
| 18 | Lodge at Moosehead Lake | | 94 |
| 19 | Maine Stay Inn | | 95 |
| 20 | Maine Stay Inn & Cottages | | 95 |
| 21 | Mira Monte Inn | | 96 |
| 22 | Newcastle Inn | | 96 |
| 23 | Ocean Gate | | 97 |
| 24 | Ocean Point Inn | | 97 |
| 25 | Spruce Point Inn | | 87 |
| 26 | Stage Neck Inn | | 88 |
| 27 | Sugarloaf | | 89 |
| 28 | York Harbor Inn | | 98 |

## MAINE

# BAR HARBOR HOTEL - BLUENOSE INN
### BAR HARBOR

Escape to the privacy of America's most beautiful island - Mount Desert. Atop a granite-terraced hillside, the Bar Harbor Hotel-Bluenose Inn offers breathtaking views of sparkling Frenchman Bay and, surrounded by Acadia National Park - a symphony of natural beauty - is only 600 yards to the famed Bluenose Ferry Terminal. Although set aside from bustling Bar Harbor, guests may enjoy a leisurely stroll to its shops, museums, concerts, boat tours, beaches, and mountains.

The Hotel is distinguished by two guest buildings: the Mizzentop and Stenna Nordica feature 97 immaculate rooms and 2-person suites with air conditioning and mini-refrigerator - many with romantic fireplaces. Also featured are the charming Rose Garden Restaurant - distinctive dining, casual attire; the magnificent Great Room & Bar; Raspbeary's Gift Shop; our elegant indoor pool; spa; fitness centre; outdoor heated pool, and rolling garden paths.

We're proud of our long-time AAA Four Diamond Award for Excellence and honoured to be the only resort in Bar Harbor to receive a Four Star rating in the Mobil Travel Guide.

90 Eden Street,
Bar Harbor,
ME 04609
•
Tel 207 288 3348
Fax 207 288 2183
Freephone in US
800 445 4077
•
Owner:
Edward & Judy
Hemmingsen
•
97 rooms
including 30 one bedroom
suites.

Doubles  $88 - $248 EP
•
Tax  7%
•
Outdoor & indoor pools,
conference facilities
Nearby: tennis, golf,
riding, sailing
•
Children welcome.
•
Non-smoking
•
VS • MC

## MAINE

# BAYVIEW HOTEL
### BAR HARBOR

Down a long winding drive The Bayview offers privacy and serenity with unsurpassed ocean views. The choice of accommodation is varied between the original Bayview Inn, built in 1930 and our modern Hotel and Townhomes built in 1985. All provide the modern luxuries you expect while maintaining the charm of a bygone era. We are small enough to be attentive to your wishes, yet your privacy is always assured.

Enjoy a delicious meal in our gourmet restaurant. Our creative chef prepares exceptional regional cuisine using only the finest ingredients. The restaurant is open daily serving breakfast and dinner.

Our location is convenient to beautiful Acadia National Park and all area attractions. Close by you will find golfing, boating, biking and sightseeing. Spend an afternoon swimming in our oceanfront pool, playing a game of tennis, or just relaxing on our secluded property. The Bayview holds the AAA Four Diamond award and is conveniently located on rt 3, one mile from downtown.

111 Eden Street,
Bar Harbor,
ME 04609
•
Tel 207 288 5861
Fax 207 288 3173
Freephone in US
800 356 3585
•
Manager: Trish Nolan
•
31 rooms
1 one bedroom suite
two and three bedroom townhomes

Doubles $95 - $240 B&B
Suite, townhomes
$135 - $440
•
Tax 7%
•
Indoor and outdoor pools,
tennis, hiking.
Nearby: golf,
horseriding, sailing
•
Children welcomed in hotel
and townhomes
•
VS • MC • Amex • Diners

## MAINE

# BLACK POINT INN RESORT
## SCARBOROUGH

The Black Point Inn is one of America's few remaining resort-inns, and still offers modified or full American meal plan. Awarded Four Diamonds by the AAA, it is unpretentious elegance, recognised the world over.

Accommodations offer spectacular views and vistas. At night you will hear the nearby ocean as waves crash against cliffs or breakers slowly roll across the beaches. A fire crackles in the main lobby.

Fifteen minutes from the centre of Portland, on historic Prout's Neck, come for the unspoiled ocean vistas, rugged cliffs, sheltered sandy beaches and wooded areas fragrant with the smell of pines and balsams.

Enjoy the finest Maine has to offer. Get away from responsibility and routine and let us cater to your every whim. Spend days on white sandy beaches, evenings enjoying gourmet dining. Discover Maine this year!

510 Black Point Road,
Scarborough,
ME 04074
•
Tel 207 883 4126
Fax 207 883 9976
Freephone in US
800 258 0003
•
Owner:
Normand Dugas
•
75 rooms
7 one bedroom suites

Doubles $250 - $375
MAP
Suites $350 - $450
•
Tax 7%. s.c. 15%
•
Indoor and outdoor pools, tennis, golf, sailing, fitness center, bikes available, boat trips, conference facilities
•
Children over 8 welcome
•
VS • MC • Amex

**MAINE**

# CAPTAIN DANIEL STONE INN
## BRUNSWICK

This outstanding 1819 Federal-style home built for Captain Daniel Stone and his family and inherited by Miss Narcissa Stone, a prominent figure in Brunswick's history, is now proudly recognized as the Captain Daniel Stone Inn.

All rooms and suites have been tastefully decorated in keeping with the Federal style of the original home. Each has different wall coverings, window treatments, plush carpeting, ceramic tile, museum prints, and fine, Federal-period furniture.

Fine dining is always a pleasure in the intimate dining room and open veranda of the Narcissa Stone Restaurant. For business meetings, functions, banquets and weddings our conference rooms can accommodate up to 150 people.

The coastal town of Brunswick is the home of Bowdoin College, its magnificent campus and art galleries. A summer theatre, several museums, two excellent libraries, many good restaurants and its classic New England architecture complete Brunswick's charming ambiance. Just a ten minute drive north of Freeport, Maine, home of L.L. Bean.

10 Water Street,
Brunswick,
ME 04011
•
Tel 207 725 9898
Fax 207 725 9898
Freephone in US
800 267 0525
•
General Manager:
William Bennett
•
34 rooms
including 4 one bedroom
suites

Doubles $109 - $139 EP
Suites $140 - $175
•
Tax 7%
•
Conference facilities.
Nearby: swimming, tennis,
riding, sailing, water skiing,
down-hill & cross-country
skiing
•
Children welcome
•
Non-smoking
•
VS • MC
Amex • Diners

**MAINE**

# CAPTAIN LORD MANSION
## KENNEBUNKPORT

The Captain Lord Mansion is an award-winning, intimate country inn overlooking the Kennebunk River from the head of a sweeping lawn. The inn is ideally situated in a quiet, residential neighbourhood but is only four blocks from lively shops and restaurants.

Each bedroom is individually and luxuriously decorated with quality antiques, comfortable seating, good lighting and air conditioning. Many rooms have lace canopy beds and working fireplaces, some also have whirlpool tubs and refrigerators stocked with soft drinks.

A complimentary full breakfast is served.
Free parking passes for area beaches; towels, mats and umbrellas are provided. Free afternoon tea and sweets are offered daily, as is early morning coffee. Maps, tourist information, local menus are always available, together with lots of helpful advice.

Awarded Four Diamonds by the AAA and Four Stars by Mobil, the inn is a member of the Independent Innkeepers Association.

P.O. Box 800,
Kennebunkport,
ME 04046
•
Tel 207 967 3141
Fax 207 967 3172
•
Innkeepers:
Bev Davis &
Rick Litchfield
•
16 rooms

Doubles $149 - $199
B&B
•
Tax 7%
•
Conference room available to accommodate 16.
Ocean and beaches nearby
•
Not particularly suitable for children
•
VS • MC • Discover

**MAINE**

# GORGES GRANT HOTEL
## OGUNQUIT

Beautiful Gorges Grant Hotel is situated on meticulously manicured grounds in the heart of Ogunquit. Catch the trolley bus in front of the hotel for an easy trip to the village, or wander down to Ogunquit's fabled white sand beach for some sun and surf. Stretch out on our sunning deck and then cool off in our outdoor heated pool or move in out of the sun beside our indoor heated pool, jacuzzi and fitness center.

Treat yourself to fine dining at Raspberri's, our own full-service restaurant open for breakfast and dinner.

You will find your accommodations truly a pleasure. We offer a variety of handsomely appointed guest rooms each with luxurious furnishings, full baths, refrigerators and remote control television with premium movie channel.

We have some connecting units, ideal for families. Indulge yourself at Gorges Grant Hotel where special vacation memories begin.

239 US Rt 1.
PO Box 2240
Ogunquit,
ME 03907
•
Tel 207 646 7003
Fax 207 646 0660
Freephone in US
800 646 5001
•
Innkeeper/Owner:
Karen J. Hanson
•
56 rooms
2 one-bedroom suites

Doubles $129 - $159  EP
Suites $149 - $179
•
Tax 7%
•
Outdoor and indoor pools, spa, fitness center. Nearby: golf, tennis, whale-watching, deep sea fishing, factory outlet shopping
•
Children welcome
•
VS • MC • Amex

**MAINE**

# HARRASEEKET INN
## FREEPORT

The Harraseeket is an AAA Four Diamond, 54 room luxury country inn, set on five beautifully landscaped acres of old fashioned gardens in the village of Freeport.

23 bedrooms have fireplaces and jacuzzi tubs. All have private baths and the amenities expected by discerning travellers. An elegant, fine dining restaurant and a casual tavern with award winning wine lists and terrace dining in season await your pleasure. Full breakfast buffet and afternoon tea are included in the room rate.

The inn is located on rt 1, just two blocks north of L.L. Bean and is within easy walking distance of 110 outlet stores for which Freeport is deservedly famous. To drive from Boston takes about 2½ hours.

162 Main Street,
Freeport,
ME 04032
•
Tel 207 865 9377
Fax 207 865 1684
Freephone in US
800 342 6423
•
General Manager:
Nancy D. Gray
•
50 rooms
4 one bedroom suites

Doubles $145 - $195
B&B
Suites $185 - $225
•
Tax 7%
•
Croquet, conference
facilities
Nearby: golf, fishing,
boating, hiking
•
VS • MC • Amex
Diners • Discover

## MAINE

# INN BY THE SEA
### CAPE ELIZABETH

Overlooking the Atlantic, the Inn occupies one of the most splendid locations along Maine's entire 3000 mile coast. In keeping with this incomparable setting the Inn is designed to blend every contemporary amenity with the understated elegance of classic resort architecture.

All accommodations in this AAA Four Diamond resort are one or two-bedroom suites furnished either with period antiques or classic Maine style with wicker and pine. Each suite has fully equipped kitchen, living/dining area and private balcony or deck, complete with rocking chair and garden or ocean views.

The Audubon Restaurant with it's spectacular setting overlooking the water, offers the freshest of local seafood. Evening turndown service features chocolate covered berries or fresh cookies. Amazingly, the city of Portland is only minutes away from the Inn's tranquil setting and you can visit fine museums, enjoy Summer theatre, ballet and concerts, the Old Port shops or take an excursion boat for a cruise of Casco Bay.

40 Bowery Beach Road,
Cape Elizabeth,
ME 04107

•

Tel 207 799 3134
Fax 207 799 4779
Freephone in US
800 888 4287

•

Owner/Innkeeper:
Maureen McQuade

•

25 one-bedroom suites
18 two-bedroom suites

Doubles $110 - $390 EP

•

Tax 7%. s.c. 3%

•

Outdoor pool,
beach, tennis,
jogging trails,
volleyball,
cross-country
skiing

•

VS • MC
Amex • Discover

## MAINE

# SPRUCE POINT INN
## BOOTHBAY HARBOR

*This newly renovated Inn, (established 1902), on a tranquil 100 acre peninsula, offers a relaxed yet sophisticated atmosphere, a short distance from the village of Boothbay Harbor; a quaint coastal fishing village. Stonewalls, flowers and well groomed lawns surround the Inn and cottages. Spectacular ocean views and breathtaking sunsets can be enjoyed from most of the accommodations and dining room. All accommodations offer early American furnishings, telephone and cable tv. Recent additions include the Admiral's Quarters executive suite and a group of Downtown suites.*

*Famous for excellence in dining, the Inn operates the Modified American Plan. During high season a "Traditional Maine Lobster Bake" is on Tuesday evenings and Thursday evening features our "Gourmet Buffet".*

*There is a heated outdoor freshwater pool and new oceanside saltwater pool along with a heated spa. Tennis, shuffleboard and a putting green are also on site. A stay at the "Spruce Point Inn" is unforgettable.*

Atlantic Avenue, Box 237,
Boothbay Harbor ME 04538
•
Tel 207 633 4152
Fax 207 633 7138
Freephone in US
800 553 0289
•
Managers: Angelo Digiulian
& Joseph Paolillo
•
65 rooms
Two and three bedroom
townhouse condominiums

Inn doubles/suites
$190 - $396 MAP for two
Apartments/cottages
$345 - $532 MAP for four
Condominiums
$242 - $532 EP
•
Tax 7%. s.c. 15%
•
2 outdoor pools,
tennis, spa.
Conference room available.
•
Children welcome
•
VS • MC

**MAINE**

# STAGE NECK INN
## YORK HARBOR

At the mouth of the York River, where the rocks, beach and ocean meet, you'll find Stage Neck Inn, a small resort which has consistently for twenty years, earned the distinctive AAA Four Diamond Award. Each of the 58 guest rooms offers a balcony or terrace overlooking the beach and ocean. Exceptional accommodations are complemented by full room service, ocean-side pool with restaurant and bar, clay tennis courts, indoor pool/jacuzzi, fitness room with sauna, and membership privileges at a private, 18-hole River-front golf course.

The Inn serves breakfast, lunch and dinner daily. Choose the casual Sandpiper Bar & Grille with outdoor terrace and piano bar or Harbor Porches Café, all of which offer varied menus including appetizers, light fare and creative entrées. Stage Neck Inn is open year-round and features excellent value off-season get-away packages.

"One of the most well-appointed hostelries in the region - dining is either casual or formal, but the fare is consistently excellent - among the best in southern Maine" - *Down East Magazine.*

PO Box 70,
York Harbor,
ME 03911
•
Tel 207 363 3850
Fax 207 363 2221
Freephone in US
800 222 3238
•
General Manager:
Phoebe Apgar-Pressey
•
58 rooms
•
Doubles $95 - $210

Tax 7%. s.c. 15%
•
Indoor and outdoor pools, tennis, fitness room with sauna.
•
Nearby: golf, horseriding, sailing, water-skiing, hiking.
•
Conference facilities
•
VS • MC
Amex • Discover

## MAINE

# SUGARLOAF
### CARRABASSETT VALLEY

Located in the North Woods, at the foot of Maine's second highest mountain - 2,600 skiable vertical drop - Sugarloaf/USA offers wonderful skiing opportunities. Some of the best snow-making equipment in the East, added to the natural snowfall, ensures that skiing, snowmobiling and snowboarding are available for most of the winter season and right into March and April. There are always excellent all-inclusive prices to cover not only accommodation but also lift tickets and ski hire.

Children are exceptionally well-catered for with programmes specially devised not only for enjoyment but also for education with the result that Sugarloaf has consistently been voted one of the top family ski resorts.

Sugarloaf village is a great community and there are shuttles to take you between various points, whether you choose to stay in the inn, the hotel or in one of the apartments or houses.

RR1 Box 5000
Carrabassett Valley,
ME 04947
•
Tel 207 237 2000
Fax 207 237 2718
Freephone in US
800 THE LOAF (8439623)
•
President
Warren Cook
•
40 inn rooms
900 one to six bedrooms units

Doubles $85 - $120 EP
Suites apartments & homes
$120 - $575
•
Tax 7% s.c. 3%
•
Outdoor and indoor pools, tennis, golf, down-hill & cross-country skiing.
•
Children welcome.
Childrens' programmes available during the winter.
•
VS • MC

**MAINE**

# ANDREWS LODGING BED & BREAKFAST
## PORTLAND

*Situated on one and three quarter acres of beautifully landscaped grounds on the outskirts of the city of Portland, our 250 year old colonial home has been completely renovated for your year-round comfort. We offer modern baths and a completely applianced guest kitchen as well as sitting rooms, solarium and outdoor decks overlooking beautiful gardens in Summer and pristine snow in Winter with an ice skating rink for your enjoyment. Breakfast is served on silver and china in our formal dining room.*

*Antique furnished bedrooms include quilts and warm comforters for chilly Maine nights. You can expect refreshments in the refrigerator, your bed turned down nightly and warm hospitality from the Andrews family as we share our home with you.*

| | | | | | |
|---|---|---|---|---|---|
| 417 Auburn Street, Portland, ME 04103 Tel 207 797 9157 Fax 207 797 9040 | Owner/innkeeper/ plus everything else! Elizabeth Andrews | 6 rooms, 1 with private bath. 1 suite with bedroom, bathroom and sitting room. | Doubles $68 - $88 B&B Suite $100 - $150 Tax 7% | Non-smoking Children over 7 welcome, not ideal for ages 2-6 | VS • MC • Amex |

# BAGLEY HOUSE
## DURHAM

*Just ten minutes from downtown Freeport situated on six acres of lovely fields and woods the Bagley House offers a comfortable retreat in a peaceful, country setting.*

*Breakfast is served round an eight-foot antique baker's table in our magnificent country kitchen with its huge brick fireplace, wide pine floors, hand-hewn beams and beehive oven. Handsewn quilts, comforters, individually controlled room heat, thick and thirsty towels and fresh flowers all add to the comfort of our five guest rooms.*

*We're happy to direct our guests along scenic byways to wonderful little museums, nearby state parks, sparkling clean beaches. On foot you can discover private cross-country ski trails in winter and abundant berry-picking in Summer.*

| | | | | | |
|---|---|---|---|---|---|
| 1290 Royalsborough Road Durham ME 04222 | Tel 207 865 6366 Fax 207 353 5878 Freephone in US 800 765 1372 | Owner/Innkeepers: Suzanne O'Connor & Susan Backhouse | 5 rooms Doubles $85 - $125 B&B Tax 7% | Nearby: indoor pool, golf, sailing, beaches, hiking, outlet shopping, summer theatre, country fairs. | Children welcome. Non-smoking VS • MC • Amex Diners • Discover |

**MAINE**

# BLUE HARBOR HOUSE
## CAMDEN

A classic village inn on the Maine coast, the Blue Harbor House welcomes guests to relax in a restored 1810 Cape home with yesterday's charms blending perfectly with today's comforts.

The beautiful town of Camden, renowned for its spectacular setting, where the mountains meet the sea, is just outside the door. The inn's inviting guest rooms are bright with country antiques and hand-fashioned quilts; several have canopy beds. Breakfasts feature such specialities as lobster quiche, cheese soufflé, and blueberry pancakes with blueberry butter. Dinner, available to guests by reservation, can be a romantic candlelit affair or an old-fashioned Down East lobster feast.

| 67 Elm Street<br>Camden<br>ME 04843<br>Tel 207 236 3196<br>Fax 207 236 6523 | Freephone in US<br>800 243 3196<br>Innkeeper/Owners:<br>Jody Schmoll &<br>Dennis Hayden | 10 rooms<br>including 1 one<br>bedroom suite. 1 two<br>bedroom suite.<br>Doubles $85 - $135<br>B&B | Suites $135 - $150<br>Tax 7%<br>Nearby: outdoor &<br>indoor pools, tennis, | golf, riding, sailing,<br>water skiing.<br>Children welcome<br>(kids programme $30<br>daily) | Non-smoking<br>VS • MC<br>Amex • Diners |

# BLUE HILL INN
## BLUE HILL

Constructed on a scenic part of the dramatic Maine coast 164 years ago, The Blue Hill Inn is set on a one acre perennial garden in the village within walking distance of the harbour, several fine galleries, antique shops, the base of Blue Hill Mountain and easy reach of Acadia National Park. An evening cocktail hour with tempting appetisers including smoked pepper mackerel canapés, assorted French cheeses and fresh lobster on crackers offers a relaxing fireside setting for guests to meet, mingle and exchange sightseeing tips. This is followed by a delicious five-course dinner presented in an intimate many-windowed dining room where service is attentive and friendly and the convivial warmth of the atmosphere is enhanced by the glow from the splendid sixteen candle chandelier. Special Event packages include sailing, chamber music concerts and wine dinners.

| PO Box 143,<br>Union Street,<br>Rt 177, Blue Hill,<br>ME 04614 | Tel 207 374 2844<br>Fax 207 374 2829<br>Innkeepers:<br>Don & Mary Hartley | 11 rooms<br>including 1 two-<br>bedroom suite | Doubles $140 - $190<br>MAP<br>Tax 7%. s.c. 15% | Nearby: Acadia<br>National Park,hiking,<br>birdwatching,<br>kayaking, cycling<br>trails, golf | Children over 13<br>welcome<br>Non-smoking<br>VS • MC |

**MAINE**

# CAPTAIN LINDSEY HOUSE INN
## ROCKLAND

Two relaxing days at the Captain Lindsey House Inn and then a three or six day cruise - let Captains Ken & Ellen Barnes offer you a real taste of Maine. At the inn, a 19th century Sea Captain's home, your stay is enhanced by comfortable beds, inviting bathrooms, a parlour with a softly glowing fire and wonderful meals at the Waterworks pub and restaurant.
The moment you step aboard the 83 foot motor yacht Pauline and relish the mahogany panelled main saloon, the fresh banana bread laid out for tea, the large open air boat-deck and the effortless glide as she leaves the cove, you will know you're in for an unforgettable experience. A longer cruise on the Stephen Taber will have you caught up in the excitement of a voyage on the oldest documented U.S. sailing vessel, as several thousand square feet of canvas unfurl to the waiting breeze.

| 5 Lindsey Street Rockland ME 04841 | Tel 297 596 7950 Fax 207 596 2758 | General Manager: Susan Barnes 9 rooms including 2 one bedroom suites at the Inn. | Doubles $95 - $160 B&B Tax 7% | Nearby: tennis, golf, sailing, water skiing, conference facilities, down-hill skiing, cross-country skiing | Children over 10 welcome. Non-smoking VS • MC • Discover |

# DOCKSIDE GUEST QUARTERS
## YORK

A small family-run resort situated on a private peninsula in York Harbor, the unsurpassed location provides a panoramic view of ocean and harbour activities. Spacious and meticulously landscaped grounds offer privacy as well as numerous recreational activities.
Accommodations are in the Maine House, a restored seacoast homestead, and modern multi-unit cottages. Most rooms have private balconies or porches with unspoiled views. The Restaurant at the resort is bi-level with floor to ceiling windows affording wonderful water views. Food is equally impressive, offering a varied menu but specialising in Maine seafood.
The York area offers beaches, beautiful scenery, outlet shopping and friendly people, only 1½ hours north of Boston. We hold the Three Diamond AAA rating.

| PO Box 205, York, ME 03909 Tel 207 363 2868 | Innkeepers: The Lusty Family Open all year | 22 rooms, only 2 with shared bath. 7 apartment suites with kitchenettes | Doubles $64 – $107 EP Suites $102 – $153 Tax 7% | Cycling, swimming, motor-boat cruises, canoeing. Nearby: tennis, golf, horseriding, sailing | Children welcome VS • MC |

**MAINE**

# GREENVILLE INN
## GREENVILLE

*In 1895 a wealthy Lumber Baron, fell in love with the dramatic vista of Moosehead Lake and Squaw Mountain - the elegant Victorian mansion he built is now the Greenville Inn and for ten years, carpenters worked to complete the unique carved embellishments and panelling found throughout. A spruce tree leaded glass window graces the stairway landing, fireplaces are ornamented with carved mantels and mosaics and individually appointed guest rooms and cottages are furnished with equal attention to detail and comfort.*

*Relish the romantic setting of our lake and mountain view dining rooms whilst enjoying our innovative menus featuring fresh Maine seafood, roast duckling, rack of lamb, steaks and other local specialities. Finish your meal with delicious home-made desserts and pastries.*

Norris Street,
PO Box 1194,
Greenville,
ME 04441
Tel 207 695 2206
Fax 207 695 2206

Freephone in US
888 695 0000
Innkeepers:
Elfi, Michael & Susie Schnetzer

12 rooms including 1 one bedroom suite & 6 cottages

Doubles $105 - $145
B&B
Suites/Cottages
$135 - $185
Tax 7 %

Nearby: tennis, golf, riding, sailing, water skiing, down-hill skiing, cross-country skiing

Children over 7 welcome.
Non-smoking
VS • MC • Discover

# KENNEBUNKPORT INN
## KENNEBUNKPORT

*The Kennebunkport Inn is in Dock Square in the heart of picturesque Kennebunkport. Steps from our door are delightful shops and galleries featuring arts, crafts, clothing and more.*
*Guest rooms of this elegant 19th Century mansion and the attached River House are thoughtfully and individually decorated with period antiques. All accommodations include colour tv. Take a swim in the pool, lounge on the deck or stroll along beautiful white sandy beaches.*
*The dining room is renowned for fresh native seafood and Maine lobster, as well as exquisitely prepared regional cuisine. Dinner is served by candlelight in relaxed elegance. For more casual fare try our Martha's Vineyard sidewalk café. Exquisite food, gracious service and charming accommodations – a memorable stay, a truly heartwarming experience. AAA Three Diamond rated.*

One Dock Square,
PO Box 111,
Kennebunkport,
ME 04046

Tel 207 967 2321
Fax 207 967 3705
Freephone in US
800 248 2621

Innkeeper:
Rick Griffin
34 rooms.
1 apartment with kitchen

Doubles $89 – $234
EP
Tax 7%

Outdoor pool.
Nearby: tennis, golf, horseriding, sailing, whale-watching.

Children welcome
VS • MC • Amex

## MAINE

# LAWNMEER INN
### WEST BOOTHBAY HARBOR

*The only thing we overlook... is the water!*
- *Old time Maine • Lighthouses • Sea breezes •*
- *Vivaldi • Rocky coast • Indian Pudding •*
- *Whales • Clam diggers • Cliffs • Coon Cat •*
- *Porches • New friends • Schooners • Racoons •*
- *Serenity • Homemade sausage • Broad lawns •*
- *Puffins • Key Lime pie • Seals • Blueberries •*
- *Retreat • Eagles • Homemade ice-cream •*
- *Fine wines • Lobsters • Lobsters • Lobsters •*

| | | | | |
|---|---|---|---|---|
| Rt 27, Southport Island, ME 04576 (mail PO Box 505, West Boothbay Harbor ME 04575) | Tel 207 633 2544 Freephone in US 800 633 7345 | Innkeepers: Jim & Lee Metzger 32 rooms., 1 cottage, 1 apartment | Doubles $75 – $130 EP Cottage etc. $130 - $170 | Off season rates available Tax 7% Children welcome | Open mid-May to mid-October VS • MC |

---

# LODGE AT MOOSEHEAD LAKE
### GREENVILLE

In a tiny town on a forty mile lake, in the northern reaches of Maine the Lodge at Moosehead Lake can be found. This eight room, AAA Four Diamond Award winning inn with its spectacular lake views, hand-carved four poster beds, fireplaces and whirlpool baths offers you unspoiled serenity and unashamed luxury.

From October to June delicious dinners are included in the rates with tempting items such as apple cider and onion soup, chicken breast sautéed with blueberries and flamed with brandy and, perhaps best of all, Chocolate Moose Maximus! Hearty breakfasts are on offer daily throughout the year and innkeepers Roger & Jennifer Cauchi keep the coffeepot going, the guest pantry stocked with cookies and are always ready with knowledgeable local advice.

| | | | | | |
|---|---|---|---|---|---|
| Upon Lily Bay Road, Box 1167 Greenville, ME 04441 Tel 207 695 4400 Fax 207 695 2181 | Owner/Innkeeper: Roger S. Cauchi 8 rooms including 3 one bedroom suites | Doubles in season $135 - $185 B&B off-season, weekdays $125 MAP weekends $160 Tax 7% | Moose safaris, hiking, dog sledding, snow mobiling, snow shoeing | Nearby: tennis, golf, riding, down-hill and cross-country skiing Does not meet the needs of children | Non-smoking VS • MC Amex • Discover |

## MAINE

# MAINE STAY INN
### CAMDEN

Relaxed, cozy and very friendly, the Maine Stay is a grand old home located in the Historic District of one of America's most beautiful seaside villages. Built in 1802 and situated on two wooded acres, the inn's eight lovely bedrooms, cozy parlours with fireplaces and tv room are tastefully and comfortably decorated with oriental rugs and period furnishings. Guests often gather to gossip round the Queen Atlantic wood and coal stove in the cozy country kitchen.
Breakfasts, delicious, and served at a long harvest table, are designed to set you up for the day and your host, Peter, a former navy captain, is a wonderful source of local knowledge. It is just a two-block walk from the inn, down tree lined streets and through the beautiful harbour park, to the shops and restaurants. This is Down East hospitality at its absolute best!

| 22 High Street<br>Camden<br>Maine 04843<br>Tel 207 236 9636<br>Fax 207 236 0621 | Owners:<br>Captain Peter Smith<br>and the twins, Donny<br>Smith and Diana<br>Robson | 8 rooms, (2 do not<br>have private bath).<br>1 one bedroom suite | Doubles $75 - $95<br>B&B<br>Suite $125<br>Tax 7% | Nearby: tennis, golf,<br>riding, sailing,<br>conference facilities,<br>down-hill & cross-<br>country skiing. | Children over 8<br>welcome.<br>Non-smoking<br>VS • MC • Amex |

# MAINE STAY INN & COTTAGES
### KENNEBUNKPORT

Beautiful 1860 Victorian-style inn and cottages, located on spacious grounds in the quiet surroundings of Kennebunkport's National Historic District, only a short walk from the delightful shops, galleries and restaurants in Dock Square and Lower Village.

The innkeepers, Carol and Lindsay Copeland and their staff are courteous, attentive and knowledgeable. They are particularly helpful to guests needing assistance in planning activities and itineraries. A full breakfast is served each morning which guests may take in the main inn or have delivered to their cottages. Afternoon tea is a popular time to meet the other guests and exchange travel experiences. The Maine Stay is rated Three Diamonds by the AAA and Three Stars by Mobil

| 4 Maine Street,<br>PO Box 500 A,<br>Kennebunkport,<br>ME 04046<br>Tel 207 967 2117<br>Fax 207 967 8157 | Freephone in US<br>800 950 2117<br>Owner/Innkeepers:<br>Carol &<br>Lindsay Copeland | 6 rooms in the main<br>house, 2 of which are<br>suites,<br>9 one bedroom<br>cottages with<br>kitchenettes. | 1 two-bedroom<br>cottage with kitchen.<br>(7 rooms have<br>fireplaces) | Doubles $125 - $165<br>B&B<br>Cottages $135 – $210<br>Tax 7%<br>Non-smoking | 1 mile from beach.<br>Nearby: golf,<br>horseriding, sailing.<br>Children welcome.<br>VS • MC • Amex |

MAINE

# MIRA MONTE INN
## BAR HARBOR

An 1864 Bar Harbor summer estate graced by porches, balconies and bay windows, the Mira Monte boasts a library, living room, formal dining room and twelve guest rooms with period furnishings, private baths, tv, phones and air conditioning.

Staff here are friendly and helpful and included in the rate is a full buffet breakfast and afternoon refreshments. Located in the historic district, the Inn is set in its own quiet acres, although only an easy walk to shops, restaurant and waterfront and five minutes to the wonders of Acadia National Park.

There is a wealth of activities to choose from, including summer theatre and music, whale watching, guided naturalist walks and sea kayaking.

| 69 Mt Desert Street, Bar Harbor, ME 04609 Tel 207 288 4263 Fax 207 288 3115 | Freephone in US 800 553 5109 Owner: Marian Burns 12 rooms 2 suites with decks and kitchenettes | 1 two bedroom suite sleeps 4 Doubles $115 – $150 B&B Suites $150 – $180 | Two bedroom suite $850 per week. (weekly rate does not include breakfast) Tax 7% | Nearby: tennis, golf, sailing, fitness center, hiking, cycling | Non-smoking Children over 8 welcome VS • MC • Amex |

# NEWCASTLE INN
## NEWCASTLE

At the Newcastle Inn you find more than a welcome, you find a welcome home! Here, by the broad and salty Damariscotta River, our door is always open. Enjoy our fine small inn and share in our tradition of genuine unpretentious hospitality. At the end of a day's journey – a warm greeting, a comfortable room and an exceptional dinner await you.

Inside, this classic New England dormered colonial offers hand-stencilled floors, beautiful antiques and artwork, an inviting river view and comfortable living rooms for relaxation and conversation.

The three and five course dinners at the inn are nationally acclaimed and have won the restaurant a four star rating. The inn also holds Three Diamonds from the AAA and Three Stars from Mobil.

| RR2 Box 24, River Road, Newcastle, ME 04553 | Tel 207 563 5685 Fax 207 563 6877 Freephone in US 800 832 8669 | Owner/Innkeepers: Howard & Rebecca Levitan 15 rooms including 1 suite | Doubles $167 – $270 MAP $95 – $200 B&B Tax 7% s.c. 15% | Nearby: tennis, golf, swimming, sailing, bird-watching, cycling Non-smoking | Does not meet the needs of children VS • MC • Amex |

**MAINE**

# OCEAN GATE
## WEST SOUTHPORT

*Escape to 85 wooded waterfront acres on beautiful Southport Island. Relax and watch the boats go by from your private porch. Smoke-free rooms, cottages and efficiencies are available.*

*A full breakfast and in-room tea and coffee are included in the rate. There is no charge for children under 12 sharing a room with parents. Ocean Gate has a Three Diamond AAA and Three Star Mobil rating and is only five minutes from charming Boothbay Harbor, within easy reach of area attractions.*

*Cross the bridge to Ocean Gate... your island home.*

| Rt 27, PO Box 140, W. Southport, ME 04576 | Tel 207 633 3321  Fax 207 633 7337  Freephone in US  800 221 5924 | General Managers: Ted & Judith Kolva | 67 rooms, plus cottages and efficiencies with kitchenettes | Doubles $80 – $140 B&B  Suites from $160 – $190  Tax 7% | Heated swimming pool, fitness center, tennis, boats, outdoor games area. Nearby: golf, fishing  VS • MC |

---

# OCEAN POINT INN
## EAST BOOTHBAY

Savour the breathtaking view of dark green islands and rock-bound shoreline from the Inn's spectacular setting, across from the Town Pier, near the tip of a peninsula jutting into the vast Gulf of Maine.

Life is easy-going in this area of summer cottages and sea breezes, join us for a relaxing stay in the main inn, lodge or motel and cottage units with colonial or modern decor. All rooms with tv, telephone, fridge, and heating. Ideal for families, the newly renovated Sea Kist Cottage offers spacious accommodation and magnificent views.

Walk run or bike along the Shore Road, watch lobster fishermen at work and sailboats at play in Linekin Bay, visit the lighthouses that beckon from nearby islands. In the evening relax in the cocktail lounge and dining room to watch the sunset and enjoy our varied menu.

| PO Box 409, Shore Road, East Boothbay, ME 04544 | Tel 207 633 4200  Fax 207 633 6040  Freephone in US  800 552 5554 | Managers: David & Beth Dudley  60 rooms, cottages & apartments, some with kitchenette & fireplace (sleep 3 or 4) | Doubles $83 - $128 EP  Cottages $78 - $135 per night  weekly rates available | Tax 7%  Outdoor heated pool Nearby: tennis, golf, sailing, boat excursions, deep sea fishing | Children very welcome  VS • MC • Amex |

**MAINE**

# YORK HARBOR INN
## YORK HARBOR

Nestled in an historic harbour village, this AAA Three Diamond inn with breathtaking water views, stands as a warm and restful sentinel. At its centre, the immaculate inn has a re-assembled, circa 1637, former fisherman's cabin from the Isles of Shoals. This rustic structure with massive stone fireplace, cosy Oriental rugs and comfortable sofas, offers a uniquely comfortable reading or sitting room.

Imaginative use of floor coverings, wallpaper and fabric create the perfect backdrop for four poster beds, paintings and antiques. Ocean views, fireplaces, classic linens, complimentary toiletries and phones are but a few of the in-room amenities to add to your comfort.

Attention to detail is a matter of pride as is exquisitely prepared cuisine and meticulous service.

| PO Box 573, Rt 1A, York Harbor, ME 03911 | Tel 207 363 5119<br>Fax 207 363 3545<br>ext 295<br>Freephone in US<br>800 343 3869 | Innkeeper:<br>Garry Dominguez<br>32 rooms | Doubles $89 – $195<br>B&B<br>Tax 7% | Tennis, golf, horseriding, sailing, beach, swimming, hot tub | Children welcome<br>VS • MC • Amex |

## COMPLIMENTARY BOOKING SERVICE

*Don't forget we offer an advisory and booking service and you can make all your reservations with just one phone call to us. The service is completely free and prices are not loaded in any way.*

**Call for a chat on**

# 01895 622233

1 REGION
4 SEASONS

# DISTINCTIVE
# INNS OF NEW
# ENGLAND

6 STATES
12 DISTINCTIVE INNS

Rabbit Hill Inn 178
Inn at Thorn Hill 139
Camden's Maine Stay 95
Newcastle Inn 96
The Manor on Golden Pond 141
Village Country Inn 198
Windham Hill Inn 181
Chesterfield Inn 137
Deerfield Inn 109
The Boulders 70
The Captain's House Inn 104
Cliffside Inn 156

*Numbers correspond to page number in Welcome Directory.*

*An Association of Independent Inns for Independent Travelers*

Visit our Web Site at
http://www.distinctiveinns.com

## Your Assurance of Quality & Hospitality.

# Massachusetts

## Massachusetts

| | | |
|---|---|---|
| **1** Addison Choate Inn | 122 | |
| **2** Blantyre | 102 | |
| **3** Boston Harbor Hotel | 103 | |
| **4** Bradford Inn | 122 | |
| **5** Cambridge House | 123 | |
| **6** Captain Nickerson Inn | 124 | |
| **7** Captain's House Inn of Chatham | 104 | |
| **8** Charles Hotel | 105 | |
| **9** Chatham Bars Inn | 106 | |
| **10** Colonnade Hotel | 107 | |
| **11** Corner House Inn | 123 | |
| **12** Dan'l Webster Inn | 108 | |
| **13** Deerfield Inn | 109 | |
| **14** Grafton Inn | 124 | |
| **15** Harbor Light Inn | 110 | |
| **16** Hawthorne Inn | 125 | |
| **17** Inn at Stockbridge | 125 | |
| **18** Isaiah Hall | 126 | |
| **19** Isaiah Jones Homestead | 126 | |
| **20** Jared Coffin House | 111 | |
| **21** John Carver Inn | 127 | |
| **22** Lenox Hotel | 112 | |
| **23** Liberty Hill Inn | 127 | |
| **24** Lighthouse Inn | 128 | |
| **25** Longfellow's Wayside Inn | 128 | |
| **26** The Marlborough | 129 | |
| **27** Mary Prentiss | 129 | |
| **28** Mostly Hall | 130 | |
| **29** Ocean Edge Resort & Golf Club | 113 | |
| **30** Onset Pointe Inn | 130 | |
| **31** Pheasant Hill Inn | 131 | |
| **32** Pleasant Bay Village Resort | 131 | |
| **33** Publick House Historic Inn | 114 | |
| **34** Queen Anne Inn | 132 | |
| **35** Red Lion Inn | 116 | |
| **36** Rocky Shores Inn & Cottages | 132 | |
| **37** Salem Inn | 117 | |
| **38** Sharon Inn | 133 | |
| **39** Thorncroft Inn | 118 | |
| **40** Village Green Inn | 133 | |
| **41** Weathervane Inn | 134 | |
| **42** Wedgewood Inn | 134 | |

NEW HAMPSHIRE

Lowell

Rockport

RHODE ISLAND

Fall River

New Bedford

Plymouth

Sandwich

Provincetown

Chatham

Martha's Vineyard

Nantucket

alewalk Inn            119
dflower Inn            135
kee Clipper Inn        120

# MASSACHUSETTS

## BLANTYRE
### LENOX

*An impeccably maintained Tudor-style mansion in 85 park-like acres in the Berkshire hills. Enjoy the Boston Symphony Orchestra at Tanglewood, theatre festivals, and attractive shopping villages or visit for the spectacular Fall foliage. Eight exquisite accommodations in the Main House, twelve newly renovated Carriage House rooms and suites, and two cottages. Baronial Great Hall accented by rich panelling, glorious floral displays, heirloom furnishings; also superb formal dining room, glass-enclosed winter garden/conservatory for complimentary continental breakfasts and ornate music salon. Small swimming pool, jacuzzi, sauna, four tennis courts and two croquet lawns all set amid extraordinarily blissful surroundings.*
*Nearby attractions are the Clark Art Institute, the Norman Rockwell Museum and Chesterwood, home of the sculptor Daniel Chester French. A member of Relais & Chateaux, Blantyre received their prestigious "International Welcome Award" in 1989; currently holds Four Stars from Mobil, and the restaurant has been awarded Four Diamonds from the AAA. Located 2 hours from Boston, 3 hours from New York City.*

Rt 20, Lenox,
MA 01240
•
Tel 413 637 3556
(Summer)
413 298 1661
(Winter)
Fax 413 637 4282
•
Managing Director:
Roderick W. Anderson
•
19 rooms
3 one bedroom suites
1 two bedroom suite

Doubles $240 - $450 B&B
Suites $300 - $650
Tax 9.7%. s.c. 10%
•
Outdoor pool, tennis,
croquet. Nearby: golf,
horseriding, sailing, water
skiing, fitness center
•
Conference facilities
for up to 25
•
Children over 12 welcome
•
VS • MC • Amex • Diners

**MASSACHUSETTS**

# BOSTON HARBOR HOTEL
## BOSTON

A distinctive twelve story arch greets travellers arriving at Rowes Wharf via water shuttle from Logan Airport. Proximity to Boston's financial District as well as the attractions of Quincy Market and Faneuil Hall, further enhances the location of Boston's only luxury waterfront hotel.

Oversized guest rooms are enhanced by full services and amenities, including a marina, in-house business centre, 24-hour room service, complimentary shoe-shine, overnight valet service, twice daily maid service, complimentary transport to local attractions and shopping, award-winning cuisine and fully equipped health club recognised nationally and internationally as one of the finest hotel health clubs in North America.

The Boston Harbor Hotel, a member of Preferred Hotels and Resorts, holds the Four Diamond award from the AAA and Four Stars from Mobil. Its unbeatable waterfront location amidst Boston's historic district is convenient and exciting with a distinctly Boston character.

70 Rowes Wharf,
Boston,
MA 02110

•

Tel 617 439 7000
Fax 617 330 9450
Freephone in US
800 752 7077

•

Managing Director:
Francois-Laurent Nivaud

•

230 rooms & suites

Doubles $250 - $415 EP
Suites $385 - $1600

•

Tax 12.45%

•

Indoor swimming pool,
fitness center, spa,
children's programmes
available

•

Parking available

•

VS • MC • Amex • Diners
Discover • Carte Blanche

## MASSACHUSETTS

# CAPTAIN'S HOUSE INN OF CHATHAM
### CHATHAM

An authentic captain's house built in 1839, this elegant AAA Four Diamond inn with sixteen bedrooms is situated on two acres of pine trees, shaded lawns and thick hedges. Located ½ mile from Chatham Center and the ocean, The Captain's House provides a romantic and quiet getaway.

The inn consists of three buildings, the Main House, Carriage House and the Captain's Cottage. Each guest room has its own bathroom and is individually stylised with antiques, fine furnishings including four-poster beds with white lace canopies, and woodburning fireplaces in five of the rooms.

Every morning Jan McMaster, an Englishwoman from Bournemouth, and her staff, serve guests an extensive homemade gourmet breakfast. In the afternoon, after a bike ride on one of the inn's courtesy bicycles or a game of croquet on the front lawn, a lovely English tea is served complete with freshly baked scones, jam tarts and cakes. The Captain's House Inn is located off rt 28 in Chatham, about 90 minutes by car from Boston.

369-377 Old Harbor Rd,
Chatham,
MA 02633
•
Tel 508 945 0127
Fax 508 945 0866
•
Owner/Innkeepers:
Jan & Dave McMaster
•
19 rooms
5 one bedroom suites

Doubles $130 - $190
B&B
Suites $185- $225
•
Tax 9.7%
•
Nearby: tennis,
golf, sailing
•
Does not meet the needs
of children
•
VS • MC • Amex

**MASSACHUSETTS**

# CHARLES HOTEL
## CAMBRIDGE

Located in Harvard Square, The Charles Hotel is home to the best and the brightest, including visiting business, entertainment and academic leaders. Goosefeather quilts grace each bed and every room offers radio, two line phones with voice mail, PC/fax capabilities and television in bathrooms as well as bedrooms.

The Charles's Four Star Rialto Restaurant, features French, Italian and Spanish cuisine. Boston Magazine's "Best Jazz" can be found at Regattabar, and Henrietta's Table serves fresh from the farm and honest to goodness New England home cooking at breakfast, lunch, supper and Sunday Brunch.

At Charles Square, Le Pli Day Spa and Salon, WellBridge Health & Fitness Center and Spence Center for Women's Health offer a wealth of health, beauty and fitness facilities. Enjoy our simply elegant accommodations as you explore Harvard University and Square, the outdoor cafés, street performers, live theatre, bookstores, museums and boutiques.

In Harvard Square,
One Bennett Street,
Cambridge, MA 02138
•
Tel 617 864 1200
Fax 617 864 5715
Freephone in US
800 882 1818
•
General Manager:
Brian Fitzgerald
•
296 rooms

Doubles $225 - $295 EP
•
Tax 12.45%
•
Indoor pool,
conference facilities
•
Parking available
$18 per day
•
Children welcome.
•
VS • MC • Amex • Diners

## MASSACHUSETTS

# CHATHAM BARS INN
### CHATHAM

`Perched gracefully atop a rise overlooking the waters of Chatham Harbor and the open Atlantic beyond, Chatham Bars Inn is Cape Cod's only luxury resort. This beautifully restored 155 room and suite turn-of-the-century resort boasts charming guest rooms located in the Main Inn as well as in 26 surrounding Cape style cottages, and enjoys a reputation for fine food and outstanding service.

Catering to a gracious clientele since 1914, this year-round resort has two award-winning restaurants as well as seasonal beachside dining. Festive beach parties at the Beach House Grill are a cherished summertime tradition. Antique shops, art galleries and boutiques are just minutes away in the delightful seaside village of Chatham. Complimentary children's programme.

A world away..... yet just 90 miles from Boston and easily accessed by major highways. Come and experience a Cape tradition.

Shore Road,
Chatham, MA 02633
•
Tel 508 945 0096
Fax 508 945 5491
Freephone in US
800 527 4884
•
General Manager:
Christopher Diego
•
135 rooms
including 20 luxury suites
•
Doubles $170 - $385 EP
Suites/Cottages $360 - $1,200

Tax 9.7%.
s.c. 17% on food &
beverages only
•
Private beach, outdoor
pool, tennis, golf,
horseback riding, sailing,
watersports, hiking.
•
Children welcome
Childrens Programmes
available during
July and August
•
VS • MC • Amex • Diners

**MASSACHUSETTS**

# COLONNADE HOTEL
## BOSTON

The Colonnade Hotel is a 285 room independently owned, luxury hotel that takes great pride in its service and ability to pay the utmost attention to every detail. Spacious and comfortable rooms are all individually detailed with works from local artists and in addition we offer 10,000 square feet of newly designed function space.

Located in Boston's historic Back Bay, the cultural hub of the city, The Colonnade is adjacent to the magnificent Copley Place shopping plaza, directly across from the new Prudential Shopping and Tower and the Hynes Convention Center and only steps away from the delights of Newbury Street, Symphony Hall, Fenway Park and Boston's fabulous museum and theatre district. Whether travelling for business or pleasure, the Colonnade looks forward to welcoming you.

120 Huntington Avenue,
Boston, MA 02116
•
Tel 617 424 7000
Fax 617 424 1717
Freephone in US
800 962 3030
•
Managing Director:
David J. Colella
•
285 rooms
8 one-bedroom suites
4 two-bedroom suites

Doubles $195 - $275 EP
Suites $450 - $1050
•
Tax 12.45%
s.c. 15% on food services
•
Roof-top swimming
pool and cafe,
fitness center, conference
facilities, children's
programmes available
•
VS • MC • Amex

## MASSACHUSETTS

# DAN'L WEBSTER INN
## SANDWICH

The Four Star Dan'l Webster Inn with beautifully landscaped grounds and swimming pool blends historic elegance with modern convenience. A Gathering Room invites one to sit a spell, relax and visit with other guests or the friendly staff. Three elegant dining rooms offer award-winning classic American cuisine and a wine list to tempt the most discerning palate. All rooms have air conditioning, phones and tv, many featuring four poster canopy beds. Fresh flowers, turndown service and suites with whirlpool tub and marble fireplace add to your enjoyment. The inn holds the prestigious DiRONA Award (Distinguished Restaurants of North America), while its wine list has been awarded the Wine Spectator "Best Of" Award for the last several years. Cape Cod Life Magazine also voted the Inn "Best Inn" and "Best Fine Dining" awards for the Upper Cape area.

Front desk staff are available 24 hours a day to help you plan your itinerary, whether to Plymouth or Provincetown, all area sights are a short drive away.

Recapture the romance, charm and heritage of this proud old inn.

149 Main Street,
Sandwich,
MA 02563
•
Tel 508 888 3622
Fax 508 888 5156
Freephone in US
800 444 3566
•
Innkeepers:
The Catania family
•
37 rooms
9 suites

Doubles $89 - $169 EP
Suites: $149 - $325
$89.50 - $190
per person MAP
•
Tax 9.7%
•
Outdoor swimming pool.
Nearby: tennis, golf,
bicycling, sailing, hiking,
sandy beaches and many
attractions
•
VS • MC•Amex • Diners

**MASSACHUSETTS**

# DEERFIELD INN
## DEERFIELD

The Deerfield is a full service country inn, set on what has been called the loveliest street in New England. Each room is individually and beautifully furnished and named after a person connected with the village's history. Modern comforts, however, include air conditioning and telephones. Our award winning restaurant uses only the freshest and finest local ingredients and some of our recipes are gathered from the old books in the village's archive library. Included in the room rate is a full country breakfast and afternoon tea.

Historic Deerfield Village was once an outpost of colonial America and maintains 14 museum houses which line the mile-long Street and encapsulate the cultural history, art and craftsmanship of the Pioneer Valley. When dusk starts to fall and horse-drawn carriages clop along the road you will find yourself transported back in time.

Nearby attractions are the world class art museum in Williamstown, historic villages of Shelburne Falls and Amherst, numerous craft shops and country walks.

The Street,
Deerfield,
MA 01342
•
Tel 413 774 5587
Fax 413 773 8712
Freephone in US
800 926 3865
•
Innkeepers:
Karl & Jane Sabo

23 rooms

Doubles $140 - $150
B&B
•
Tax 9.7%. s.c 10%
•
Nearby: boating trips,
white-water rafting
•
Children welcome
•
VS • MC
Amex • Diners

**MASSACHUSETTS**

# HARBOR LIGHT INN
## MARBLEHEAD

Winner of numerous national awards for excellence, the Harbor Light, now in its tenth year, offers first class accommodation and amenities in two elegantly furnished, side by side, period Federalist mansions in the heart of Marblehead - within walking distance of all the local attractions.

Formal fireplaced parlours, dining room and bed chambers, sparkling private baths, double jacuzzis, sundecks, patio, quiet garden and outdoor heated pool along with an extensive continental breakfast buffet, combine to ensure the finest in New England hospitality. Breakfast includes bagels, muffins, cakes, fruit breads, fruits in season, yogurts, fresh squeezed juice, tea and fresh brewed coffees. Located in the Historic Harbor District which includes many fine shops, art galleries and restaurants, the inn welcomes guests year round.

58 Washington Street
Marblehead
MA 01945
•
Tel 781 631 2186
Fax 781 631 2216
•
Owner:
Peter C. Conway
•
21 rooms
including
1 one bedroom suite
•
Doubles $95 - $245 B&B
Suite $150 - $175

Tax 12.45%
•
Outdoor pool,
conference facilities
•
Nearby: tennis, golf,
sailing
•
Children over 8
welcome.
•
Non-smoking
•
VS • MC•Amex

**MASSACHUSETTS**

# JARED COFFIN HOUSE
## NANTUCKET

*The Jared Coffin House, a stately 1845 three-storey brick mansion built for a successful ship owner, is the centrepiece of the inn, a collection of six buildings in all. Comfortably elegant public areas and guest rooms combining period decor with modern amenities, offer you an ideal base for exploring Nantucket, the faraway island that takes you back in time to a gentler past.*

*Sense the history, as you walk along cobblestoned streets by grey shingled cottages and restored nineteenth century mansions. Dine on creative local cuisine, fresh seafood from the docks and traditional New England fare at Jared's our signature restaurant or relax in our Tap Room, a favourite gathering place for Nantucketers and visitors alike.*

*Springtime is glorious, as daffodils blanket the town in yellow. Summer is Nantucket's "season" with sailboats, beaches and wild roses on white picket fences. Autumn is coloured by russet heathlands, cranberry bogs and vivid blue skies while Winter is a time of quiet escape. We look forward to welcoming you to Nantucket and the Jared Coffin House.*

29 Broad Street
Nantucket, MA 02554
•
Tel 508 228 2400
Fax 508 228 8549
Freephone in US
800 248 2405
•
Innkeepers:
Phil & Peg Read
General Manager:
Jonathan Stone
•
60 rooms

Doubles $150 - $200
B&B
•
Tax 9.7%
•
Conference facilities
Nearby: golf, sailing,
water skiing
•
Children welcome.
•
VS • MC
Amex • Diners
Discover

**MASSACHUSETTS**

# LENOX HOTEL
## BOSTON

Nearly 100 years after its founding, The Lenox enjoys a privileged position in the society of Boston hotels. Old-world Boston charm and elegance are paired with the latest conveniences in this 214-room landmark.

Located in historic Back Bay, steps away from the finish line of the Boston Marathon, The Lenox is convenient to boutique and department stores, art galleries, and the sidewalk cafés of Newbury Street. Just blocks away is the music of Symphony Hall and the collections and exhibitions at the Museum of Fine Arts.

The newly renovated, award-winning guest rooms are appointed with Italian marble bathrooms and terry bathrobes. Included are such modern amenities as a fax machine, personal voice mail, and a modem port. Simpler needs may be filled by a crackling fire in one of the hotel's select rooms with fireplaces, or a complimentary newspaper waiting at the door each morning. The hallmark service of the family-owned Lenox Hotel ensures a carefree holiday in Boston with the professional staff taking pride in providing every guest with warm, personal attention.

710 Boylston Street
Boston
MA 02116
•
Tel 617 536 5300
Fax 617 267 1237
Freephone in US
800 225 7676
•
General Manager:
Leszlie A. Purstell
•
214 rooms including
3 one bedroom suites
Doubles  $210 - $275 EP
Suites $475 EP

Tax 12.45%
•
Conference facilities,
exercise room
•
Parking available
$26 per day
•
Children welcome
•
Non-smoking
•
VS • MC • Amex
Diners • Discover
JCB • EnRoute

112

## MASSACHUSETTS

# OCEAN EDGE RESORT & GOLF CLUB
### BREWSTER

*Ocean Edge was built in 1890 as a private mansion. Today, guests have the choice of staying in the handsomely renovated hotel or in spacious, fully equipped, beautifully furnished, private bayside or golf course villas with a choice of casual or gourmet dining featuring fresh regional ingredients.*

*The resort's 18-hole championship course, named by Golf Illustrated as one of the top ten conference golf destinations in the country, is the New England site of the prestigious Golf Digest Golf Schools. Ocean Edge is also a popular tennis destination featuring clay and plexi-pave courts. PGA and USPTA pros are available for coaching.*

*A private beach and six swimming pools are available throughout the property. Guests also enjoy jogging and cycle paths leading to the beautiful Cape Cod National Seashore. Nature lovers will appreciate the Audubon Wildlife refuge nearby or taking a whale-watching trip. A few minutes drive brings you to excellent museums, art galleries and theatres.*

2907 Main Street,
Brewster, MA 02631
•
Tel 508 896 9000
Fax 508 896 9123
Freephone in US
800 343 6074
•
General Manager:
Kevin M. Howard
•
88 rooms including
2 one bedroom suites
One, two and three bedroom
apartments and villas.
(Daily maid service)

Doubles $199 - $350 EP
Appts and villas
$190 - $775
Off-season rates available
•
Tax 9.7%
s.c. 18%
•
Private beach, tennis, golf,
fitness center, hiking, spa.
Childrens' programmes
available during
the Summer
•
VS • MC • Amex
Diners • Discover

## MASSACHUSETTS

# PUBLICK HOUSE HISTORIC INN
### STURBRIDGE

The Publick House, established by Colonel Ebenezer Crafts over 220 years ago, is today, a 60 acre resort offering a choice of accommodations ranging from the Publick House Inn itself, featuring colonial style furnishings to the 96-room Country Motor Lodge ideal for families, or the Chamberlain House, for authentic historic lodging.

In the dining room, with wide planks held fast by cast nails, winter breakfast buffets are served at the enormous original open hearth. Other dining choices include Ebenezer's Tavern, a menu of lighter fare and Charlie Brown's Steakhouse or visit the Publick House Bake Shoppe to sample their famous sticky buns. When the weather and the seasons are right, sheep leave their pens to graze on the meadows, extending to the bordering woods.

An ideal stopping point between New York and Boston and for a visit to Old Sturbridge Village, the Publick House maintains a programme of preservation and renovation, which assures both colonial atmosphere and contemporary conveniences.

Rt 131, PO Box 187,
Sturbridge,
MA 01566-0187
•
Tel 508 347 3313
Fax 508 347 5073
Freephone in US
800-Publick
•
Innkeeper:
Lenora Bowen
•
126 rooms
including 9 period suites
& 21 period bedrooms

Doubles $55 - $135 EP
•
Tax 9.7%
•
Outdoor swimming, tennis, golf, fitness center, conference facilities.
•
Children welcome.
•
VS • MC
Amex • Diners

## Experience 1830s Rural New England

Join costumed villagers as they go about their daily chores in their homes, farms, shops and meeting houses in New England's largest outdoor history museum. Enjoy the gardens! Participate in 19th century activities.

Savour traditional New England fare in the Bullard Tavern, and visit the Museum Gift Shop full of treasures, including some made by our own artisans.

A SAVING OF $1 is offered to holders of the Welcome Card or on presentation of a copy of **Selected Hotels & Inns, East Coast North America.**

# Old Sturbridge Village

Old Sturbridge Village
1 Old Sturbridge Village Road, Sturbridge, MA 01566
Tel 508 347 3362   Fax 508 347 9012

We are just a one hour drive west of Boston on the Massachusetts Turnpike. Take exit 9, then Rt 20 West.

**MASSACHUSETTS**

# RED LION INN
## STOCKBRIDGE

The Red Lion Inn, a member of Historic Hotels of America, offers comfortable lodging and excellent food in a landmark setting, where nineteenth century atmosphere is combined with twentieth century efficiency. Warmth and charm welcome guests as they step into the main parlour. The inn has a fine collection of antique furniture and china. There is nowhere better than the long flower-filled verandah, with its rocking chairs, for sitting and watching the world go by.

Most guest rooms have television and all have air conditioning and phones. Dine in the elegant dining room or in the more intimate atmosphere of the Widow Bingham Tavern with its dark panelling. There is evening entertainment in the Lion's Den and in warm weather the courtyard is a delightful place for a meal.

The Red Lion is ideally situated for all Berkshire attractions; visit the Norman Rockwell museum, the Berkshire Playhouse or enjoy a concert on the lawn at Tanglewood. The Inn is a member of the Independent Innkeepers Association.

Main Street,
Stockbridge,
MA 01262
•
Tel 413 298 5545
Fax 413 298 5130
•
General Manager:
C. Brooks Bradbury
•
111 rooms
8 one bedroom,
2 two bedroom suites

Doubles $65 - $155 EP
Suites $165 - $235
•
Tax 9.7%
•
Outdoor swimming pool, exercise room, conference facility for up to 75 people
•
VS • MC
Amex • Discover

## MASSACHUSETTS
# SALEM INN
## SALEM

*Located in the heart of one of America's oldest seaport cities and only 17 miles from Boston, the lovely Federal-style Salem Inn was built in 1834 by sea captain Nathaniel West. It is within walking distance of the harbour and Salem's many museums, restaurants and historic sights.*

*The inn's accommodations include 31 spacious, comfortable, and individually decorated guest rooms featuring antiques, period detail and homey touches. Guest suites, complete with equipped kitchens are ideal for families. All rooms have a queen or dual-king bed, air conditioning, phone, tv and private bath. The inn's restaurant, Courtyard Café, offers two intimate dining rooms and, in warm weather, our secluded brick patio is the perfect place for enjoying a refreshing beverage or a delightful meal. A delicious, hearty continental breakfast is included in the room rates. The inn holds the AAA Three Diamond award.*

7 Summer Street,
Salem, MA 01970
•
Tel 978 741 0680
Fax 978 744 8924
Freephone in US
800 446 2995
•
Innkeepers:
Diane & Richard Pabich
•
39 rooms
11 one bedroom suites
with kitchens

Doubles $99 - $175
B&B
Suites $119 - $175
•
Tax 9.7%
•
Facilities for
small conferences
(up to 20 people)
•
VS • MC • Amex
Diners • Discover

**MASSACHUSETTS**

# THORNCROFT INN
## MARTHA'S VINEYARD

Thorncroft Inn comprises three buildings on three and a half acres of treed grounds, on a peninsula on the lovely island of Martha's Vineyard. It is a secluded, first class country inn, with the Island's only ★★★★ Mobil Rating and only ♦♦♦♦ Award from the AAA. The inn is a couples oriented, honeymoon, anniversary and special occasion destination.

Rooms have private bath, antique furnishings, air conditioning, phone and colour cable tv. Buildings and grounds are completely non-smoking. Rates include full country breakfast in our dining room or, if you prefer, breakfast in bed; afternoon tea and pastries, evening turndown service, free parking and the Boston Globe delivered daily. Most rooms have working, wood-burning fireplaces and canopied beds. Some have furnished balconies or porches, private exterior entrances, two person whirlpool tubs or private 300 gallon hot tubs. There is a self-contained cottage with garage for the guest who prefers absolute privacy.

PO Box 1022, Main Street,
Vineyard Haven,
MA 02568
•
Tel 508 693 3333
Fax 508 693 5419
Freephone in US
800 332 1236
•
Proprietors/Innkeepers:
Lynn & Karl Buder
•
14 rooms
including a one bedroom
cottage (no kitchen)

Doubles $200 - $450
B&B
$160 - $375 (off season)
•
Tax 9.7%
•
Nearby: Atlantic ocean!
Indoor pool, tennis, golf,
riding, sailing, water skiing.
•
Does not meet the
needs of children
•
Non-smoking
•
VS • MC • Amex
Diners • Discover

**MASSACHUSETTS**

# WHALEWALK INN
## CAPE COD

The owners of the Whalewalk, Dick and Carolyn Smith, promise their guests a spoiled vacation in the unspoiled environment of outer Cape Cod, considered by many to be one of the country's most beautiful places.

The Whalewalk, an 1830's whaling master's home has been authentically restored and creatively redecorated with English, French and Danish antiques. It is set on 3 acres of lawns, gardens and trees on a back road, only minutes by car or bike to beaches or Orleans Village. The guest rooms provide a range of individual air conditioned accommodations, and there are 4 large suites or a delightful saltbox self-contained studio cottage, all with wet bars and fireplaces.

The hallmark of this award-winning inn is the warmth and friendship that prevails. Each day begins with a full breakfast served in the sunroom or on the patio, in the evening you can join other guests for a "happy hour" with complimentary hors-d'oeuvres. The inn is about two hours from Boston.

220 Bridge Road,
Eastham,
MA 02642
•
Tel 508 255 0617
Fax 508 240 0017
•
Innkeepers:
Carolyn & Richard Smith
•
11 rooms
5 one bedroom suites
(a two-bedroom suite can
be made available.)

Doubles $140 - $290
B&B
Suites $165 - $190
•
Tax 9.7%
•
Nearby: beaches,
cycling trails.
Small conference facility
•
Children over 12
welcome
•
VS • MC

**MASSACHUSETTS**

# YANKEE CLIPPER INN
## ROCKPORT

Family owned and operated for 50 years and offering gracious hospitality, this resort inn consists of four beautifully converted buildings; two of which are directly on the ocean. Landscaped gardens lead right down to the water and many rooms offer spectacular ocean views. Enjoy a full-service ocean-front restaurant, serving breakfast and gourmet dinner; heated saltwater pool, whirlpool and sauna and movie theatre. Additionally there is a fully equipped, completely private house for weekly rent, set on a hilltop with distant views to the open sea.

Located in a residential section of this delightful, quintessentially New England, seacoast village with its many galleries and shops, the Yankee Clipper is only one hour drive, but a world away from Boston. Our helpful concierge service is always more than delighted to assist with bookings for all local points of interest such as the Gloucester Stage Company, Rockport Art Association, a tour of the North Shore Lighthouses or an unforgettable whale-watch expedition from Cape Ann.

96 Granite Street,
Rockport,
MA 01966
•
Tel 978 546 3407
Fax 978 546 9730
Freephone in US
800 545 3699
•
Innkeepers:
Bob & Barbara Ellis
•
22 rooms
3 one-bedroom,
2 two-bedroom suites
3 bedroom house

Doubles $149 - $239 B&B
Suites $239
3 bedroom house
$2400 per week
(off season $1800
per week)
•
Tax 9.7%
•
Heated saltwater
outdoor pool.
Nearby: tennis, golf,
horseriding, hiking, spa
•
VS • MC
Amex • Discover

# Visit New England
## Circa 1627

Experience life in 17th-century Plymouth. Wander through timber frame homes, grainfields, and garden plots. Talk with Pilgrims and Wampanoag Indians as they go about their daily chores. Visit the 1627 Pilgrim Village, Hobbamock's *(Wampanoag Indian)* Homesite, Crafts Center, and on the harbor, *Mayflower II*.

## PLIMOTH PLANTATION
### PLYMOUTH, MASSACHUSETTS

(508) 746-1622

One hour from Boston. Near Cape Cod. Open April through November. Write for information at P.O. Box 1620, Plymouth, MA 02362

*Produced in cooperation with Plymouth County Development Council.*

**MASSACHUSETTS**

# ADDISON CHOATE INN
## ROCKPORT

Experience the charm and hospitality of coastal New England at the Addison Choate Inn. Set on the tip of Cape Ann, where an ever-changing seascape provides a backdrop for the town's inviting array of artists' galleries, quaint shops, tantalising restaurants, and lazy, serene beaches with Boston only an hour away by train or car. An inn for over 30 years, the charming, late Greek Revival house offers comfortable guest rooms, all with private baths and king, queen, or twin beds. Buffet breakfast, served in the dining room, features freshly ground, private blend coffee, tea, juice, homebaked breads and coffee cakes, "house recipe" granola, cereals and fresh fruits.

It's the little things at the Addison Choate that make for a memorable stay. The awning-shaded, table and chair lined porch overlooking the perennial garden, the pool inviting you for a cooling splash on a hot summer day or a blazing fire on the living room hearth, warming you on a cold winter's evening.

| 49 Broadway, Rockport, MA 01966 Tel 978 546 7543 Fax 978 546 7638 | Freephone in US 800 245 7543 Owners/Innkeepers: Shirley & Knox Johnson | 8 rooms including 1 two room suite, 2 apartments with kitchen Doubles $101 - $110 B&B | Suite & Apartments $130 - $140 weekly rate available for apartments Tax 9.7% | Outdoor pool Nearby: tennis, horse riding, golf, sailing, bicycles, walking, whale-watching, museums, kayaking | Children over 12 welcome Non-Smoking VS•MC•Novus |

---

# BRADFORD INN
## CHATHAM

The AAA Three Diamond Bradford Inn, on two secluded acres in the picturesque seaside village of Chatham, is a short step away from shops, theatre, restaurants, beach, golf and tennis facilities. Guestrooms, furnished for comfort and enjoyment are in seven different buildings. Breakfast is memorable – complimentary, prepared to order and served overlooking the swimming pool and flower-filled gardens. Start your day a special way – our full menu offers long-time New England favourites, along with some specialities of our own. Our fireplaced lounge area is a wonderful place to create or renew friendships, and a meal in our award-winning restaurant, Champlains, open for dinner, mid-May until mid-October, should not be missed. Each season here has its own special ambience...do come... share... and then savour the memories until you return.

| 26 Cross Street, Chatham, MA 02633 Tel 508 945 1030 Fax 508 945 9652 | Freephone in US 800 562 4667 Resident Owners: William & Audrey Gray | 29 rooms and suites, some with kitchens. 1 two-bedroom fully equipped house | Doubles/suites $139 – $199 B&B (lower rates off-season) Suites $179 - $249 | Tax 9.7% Outdoor pool. Nearby: tennis, golf, sailing, water skiing, beaches | Does not meet the needs of children under 7 VS • MC • Amex |

## MASSACHUSETTS

# CAMBRIDGE HOUSE
## CAMBRIDGE

Our 1892 colonial revival inn is unique for its attention to perfect period detail and unparalleled personalized service. Guests are treated to gourmet breakfasts of soufflé omelets surrounded by vibrant berry sauces, home-made sausage and oversized waffles. Fresh fruits and baked goods are available throughout the day, and on winter evenings guests gather for wine, cheese and hot hors-d'oeuvres served by a crackling fire in the inn's welcoming antique-filled parlour.

Ideally situated for sightseeing, close to Harvard Square and 5 minutes walk to the subway which takes you into the heart of downtown Boston. Your hosts, long-time Cambridge residents have an inexhaustible knowledge of the area and all it has to offer and extend to you the warmest of invitations.

| 2218 Massachusetts Avenue, Cambridge, MA 02140-1836 | Tel 617 491 6300 Fax 617 868 2318 Freephone in US 800 232 9989 | Owner: Ellen Riley 16 rooms, 10 with bath en-suite, 4 with shared bath | Doubles $99 - $250 B&B Tax 12.45% | Non-smoking Children over 6 welcome | Complimentary off-street parking VS • MC • Amex |

# CORNER HOUSE INN
## NANTUCKET

To travel to Nantucket Island and to Corner House is to step back in time to the romantic early 19th Century whaling era. At this attractive and historic village inn, brought gently into the 20th Century, enjoy civilized comforts including private baths, down comforters, pillows piled on handsome firm beds and some rooms with tv and refrigerator. Other joys include attractive sitting rooms, cosy fires on chilly days, a screened porch overlooking a charming garden terrace, homebaked continental breakfast and afternoon tea. The superb location is a short walk to ferries, shops, restaurants, theatres, museums, beaches and tennis. A car is not necessary! Resident owners John and Sandy Knox-Johnston are happy to share their favourite restaurants, quiet beaches, bicycle routes, birding walks or whatever your soul is seeking.

| 49 Centre Street, Box 1828, Nantucket, MA 02554 | Tel 508 228 1530 Innkeepers: John & Sandy Knox-Johnston | 15 rooms 1 one bedroom suite 1 small apartment, sleeps three people | Doubles $105 - $185 B&B Suites $175 - $210 (lower rates off season) | Tax 9.7% 60 miles of beaches surround Nearby: tennis, golf, sailing, fitness center | Children over 8 welcome VS • MC Discover |

**MASSACHUSETTS**

# CAPTAIN NICKERSON INN
## SOUTH DENNIS

Delightful 1828 sea captain's home with white wicker rockers on the comfortable front porch. Guest rooms are decorated with period four poster or white iron queen beds and oriental or hand woven rugs. The welcoming, fireplaced living room has a cable tv, vcr and stained glass windows and popular board games are available for guests, as are a selection of video movies.

Bicycles can be hired for a small fee and the inn is itself located on a bike path with the Cape Cod 20 mile bike Rail Trail ½ a mile away. Other area attractions include championship public golf courses, world class beaches, paddle boats, horseback riding, museums, Cape Playhouse, fishing, craft shops and a local church which houses the oldest working pipe organ in the U.S. Children of all ages are very welcome. Full breakfast is satisfying with homemade muffins and a hot entrée.

| 333 Main Street South Dennis, Cape Cod MA 02660 | Tel/Fax 508 398 5966 Freephone in US 800 282 1619 | Owner/Innkeeper: Patricia York 5 rooms, 3 with private bath. | Doubles $60 - $90 B&B Tax 9.7% Bicycles available | Nearby: tennis, golf, riding, sailing, 2 miles from beach. Children welcome. | Non-smoking. Smoking allowed on porch. VS • MC • Discover |

---

# GRAFTON INN
## FALMOUTH

Experience a true breath of Old Cape Cod, in this Victorian style inn set right on the ocean at Falmouth Heights. Enhancing your seaside stay are bright and airy guest rooms comfortably furnished with thoughtful extra touches such as ceiling fans, fluffy towels, French milled soaps, extra pillows, fresh flowers and even homemade chocolates on the nightstand.

The view is glorious, you can watch the ever changing panorama of cruise ships, windsurfers and sailing vessels or explore miles and miles of Falmouth beaches. When darkness falls, enjoy the moon shimmering on the ocean and the lights of Martha's Vineyard spread before you. Full breakfast, served on the sun porch, begins with fresh fruit and juices and may be followed by delicious herb omelettes, blueberry pancakes, Hawaiian toast with real maple syrup or Belgian Waffles. Just the thing for appetites whetted by the sea air!

| 261 Grand Avenue South, Falmouth, MA 02540 | Tel 508 540 8688 Fax 508 540 1861 Freephone in US 800 642 4069 | Owners/Innkeepers: Liz & Rudy Cvitan 11 rooms Doubles $95 - $169 B&B | Tax 9.7% Ocean swimming, sailing, water-skiing Nearby: tennis, golf, horse riding | Not suitable for children under sixteen | Non-smoking VS•MC•Amex Travellers cheques |

**MASSACHUSETTS**

# HAWTHORNE INN
## CONCORD

Just 45 minutes from Boston and located in the historic area of Concord, the Hawthorne is steeped in history and literary associations standing as it does on land that once belonged to Ralph Waldo Emerson, the Alcotts and Nathaniel Hawthorne. Our rooms are appointed with antique furnishings, beautifully designed hand-made quilts, and wood floors graced with oriental and rag rugs all highlighted by wonderful colours that rest the soul and warm the heart.

Each morning at a common table our guests enjoy a continental breakfast – raspberries from our patch, grapes from our vines and soon, if the bees keep working, our own honey for your enjoyment.

Our town is alive with history, beauty and peacefulness. We at the Hawthorne Inn hope we have captured a small part of what is Concord.

| 462 Lexington Road, Concord, MA 01742 | Tel 508 369 5610 Fax 508 287 4949 | Innkeepers: Gregory Burch & Marilyn Mudry 7 rooms | Doubles $125 - $185 B&B Tax 9.7% | Nearby: swimming in Walden Pond, tennis, golf, boating, cross country skiing | Non-smoking Children welcome VS • MC • Amex |

# INN AT STOCKBRIDGE
## STOCKBRIDGE

Just a mile from Main Street Stockbridge, a country lane leads into the circular drive of the twelve acre, owner-occupied, Inn at Stockbridge, an elegant Georgian colonial mansion.

Rooms are individually decorated with wonderful views over meadows and hills. Spacious public areas include living room with grand piano, library and tv room with board-games and puzzles. Relax on the wicker furnished porch, soak up the sun around the pool, or take a stroll in the woods.

An abundant breakfast is served round a sixteen place mahogany table, beautifully set with silver and china. Tanglewood, Summer theatre and the Norman Rockwell Museum are all nearby. The Inn holds the Three Star Mobil award.

| Rt 7 (north), Stockbridge, MA 01262 | Tel 413 298 3337 Fax 413 298 3406 Innkeepers: Alice & Len Schiller | 8 rooms Doubles $115 – $235 B&B Tax 9.7% s.c. 5% | Outdoor swimming pool. Nearby: tennis, golf | Non-smoking Children over 12 welcome | VS • MC Amex |

**MASSACHUSETTS**

# ISAIAH HALL
## DENNIS

*The warmth of true country ambience and hospitality in the heart of Cape Cod. On a quiet historic street, this lovely 1857 farmhouse offers relaxation in beautiful gardens or comfortable antique furnished parlour scattered with oriental rugs. Guest rooms are decorated with care and charm, and a delicious breakfast is served around the farmhouse table.*

*Take a leisurely walk to the beach or the village with its restaurants, shops, theatre and fine arts museum. Enjoy bike trails, tennis, golf and whale watching, take a day trip to Provincetown, Plymouth or the Islands.*

*Awarded AAA Three Diamonds and selected by various media as one of the best places to stay on the Cape, we invite you to join us for a while.*

| 152 Whig Street, P.O. Box 1007, Dennis, MA 02638-1917 | Tel 508 385 9928 Fax 508 385 5879 Freephone in US 800 736 0160 | Owner/Innkeeper: Marie Brophy 11 rooms all except 1 with private bath | Doubles $85 – $122 B&B Tax 9.7% | Nearby: golf, tennis, horseriding, beaches, sailing, water skiing | Best meets the needs of children over 7 VS • MC • Amex |

# ISAIAH JONES HOMESTEAD
## SANDWICH

*This beautifully restored, 1849 Italianate Victorian home in historic Sandwich Village is steps away from most points of interest, and a short drive to many other historic attractions. Guests enjoy beautifully furnished rooms, taking them back to a gentler more romantic time, pampered with luxurious baths, some with oversize whirlpool tubs, robes, candles and other amenities.*

*Three guest rooms and the gathering room have fireplaces for a cosy retreat in cooler weather.*

*After a delicious full breakfast, served by candlelight, stroll through the charming village, enjoying its white steepled church, 1630 grist mill, Hoxie House and Sandwich Glass Museum. Beaches, Plimoth Plantation, Heritage Plantation, Provincetown and ferries to the Islands are nearby, as are fine restaurants, golf courses, antiquing and biking. Sandwich is just 65 miles from Boston.*

| 165 Main St, Sandwich, MA 02563 | Tel 508 888 9115 Freephone in US 800 526 1625 | Innkeepers: Shirley & Bud Lamson 5 rooms | Doubles $75 - $155 B&B Tax 9.7% | Nearby: tennis, golf, conference facilities, biking Children over 12 welcome | Non-smoking VS • MC Amex • Discover |

## MASSACHUSETTS

# JOHN CARVER INN
## PLYMOUTH

*In the heart of Plymouth, just 45 minutes from Boston/Logan Airport, sits the lovely John Carver Inn. From stately entrance to spacious overnight rooms, the staff of this quaint family-owned and operated Inn immediately makes you feel welcome. Guest rooms are thoughtfully and tastefully decorated with warm colonial furnishings. Delicious New England cuisine is served daily in the Hearth 'n' Kettle Restaurant with moderately priced meals sure to please all appetites, or sit in our pub for a drink after a day of sightseeing. We are steps from beaches, whale-watching and a host of historical and recreational attractions such as the historic Plimoth Plantation. Our front desk staff will be delighted to help you plan your excursions, share their favourite spots and even sell you discounted tickets right at the John Carver Inn.*

| 25 Summer Street, Plymouth, MA 02360 | Tel 508 746 7100 Fax 508 746 8329 Freephone in US 800 274 1620 | Innkeepers: The Catania Family 79 rooms incl. 2 suites Doubles from $75 EP | MAP rates also available Tax 9.7% Outdoor pool | Nearby: tennis, golf, sailing, hiking, cycling, Plimoth Plantation and The Mayflower | Ideal with or without children VS • MC Amex • Diners |

# LIBERTY HILL INN
## YARMOUTH PORT

*A comfortably elegant bed and breakfast welcomes travellers to Yarmouth Port, a delightful seaside village near Cape Cod Bay. Traditionally appointed spacious rooms pamper you with canopy beds, air conditioning, romantic fireplaces, cable tv, even an oversized whirlpool. Built as a private home for a whaling tycoon in 1825, the inn is in a park-like setting, surrounded by gardens and conveniently located on Main Street.*
*Liberty Hill Inn's central position on the Cape, just ninety minutes from Boston, is ideal for exploring all area attractions and Jack and Beth are always happy to help with maps, directions, and recommendations. Stroll to village shops and first class restaurants; take a run on the beach; explore marked nature trails or enjoy countless miles of peaceful country lanes, many with breathtaking views of the Cape's beautiful shoreline. Discover Liberty Hill, where yesterday and today meet to create your memories of tomorrow.*

| 77 Main Street, Yarmouth Port, MA 02675 Tel 508 362 3976 Fax 508 362 6185 | Freephone in US 800 821 3977 Owners/Innkeepers: Jack & Beth Flanagan | 9 rooms including 1 two bedroom suite | Doubles $85 - $185 B&B Tax 9.7% | Nearby: outdoor & indoor pools, tennis, horse riding, water-skiing, summer theatre, craftshops, golf, sailing | Children welcome Smoking in designated areas VS•MC•Amex |

## MASSACHUSETTS

# LIGHTHOUSE INN
## WEST DENNIS

The Stone family warmly welcomes you to an oceanfront, country inn complex, located on nine secluded acres on the shore of Nantucket Sound, ideal for relaxation whilst still being central to all points of interest on beautiful Cape Cod. Enjoy the soothing sounds of the ocean, our private beach, the warm salt water of the Sound, and the sight of your child enjoying new-found friends in the childrens' programme. We offer a wide selection of accommodations, in cottages with fireplaces, Cape-style houses with guest rooms, individual suites, and rooms, in the Main House. In our dining room savour the five-course menu featuring a variety of fresh fish caught in Cape Cod waters. Each morning our full, American breakfast gets your day started on the right foot! For your next vacation, experience the rejuvenating spirit of old Cape Cod ... Lighthouse Inn!

| | | | | | | |
|---|---|---|---|---|---|---|
| 1 Lighthouse Inn Road, West Dennis, MA 02670 Tel 508 398 2244 Fax 508 398 5658 | General Manager: Patricia Stone 61 rooms including 5 one bedroom suites, | 5 two bedroom suites & cottages Doubles & suites $124 - $336 B&B, $214 - $648 MAP | Cottages $850 weekly Tax 10.2% s.c. included. | Outdoor pool, 300 feet of private ocean, tennis Nearby: golf, riding, sailing, water skiing | Children welcome. Childrens' summer programme. VS • MC |

# LONGFELLOW'S WAYSIDE INN
## SUDBURY

Immortalized in 1863 by Longfellow in his Tales of the Wayside Inn, this National Historic Site is the oldest operating inn in America. Situated on more than 100 landscaped acres just west of Boston, the site includes the original inn with ten guest rooms, seven separate dining areas, museum rooms, a working grist mill (open Apr-Nov), a beautiful steepled chapel, and the Redstone Schoolhouse of Mary Had a Little Lamb fame.
Taste America's first cocktail, the cow-wow, while seated beside the roaring fireplace in the old bar, then feast on sumptuous yankee fare in our fireplaced dining rooms - complete with fresh corn muffins courtesy of the Grist Mill.
The Redstone Schoolhouse, rebuilt on the site by one time owner Henry Ford, is visited by thousands of school children every year, and hundreds of weddings take place at the Martha-May chapel.

| | | | | | |
|---|---|---|---|---|---|
| Wayside Inn Road, Sudbury, MA 01776 | Tel 508 443 1776 Fax 508 443 2312 Freephone in US 800 339 1776 | Innkeeper: Robert Purrington 10 rooms Doubles $90 - $120 B&B | Tax 5.7% Nearby: golf, fishing, cross-country skiing | Parking available free of charge. Children welcome. | Non-smoking VS • MC • Amex Diners • Discover |

## MASSACHUSETTS

# THE MARLBOROUGH
## WOODS HOLE

Romantic Cape Cod cottage complete with picket fence, trellis and garden, set on a hill among beautiful old maple trees. Rooms, all with private bath, are individually decorated with quilts, co-ordinated scented linens and collectibles. Our large comfortable parlour is ideal for conversation, reading or television. Full gourmet breakfast with wonderfully brewed tea and our house blend of coffee. Informal afternoon tea with our own fresh home baked muffins is a great way to relax after a busy day on the Cape. AAA 3 Diamond and 3 Star Mobil rated. Excellent restaurants nearby, plus ferries to Martha's Vineyard. Woods Hole Oceanographic Institute and the National Marine Biology Laboratories, quaint shops, beaches, golf course and bike paths are only minutes away. The Inn owner, Al, will do his best to point out hidden points of interest.

| | | | | | | |
|---|---|---|---|---|---|---|
| 320 Woods Hole Road, PO Box 238, Woods Hole, MA 02543-0238 | Tel 508 548 6218 Fax 508 457 7519 Freephone from the UK 0800 96 22 79 | Owner: Al Hammond Innkeeper: Richard Hunt 5 rooms | Doubles $85 - $125 B&B (off season $65-$95) Tax 9.7% | Non-smoking Outdoor pool, paddle tennis Nearby: golf, bike path | Does not meet the needs of children under 2 VS • MC • Amex |

# MARY PRENTISS INN
## BOSTON

One hundred and fifty years ago the Mary Prentiss Inn was a country estate. Today it is surrounded by universities, museums, theatres, shops and restaurants. Conveniently located just off Massachusetts Avenue and a few blocks from Harvard University, the centre of Boston is easily accessed by subway, with the station a few minutes from the Inn.

Relax in comfortable spacious rooms, each individually decorated, many with working fireplaces and all appointed with carefully chosen vintage furnishings and your choice of down or hypoallergenic pillows. Enjoy your continental buffet breakfast, an array of juices, baked breads, home made jams and muffins with steaming pots of freshly brewed coffee and fine teas, in the parlour or on the outdoor deck.

| | | | | | |
|---|---|---|---|---|---|
| 6 Prentiss Street, Cambridge, MA 02140 | Tel 617 661 2929 Fax 617 661 5989 Manager: Jennifer Rei Lewis | 18 rooms, 16 of the rooms have wet bars, sinks, microwaves and refrigerators | Doubles $89 – $199 Suites $139 - $199 Tax 9.7% Non-smoking | Limited free parking available on site, spaces should be reserved ahead of time | Children welcome VS • MC |

**MASSACHUSETTS**

# MOSTLY HALL
## FALMOUTH

Built in 1849, a sea captain's wedding gift, the plantation-style house with wrap-around porch, lofty ceilings, tall shuttered windows and dramatic central hallway (hence the name!) is set in a landscaped park in Falmouth's historic district. The enclosed widow's walk, fitted out as a guest den with tv and travel library, and the garden gazebo are special places to relax.
Spacious air-conditioned guest rooms feature private baths, four poster queen size canopy beds, floral wallpapers, reading areas and antiques. Rates include full breakfast, afternoon refreshments and use of bicycles. A very special complimentary honeymoon package is available for a minimum stay of three nights. Close to restaurants, shops, beaches and ferries, and only 90 minutes from Boston, the inn is an ideal base from which to explore the Cape.

| 27 Main Street, Falmouth, MA 02540 | Tel 508 548 3342
Fax 508 457 1572
Freephone in US
800 682 0565 | Owner/Innkeepers:
Caroline & Jim Lloyd
6 rooms | Doubles $95 - $130
B&B
Tax 9.7% | Non-smoking
Nearby: tennis, golf, beaches, sailing | Does not meet the needs of children
VS • MC
Amex • Discover |

---

# ONSET POINTE INN
## ONSET

The Onset Pointe Inn is the unspoiled Cape you've always imagined. Quiet walks, romantic evenings, the lap of the surf, boats moored at the door, a wicker rocking chair, a bay-view from your own private balcony.

Our beautiful bed and breakfast inn offers accommodations directly on the beach. Days start with a delicious breakfast, available in the waterfront dining room or on the verandah.

Then the hours are yours to do as you please – shop, sightsee, play golf or tennis at nearby facilities, or just lounge on our own sandy beach.

At day's end the sun sets into the bay with a spectacular array of colours – this is truly Cape Cod life at its best!

| 9 Eagle Way, Onset, MA 02558-1450 | Tel 508 295 8442
Fax  508 295 5241
Freephone in US
800 35 ONSET | Innkeepers:
Debi & Joe Lopes | 14 rooms, 7 in the Mansion and 7 in the Carriage House and Guest Cottages.
3 have kitchens | Doubles $75 – $150
B&B
Tax 9.7%
Non-smoking | Children welcome in guest cottages
VS • MC • Amex |

**MASSACHUSETTS**

# PHEASANT HILL INN
## MARBLEHEAD

On the crest of a hill overlooking the Atlantic Ocean is this turn of the century shingle-style intimate bed and breakfast inn offering comfort, New England charm, a seaside town atmosphere and the convenience of being just fifteen miles from Boston.

Originally built as a summer retreat, Pheasant Hill has the ambience of a more relaxed and gracious era and you can choose a quiet spot to read and relax, stroll a couple of blocks to Devereux beach, explore the shops, galleries and restaurants of Marblehead, or take a trip into the city.

The Garden Suite has its own private wing of the house with a separate parlour, working fireplace and outdoor deck, while Tree Tops has two beds and an adjacent den with sofabed. Bird's Nest has its own private entrance and sitting room, all bedrooms are air conditioned.

71 Bubier Road, Marblehead, MA 01945

Tel 617 631 0956
Owners/Innkeepers: Bill & Nancy Coolidge

3 one bedroom suites

Doubles $95 - $145 B&B

Nearby: golf, sailing, lawn games
Children over 12 welcome

Smoking in designated areas
VS•MC•Amex

---

# PLEASANT BAY VILLAGE RESORT
## CHATHAM

We have made it our goal over the years to offer the most distinctive and beautiful resort in Chatham. Accommodations are tastefully decorated with contemporary furnishings. Efficiencies and suites with one or two bedrooms offer fully equipped kitchens ideal for family or friends. Exotic gardens nestle among six acres of private woodlands on this lovely part of the Cape. In the centre of our grounds a cascading waterfall crowns an ornamental pond. Nothing is spared in the preparation of gourmet breakfasts right down to the pure maple syrup and freshly squeezed juices. In July and August, lunch is served poolside from the grill. From the Cape, take a whale-watch tour, a day trip to Martha's Vineyard or Nantucket or charter a sport fishing boat.

PO Box 772, Chatham, MA 02633
Tel 508 945 1133
Fax 508 945 9701

Freephone in US 800 547 1011
Proprietor: Howard L. Gamsey

58 rooms/efficiencies
Suites: 2 one-bedroom, 8 two-bedroom. Many offer self-catering facilities.

Doubles $135 - $215 EP
Suites $315 - $375
Tax 9.7% s.c. 5%

Outdoor heated pool
Nearby: tennis, golf, sailing

Children welcome
VS • MC • Amex

**MASSACHUSETTS**

# QUEEN ANNE INN
## CHATHAM

Over 150 years old and welcoming guests since 1874, while all rooms have today's amenities; private bathrooms, phones, and tv, many of the antiques have never left the inn. Rooms overlooking the garden have large private balconies and a beautiful view. Working fireplaces and private whirlpools add to the comfort of other rooms. A large, heated, outdoor pool, an indoor spa and three beautiful private clay tennis courts are at our guests' exclusive disposal. Our popular restaurant serves dinner from May 1 through January 1. Tucked away from the hectic life, Chatham sits between the Atlantic and the still waters of Nantucket Sound. Quiet lanes lead through clusters of shingled cottages. Others lead you to the bustling activity of the fish piers. We love Chatham and are sure you will too.

| | | | | |
|---|---|---|---|---|
| 70 Queen Anne Road, Chatham, Cape Cod, MA 02633<br>Tel 508 945 0394<br>Fax 508 945 4884 | Freephone in US<br>800 545 4667<br>Innkeeper:<br>Guenther Weinkopf | 31 rooms<br>Doubles<br>$167 - $295 B&B<br>Tax 9.7% | Outdoor pool, indoor whirlpool, spa, tennis, conference facilities for 30. | Mountain bikes & boat excursions can be arranged by the inn. Nearby: golf, riding, sailing, water skiing. | Children welcome.<br>VS • MC • Amex<br>Diners • Discover |

# ROCKY SHORES INN & COTTAGES
## ROCKPORT

A turn of the century hilltop mansion with panoramic Atlantic views, each bedroom has its own particular flavour, some reflecting a summery mood – white wicker and light colours, others with a period feel. Fresh flowers and sweets add to the sense of welcome, while complimentary buffet-style continental breakfast is served in the dining room.

The fully equipped clapboard-style cottages with their delightful rustic decor and garden or ocean views are ideal for families with children, seeking self-catering facilities,

Enjoy gazing at the natural beauty of the scenery from the huge outdoor porch which runs the entire length of the house or strolling around the three acres of landscaped lawns. Sandy beaches are only a ten minute walk away.

| | | | | |
|---|---|---|---|---|
| 65 Eden Road, Rockport, MA 01966 | Tel 508 546 2823<br>Freephone in US<br>800 348 4003 | Owners:<br>Renate &<br>Gunter Kostka | 11 rooms<br>11 cottages | Doubles $93 – $120 B&B<br>Cottages $93– $130<br>Tax 9.7% | Cottages ideal for children of any age<br>VS • MC • Amex |

**MASSACHUSETTS**

# SHARON INN
## SHARON

*City convenience, country charm – Phyllis and Ed Raider, are the third generation in more than 50 years to provide hospitality to travellers in their AAA Three Diamond rated motor inn with its beautifully tended lawns and inviting swimming pool. Special touches include complimentary tea and coffee in the rooms; availability of microwaves, refrigerators and vcrs, add to the welcome extended by the owners and their friendly, attentive staff.*
*From May through October two people can stay for two nights and enjoy a full day escorted tour of Boston (only 20 miles away) without having to drive in the city, an ideal way of sightseeing without hassle.*
*With easy access to Southern New England's most famous attractions, enjoy our "Close to the comforts of home" hospitality on your next trip.*

| 775 Providence Highway, (Exit 9 off I-95,) Sharon, MA 02067 | Tel 617 784 5300 Fax 617 784 4862 Freephone in US 800 879 5432 | Owners/Operators: Phyllis & Ed Raider 51 rooms | Doubles $69 – $89 EP Tax 9.7% | Outdoor swimming pool | Children welcome VS • MC • Amex |
|---|---|---|---|---|---|

# VILLAGE GREEN INN
## FALMOUTH

*The Federal style Village Green Inn, tastefully decorated in soft colours, antiques and reproductions, creates a comfortable and restful atmosphere in which to relish your Cape Cod stay. Guest rooms are large, immaculately clean and have air conditioning, private baths, cable tv and some have working fireplaces. In the lovely formal parlour, enjoy complimentary sherry, area restaurant menus and often, stimulating conversation while the gentle Cape Cod breeze fills the air with the scent of salt water. Large porches with white wicker furniture and hanging geranium plants invite you to relax with lemonade and freshly baked cookies, while enjoying the view of the historic Village Green. Fine restaurants, beaches, tennis, bike path and ferry within walking distance. Come, be pampered, enjoy the hospitality of the Village Green Inn.*

| 40 Main Street, Falmouth, Cape Cod MA 02540 | Tel 508 548 5621 Fax 508 457 5051 Freephone in US 800 237 1119 | Co-owners: Diane & Don Crosby 5 rooms including 1 one bedroom suite | (accommodates 3 people, $25 additional person) Doubles & suite $85 - $140 B&B | Tax 9.7 % Nearby: Beaches, tennis, golf, riding, sailing. | Children over 12 welcome. Non-smoking VS • MC • Amex |
|---|---|---|---|---|---|

## MASSACHUSETTS

# WEATHERVANE INN
### SOUTH EGREMONT

The Weathervane Inn began life as a 1785 farmhouse and still has the original fireplace with its beehive bake oven, rarely seen today, but a necessity in bygone days for both cooking and heating. Since purchasing the ten acre property in 1980, Anne and Vincent Murphy have completely renovated the old buildings to create the elegantly comfortable ambience today's guests enjoy.

Comfortably furnished guest rooms with plenty of common areas add to your enjoyment, as does the 20 x 40 ft swimming pool in the grounds. Located just 20 minutes from Tanglewood, summer theatre and the Jacob's Pillow Dance Festival, the inn is in an ideal location for enjoying all that Western Massachusetts has to offer.

Route 23
P.O. Box 388
South Egremont
MA 01258
Tel 413 528 9580
Fax 413 528 1713

Freephone in US
800 528 9580
Owner/Innkeeper:
Vincent & Anne Murphy

12 rooms including 1 one bedroom suite.

Doubles $95 - $135 B&B
$185 - $220 MAP
Suites $200 - $245
Tax 5.7% s.c. 4.3%

Outdoor pool
Nearby: tennis, golf, riding, skiing
Children over 7 welcome.

Non-smoking
VS • MC
Amex • Discover

---

# WEDGEWOOD INN
### YARMOUTH PORT

A handsome, 1812 Greek Revival on two acres of lawn on the Cape's north side, ideal for those who appreciate stately colonial architecture, old maple and chestnut trees, a non-commercialised atmosphere and a warm welcome.

Guest rooms offer private bath and air-conditioning, most have working fireplaces, wide board floors and canopy beds. Fresh fruit and afternoon tea tray are thoughtfully placed in each room. The sunny bay-windowed dining room provides a pleasant setting for a delightful continental breakfast. The inn holds the AAA Three Diamond rating.

Yarmouth Port offers antique shops, historic sights, fine dining and whale-watching cruises. The Inn is ideally located just ten minutes from Hyannis and the island ferries.

83 Main Street,
Yarmouth Port,
MA 02675

Tel 508 362 9178/5157
Fax 508 362 5851
Innkeepers:
Milt & Gerrie Graham

9 rooms including 2 full suites and a junior suite offering private sitting areas and screened porches

Doubles $115 – $150 B&B
Suites $115 – $160

Tax 9.7%
Does not meet the needs of young children

VS • MC • Amex

**MASSACHUSETTS**

# WILDFLOWER INN
## FALMOUTH

The Wildflower Inn, where rocking chairs line the porch and a riot of vibrant flowers bloom in the gardens, is located on beautiful Cape Cod, just 70 miles south of Boston. Built in 1910, the newly renovated inn is located in the heart of Falmouth's historic district.

Guests enter through the fireplaced gathering room, from which a staircase winds its way to the upstairs guest rooms, beautifully decorated and each with its own distinct personality. An attached cottage, with its own private entrance and porch provides a full kitchen, living room and spiral staircase leading to a romantic loft bedroom (honeymooners take note!). A homemade breakfast, served each morning in the gathering room, on the wraparound porch or delivered to your room is included in the rates.

| | | | | | |
|---|---|---|---|---|---|
| 167 Palmer Avenue Falmouth, Cape Cod, MA 02540 | Tel/Fax 508 548 9524 Freephone in US 800 294 5459 Owner/Innkeeper: Donna Stone | 5 rooms 1 cottage with loft bedroom & full kitchen | Doubles $80 - $135 B&B 1 bedroom cottage plus sofabed $125 - $150 (weekly rate $600) | Tax 9.7 % Nearby: 7 miles of beaches, golf, short walk to ferry for Martha's Vineyard | Children welcome in cottage Non-smoking VS • MC • Amex |

---

## *Heritage Plantation of Sandwich*

A diversified museum of Americana and gardens on 76 acres. The Shaker Round Barn houses more than 35 antique and classic autos. The Military Museum has antique firearms, the Art Museum's working carousel hails from 1912. Museum, garden shops and cafe on site. Open May - October.

Grove & Pine Streets, Sandwich, Cape Cod, MA 02563
Tel. 508 888 3300 Fax 508 833 2917 E-mail museumcc@aol.com
*Located just three miles from Cape Cod's Sagamore Bridge.*

# New Hampshire

1. Adair — 145
2. Balsams — 145
3. Buttonwood Inn — 146
4. Chesterfield inn — 137
5. Colby Hill Inn — 146
6. Dexter's Inn & Tennis Club — 147
7. Ellis River House — 147
8. Forest, A Country Inn — 148
9. Foxglove — 148
10. Franconia Inn — 149
11. Hancock Inn — 149
12. Inn at Thorn Hill — 139
13. Inn of Exeter — 140
14. Inns at Mills Falls & Bay Point — 138
15. Manor on Golden Pond — 141
16. New London Inn — 150
17. Notchland — 150
18. Olde Orchard Inn — 151
19. Sise Inn — 142
20. Snowvillage Inn — 143
21. Sugar Hill Inn — 151
22. Village House — 152
23. Waterville Estates Resort — 144

## NEW HAMPSHIRE

# CHESTERFIELD INN
### CHESTERFIELD

Originally a 1787 New Hampshire farm, now a luxurious Country Hotel and AAA Four Diamond award winning property with 13 guest rooms, stunning dining and entertaining facility and beautifully landscaped grounds offering sweeping views of the Vermont mountains.

Our guest rooms put comfort and privacy first. All are spacious, beautifully decorated, with plush bathrooms, self controlled heating and air conditioning, phone, tv and refrigerator. Many have fireplaces and/or garden terraces.

We love imaginative, delicious food with unique flavour combinations and create contemporary cuisine based on regional ingredients. Seafood is fresh from Boston, herbs from our garden and produce from local farmers. Bon appetit! The parlour, dining room and terrace provide a gracious setting for intimate dining as well as weddings and celebrations. The setting sun, panoramic views, fresh flowers and candlelight, provide the perfect backdrop for an incredible dining experience.

Rt 9, PO Box 155
Chesterfield
NH 03443
•
Tel 603 256 3211
Fax 603 256 6131
Freephone in US
800 365 5515
•
Innkeeper:
Phil & Judy Hueber
•
13 rooms
including 2 one bedroom suites.

Doubles $115 - $170
B&B
•
Tax 8%
•
Conference facilities
•
Children welcome
•
Non-smoking
•
VS • MC
Amex • Diners

## NEW HAMPSHIRE

# THE INNS AT MILL FALLS AND BAY POINT
### MEREDITH

One quaint New England village, two charming, multifaceted inns:

The Inn at Mill Falls envelopes guests in an atmosphere of warmth, comfort, and easy relaxation. By combining old-world charm with contemporary comforts such as spacious guest rooms, indoor pool and sauna and private deck - Mill Falls redefines the traditional country inn. A glass-enclosed heated bridge leading from the inn to eighteen delightful shops, galleries and restaurants allows you to shop, dine or explore.

Adjacent to Mill Falls, surrounded by over 2,000 feet of manicured lakefront park, The Inn at Bay Point sits directly on magnificent Lake Winnipesaukee offering the ultimate in accommodations and location. Guest rooms were designed with luxurious comfort in mind and many offer balconies, cozy fireplaces and personal whirlpool spas. All offer spectacular views of the lake and Gunstock Mountain beyond. Dine at your lakeside table, watch the colour of the distant mountains change, or, better yet, pamper yourself with a romantic dinner served on your private balcony.

Rt 3,
Meredith,
NH 03253
•
Tel 603 279 7006
Fax 603 279 6797
Freephone in US
800 622 6455
•
President & General Manager:
Rusty McLear
•
54 rooms at Mill Falls
24 rooms at Bay Point

Doubles $69 - $235 EP
•
Tax 8%
•
Indoor pool, golf, horseriding, sailing, water skiing, fitness center, hiking, spa
•
Children welcome
•
VS • MC
Amex • Diners

**NEW HAMPSHIRE**

# INN AT THORN HILL
## JACKSON

*"A masterpiece among country inns"*, the Inn at Thorn Hill is a smokefree 1895 inn set on a knoll overlooking charming Jackson village, with spectacular views of the White Mountains. It is the perfect choice for honeymooners, romantics and those seeking adult sanctuary. The area offers numerous diversions throughout the year including swimming, golf and hiking in Summer; tobogganing, outdoor hot tub, cross-country and down-hill skiing, sleigh rides and ice skating in Winter.

Relax in the wicker furniture on the spacious porch, or in the fireplaced common rooms. The pub is intimate, the dining elegant with expertly prepared food and attentive service. There are 19 uniquely decorated, air-conditioned bed chambers in the Main Inn, Carriage House or Cottages where guests rest comfortably in their mountain quiet. Recommended by many Inn guides and Gourmet and Bon Appetit magazines, the Inn holds the Three Star Mobil and Three Diamond AAA awards. Special seasonal packages are available.

P O Box A,
Thorn Hill Road,
Jackson, NH 03846
•
Tel 603 383 4242
Fax 603 383 8062
Freephone in US
800 289 8990
•
Innkeepers:
Jim & Ibby Cooper
•
16 rooms
3 two bedroom suites

Doubles $150 - $250 MAP
Suites $230 - $275
•
Tax 8%. s.c. 15%
•
Outdoor swimming pool, cross country skiing from the door, outdoor hot tub
•
Conference facility for up to 45 people
•
VS • MC • Amex .
Diners • Discover

**NEW HAMPSHIRE**

# INN OF EXETER
## EXETER

*The hospitality at the Inn Of Exeter has been a tradition since the Inn was built in 1932.*

*A fine example of Georgian style architecture, the inn houses a variety of guest rooms and family suites with a blend of period antiques and all of the modern amenities a guest or business traveller could require.*

*Casually elegant dining at our Terrace Restaurant is another tradition. Full meal service is also provided in our comfortable and rustic lounge. For business or pleasure, the inn is a marvelous meeting place for lunch or dinner.*

*Conferences and social functions are memorable events and a beautiful courtyard, complete with old fashioned gazebo, is the perfect setting for wedding ceremonies and reunions.*

*Situated on the Campus of the renowned Phillips Exeter Academy, the inn is located within easy walking distance to many historical sites and shops.*

90 Front Street
Exeter, NH 03833
•
Tel 603 772 5901
Fax 603 778 8757
Freephone in US
800 782 8444
•
Innkeeper: Carl G. Jensen
•
47 rooms
including 1 one bedroom suite
•
Doubles $83 - $115 EP
Suite $160 - $175 EP

Tax 8%
•
Conference facilities
Nearby: golf, riding, sailing, cross-country skiing
•
Parking available
free of charge.
•
Children welcome.
•
Non-smoking
•
VS • MC
Amex • Diners

**NEW HAMPSHIRE**

# MANOR ON GOLDEN POND
## HOLDERNESS

The Manor was originally built as a private estate and still provdes the warmth and charm of a country home, reflected in individually decorated bedrooms; most with wood burning fireplaces and views, and some whirlpools for two. Magnificently carved mouldings and rich wood panelling in the dining room provide a setting of classical elegance for nationally acclaimed cuisine. The Manor is an unforgettable romantic hideaway.

Situated in the village of Holderness, and set on the gentle slopes of Shepard Hill, rising above the western shore of pristine Squam Lake (site of the film On Golden Pond) the estate commands a panoramic 65-mile view of the Lake and surrounding mountains. Spacious 13-acre grounds provide a tranquil yet dramatic background for the mansion.

Your hosts, David and Bambi Arnold have dedicated themselves to providing guests with the ultimate in comfort, service and cuisine. They look forward to meeting you.

PO Box T, Rte. 3,
Holderness, NH 03245
•
Tel 603 968 3348
Fax 603 968 2116
Freephone in US
800 545 2141
•
Innkeepers/Owners:
Bambi & David Arnold
•
17 rooms, 4 two bedroom cottages with kitchens and screened in porches. Ideal for families.

Doubles $190 - $325 MAP
Cottages $950 - $1725
weekly 2 - 4 people EP
•
Tax 8% s.c. 15%
•
Tennis, swimming, boating
Nearby: golf, horseriding, skiing
•
Children over 12 welcome at the Manor House
•
Non-smoking
•
VS • MC • Amex

**NEW HAMPSHIRE**

# SISE INN
## PORTSMOUTH

Located in the heart of historic Portsmouth, New Hampshire, Sise Inn was originally the home of prosperous businessman and merchant John E. Sise and his family. The 1881 Queen Anne home enjoyed single ownership status until the mid-1930's.

The inn is located on the seacoast, just one hour north of Boston. Rooms and suites have been decorated in the Victorian style using antiques, period reproductions and museum prints. No two rooms are alike.

A complimentary light breakfast is available in the Breakfast Room daily.

The luxurious decor of the inn is reflected in the Sise Room, the Oak Room and the Boardroom, providing the right atmosphere for a serious business meeting or a gourmet dinner party.

Within walking distance from the inn are many fine restaurants, shops, museums and live entertainment. For the outdoor enthusiast, coastal beaches, forested state parks, cross-country skiing, harbour cruises and golf courses are within a ten minute drive.

40 Court St,
Portsmouth,
NH 03801
•
Tel 603 433 1200
Freephone in US
800 267 0525
•
General Manager:
Chris Passero
•
34 rooms
including 7 one bedroom
suites, 4 two bedroom
suites

Doubles $105 - $175 B&B
Suites $125 - $175
•
Tax 8%
•
Conference facilities
Nearby: outdoor pool,
tennis, golf, riding, sailing,
water skiing, skiing
•
Children welcome.
•
Non-smoking
•
VS • MC
Amex • Diners

**NEW HAMPSHIRE**

# SNOWVILLAGE INN
## SNOWVILLE

Located on a hillside with a sweeping view of the White Mountains, Snowvillage Inn is an ideal romantic getaway. No traffic, no noise. Just birds, crickets and the wind playing in the pines. Generous lawns, bordered with stone walls and brightened with award winning gardens offer chairs for mountain-gazing, reading and chatting while secluded hammocks provide excellent retreats for pure relaxation. In Spring and Summer, swimming and canoeing are available in nearby lakes and rivers.

All eighteen rooms at the inn are named after writers - the Robert Frost room with its twelve windows has a breathtaking view of Mount Washington - and are furnished with country antiques, fluffy comforters, quilts and comfortable chairs. Books and cosy places in which to read them, abound.

What makes this inn special? Guests rave about the view, the cuisine, the excellent service and the friendliness of the innkeepers, but most of all they treasure the sense of warmth and serenity experienced the moment they walk through the door.

PO Box 68
Snowville,
NH 03832
•
Tel 603 447 2818
Fax 603 447 5268
Freephone in US
800 447 4345
•
Innkeeper/owners:
Barbara & Kevin Flynn
•
18 rooms
•
Doubles $129 - $219 MAP

Tax 8% s.c. 15%
•
Cross-country skiing, hiking.
Nearby: beach with lake swimming, indoor pool, tennis, golf.
•
Children over 6 welcome.
•
Non-smoking
•
VS • MC • Amex
Diners • Discover

**NEW HAMPSHIRE**

# WATERVILLE ESTATES RESORT
## CAMPTON

Described as "the best kept secret in the White Mountains" Waterville Estates Resort, just two hours drive from Boston, offers a unique choice of lodging options ideal for family or friends travelling together, with the added freedom of self-catering. Choose from private, beautifully designed, fully furnished and equipped contemporary homes or comfortable condominiums ranging in size from one to four bedrooms many with additional sleeping areas.

Year-round enjoy our beautiful new sports centre with tennis, indoor and outdoor pools, fitness centre, white sandy beach, restaurant, mountain bike trails and trout fishing in the crystal clear Mad River. The ski area (lighted for evenings) with double chairlift, offers cross-country skiing with numerous other ski options at a choice of nearby resorts.

Waterville Estates Realty,
71 Waterville Estates,
Campton, NH 03223-9707

- 

Tel 603 726 3716
Fax 603 726 4503
Freephone in US
800 222 5064

- 

Owner: Tom Mullen

- 

10 homes,
24 condominiums

- 

One-bedroom units
from $96 - $120 EP

Four-bedroom units from $180. Special rates available for visits of over 3 nights.

- 

Tax 8% s.c. 7%

- 

Indoor, outdoor pools, tennis, fitness centre, conference facilities, children's summer and winter programmes. Nearby golf, sailing, water skiing

- 

Children welcome

- 

VS • MC

## NEW HAMPSHIRE

# ADAIR
## BETHLEHEM

*Relax at Adair. Choose a quiet stroll through the Olmsted Gardens and wooded trails or enjoy a scenic drive through the spectacular White Mountains of New Hampshire. Wander through unique antique shops or simply curl up with a good book in front of a fire. Linger over delightful breakfasts with hot popovers every morning and enjoy a traditional afternoon tea.*

*Built in 1927 as a wedding gift for Dorothy Adair Hogan by her father, Adair is now a luxury country inn resting on 200 acres and surrounded by dramatic views of the Presidential Mountain Ranges. Its extensive gardens were originally landscaped by the Olmsted Brothers, famous for New York's Central Park and Boston's Emerald Necklace. Step back in time and indulge yourself in spacious guest rooms, fireplaces, gardens, tennis, strolling paths and memorable dining. Enjoy the quiet elegance that has earned Adair the AAA Four Diamond Award.*

| | | | | |
|---|---|---|---|---|
| 80 Guider Lane, Bethlehem, NH 03574  Tel 603 444 2600  Fax 603 444 4823 | Freephone in US 888 444 2600  Owners: Pat, Hardy & Nancy Banfield | 9 rooms, including 2 one bedroom suites  Doubles $135 - $155 B&B | Suites $185 - $220  Tax 8% | Tennis, snowshoeing Nearby: cross-country skiing, golf, down-hill skiing, antiquing, hiking | Children over 12 welcome  Non-smoking  VS•MC•Amex |

# BALSAMS GRAND RESORT HOTEL
## DIXVILLE NOTCH

*The Balsams is a fifteen thousand acre estate set in the Great North Woods region of the White Mountains. This Four Star resort overlooking Lake Gloriette offers world-class recreational facilities throughout the year. The heritage of this grand old resort and appropriate use of the beautiful natural environment, are of the greatest importance to the management and staff, many of whom have followed parents and grandparents into employment here. Not surprisingly, courteous and caring guest service is a key contributor to a splendid reputation enjoyed since the Balsam's 1866 opening. Designated an Historic Hotel of America, the resort is outstanding value for family vacations.*

*Rates are American plan and include three choice-of-menu award-winning meals each day, unlimited free use of resort activities, movies and three rooms of entertainment each night providing music and dancing. Summer activities include twenty-seven holes of golf, tennis, hiking, biking, fly-fishing and boating. Winter pastimes include alpine and cross-country skiing, snowboarding, snowshoeing and skating.*

| | | | | |
|---|---|---|---|---|
| Route 26, Dixville Notch, NH 03576  Tel 603 255 3400  Fax 603 255 4221 | Freephone in US 800 255 0600  General Manager: Warren Pearson | 200 rooms, including 20 one and two bedroom suites | Doubles $250 - $430 AP  Suites $550 - $600  Tax 8% s.c. 15% | Outdoor pool, tennis, cross-country and down-hill skiing, golf, snowshoeing, fly-fishing, mountain biking, hiking | Children over 6 months welcome  Smoking in designated areas  VS•MC•Amex•Discover |

145

## NEW HAMPSHIRE

# BUTTONWOOD INN
## NORTH CONWAY

Allow us to pamper you with personal service. As native New Englanders we help you with knowledgeable travel tips. Located on five wooded acres at the end of a no-through road on the side of a little mountain, we're only two miles from the village of North Conway. The nearby White Mountain National Forest's 780,000 acres offer unlimited outdoor activities year round.

Of our five acres, three are lawns and award-winning gardens, ideal for a summer stroll, finishing with a refreshing dip in the pool. Cross-country ski from our back door, Alpine skiing a mile away. We're happy to suggest hikes or walks and ensure you're fully equipped. Early risers enjoy hot coffee or tea from 7.00 am. Breakfast specials include To Die For French Toast, whilst for the faint-hearted, eggs and cold cereals are always available.

| | | | | | |
|---|---|---|---|---|---|
| PO Box 1817, Mount Surprise Road North Conway NH 03860 Tel 603 356 2625 Fax 603 356 3140 | Freephone in US 800 258 2625 Innkeepers: Peter & Claudia Needham | 9 rooms, 5 with private bath. including 1 two bedroom suite | Doubles $70 - $150 B&B Suite $135 - $150 Tax 8% | Outdoor pool Nearby: indoor pool, tennis, golf, riding, down-hill & cross-country skiing. | Children over 3 welcome. Non-smoking VS • MC • Amex |

# COLBY HILL INN
## HENNIKER

*Congenial inn-dogs Bertha and Delilah await with a handshake, and the cookie jar beckons at this rambling 1797 inn, a complex of farmhouse, carriage house, and barns. Enjoy the antique-filled guestrooms, some with working fireplaces, each with private bath and telephone and the comfortable common rooms which are a popular gathering place for visitors.*

*Five acres are lush with perennial gardens and feature a gazebo tucked between ancient apple trees for a quiet retreat. Memorable food begins and ends the day from the bountiful country breakfast to the acclaimed candlelit dinner served every night in the gardenside dining room*

*Classic New England scenery abounds in this delightful village on the river, just 90 minutes from Boston.*

| | | | | | |
|---|---|---|---|---|---|
| 3 The Oaks, PO Box 779 Henniker, NH 03242 Tel 603 428 3181 Fax 603 428 9218 | Freephone in US 800 531 0330 Innkeepers: Ellie & John Day, Laurel Day Mack | 16 rooms Can configure to have 2 three room suites Doubles $85 - $175 B&B | Suites vary according to total of 3-room rate. Tax 8% s.c. 10% | Outdoor pool, winter ice-skating, conference facilities Nearby: tennis, golf, Canterbury Shaker Village. | Children over 7 welcome Non-smoking VS • MC Amex • Diners |

146

**NEW HAMPSHIRE**

# DEXTER'S INN & TENNIS CLUB
## SUNAPEE

*Located on twenty acres in the lovely Sunapee Region of lakes and mountains, Dexter's embodies the essence of a true New England Country Inn. Warm, friendly, and unassuming hospitality is as much in evidence now as it has been for 45 years. Bountiful breakfasts and dinners are served daily and there are three all-weather world-class tennis courts with our resident professional available for tuition should you require.*

*Relax in the pool, stroll along country lanes, read on the terrace, or enjoy croquet, horseshoes or shuffleboard. We are ideally located for day trips to some of the most beautiful and interesting parts of New England. You will find Dexter's an idyllic setting evoking a charming reminder of a time and way of life that has never left this special inn.*

| | | | | |
|---|---|---|---|---|
| PO Box 703 MM, Stagecoach Road, Sunapee, NH 03782 | Tel/Fax 603 763 5571 Freephone in US 800 232 5571 | Innkeepers: Michael W. Durfor, Holly Simpson-Durfor 17 rooms Holly Cottage sleeps 4 | Doubles $135 - $190 MAP Cottage $380 B&B rates available on request | Tax 8% s.c. 15% Outdoor pool, tennis courts, conference facilities | Nearby: golf, sailing Children welcome VS • MC • Discover |

# ELLIS RIVER HOUSE
## JACKSON

*An enchanting, family run, country inn set on three acres overlooking the river and at the base of spectacular Mt Washington, the highest peak in the Northeast. Views from the inn are breathtaking. Amenities include: romantic fireplace guest rooms, spacious two room family suites, an indoor jacuzzi spa, outdoor swimming pool, delicious full country breakfast. Scenic balconies, outdoor patios and comfortable common rooms encourage conversation.*

*In Winter there are 160 kms of world class groomed trails outside the back door, with four major downhill slopes minutes away. Summer activities include hiking, cycling, swimming and factory outlet shopping, while Fall offers spectacular foliage colours. Only three hours from Boston — join us for a taste of Old New England!*

| | | | | |
|---|---|---|---|---|
| Rt 116, PO Box 656, Jackson, NH 03846 Tel 603 383 9339 Fax 603 383 4142 | Freephone in US 800 233 8309 Innkeeper/Owner: Barbara Lubao | 16 rooms, all with private bath. 1 cottage, 4 suites. | Doubles $79 – $229 B&B Cottage/suites $109 – $229 | Tax 8% s.c. 10% Non-smoking Outdoor swimming pool, golf, horseriding | Children welcome VS • MC • Amex |

## NEW HAMPSHIRE

# THE FOREST, A COUNTRY INN
## NORTH CONWAY

On a winding country road, midway between North Conway and Jackson, The Forest, a classic three storey Victorian, began operating in 1890 and has welcomed vacationers ever since. The front yard is enclosed by a low picket fence, while across the gravelled driveway is a small stone guest cottage with fireplace - perfect for that special getaway. The inn carries a Three Diamond rating from the AAA.

With only eleven charming, fireplaced, guest rooms, you're assured of personal, friendly attention. Our beautifully served complimentary breakfast includes fresh fruits, juices and an array of homemade baked goods – spiced belgian waffles, apple pancakes, and more! Tea and refreshments are served each afternoon. Enjoy our large screened verandah, heated outdoor pool, tennis court and lovely gardens.

| | | | | | |
|---|---|---|---|---|---|
| Rt 16A, (at the Intervale), North Conway, NH 03860 Tel 603 356 9772 Fax 603 356 5652 | Freephone in US 800 448 3534 Owner/Innkeepers: Bill & Lisa Guppy | 11 rooms, 9 with private bath. Garden Cottage | Doubles $80 – $130 B&B Cottage $100 – $160 | Tax 8% Outdoor swimming pool, tennis | Non-smoking Children welcome VS • MC • Amex |

---

# FOXGLOVE
## SUGAR HILL

Elegance atop Sugar Hill. Newly renovated, designer-decorated, turn-of-the-century country home. Cosy romantic bedrooms and suites, private baths. Crackling fires, park-like woodland setting, hideaway porches, terraces and quiet glades.

Trickling fountains, soft music, swaying hammocks fabulous sunsets. Foxglove offers guests a tranquil and impeccable setting from which to explore and enjoy the charm of this historic mountain village with its magnificent views - Franconia Notch, the White Mountains, The Upper Connecticut River and Mount Washington Valley. Foxglove is open year round and surrounded by a myriad of all-seasons sports and activities.

Rooms for two include a sumptuous breakfast with silver, china, crystal and other amenities. Casual comfort and attention to detail prevail.

| | | | | | |
|---|---|---|---|---|---|
| Route 117 at Lovers Lane, Sugar Hill, NH 03585 | Tel 603 823 8840 Fax 603 823 5755 Owner/Innkeeper: Janet G. Boyd | 6 rooms including 1 one bedroom suite, 1 two bedroom suite | Doubles $85 - $145 B&B $135 - $195 MAP Tax 8%. s.c. 5% (15% on dinner) | Nearby: outdoor pool, tennis, golf, riding, sailing, water skiing, down-hill & cross-country skiing | Children over 12 welcome Non-smoking VS • MC |

148

**NEW HAMPSHIRE**

# FRANCONIA INN
## FRANCONIA

*Not just a Winter Ski Lodge...
as the snow melts in Spring, four beautiful red clay tennis courts and a large, sunny swimming pool appear. Skis, boots and poles disappear, replaced by horses, saddles and stirrups. Cross-country trails become scenic bridle paths. Where snowbanks once reigned, gardens flourish. The formidable snowcapped White Mountains shed their snow blanket to become a hiker's paradise.*

On 107 acres in the Easton Valley, the inn affords the same magnificent view of Franconia Notch that inspired Robert Frost's poem "The Road Not Taken". Guest and common rooms invite relaxation and become part of your home when you stay with us.

Located 2½ hours north of Boston, we hold the AAA Three Diamond and Mobil Three Star ratings.

| | | | | | |
|---|---|---|---|---|---|
| 1300 Easton Valley Road, Franconia, NH 03580 | Tel 603 823 5542 Fax 603 823 8078 Freephone in US 800 473 5299 | Owners: Alex & Richard Morris 34 rooms | Doubles $140 – $170 MAP Tax 8% | Outdoor swimming pool, tennis, horseriding, cycling, hiking, skiing, sleigh-rides | Children welcome VS • MC • Amex |

# HANCOCK INN
## HANCOCK

*Retreat to the authenticity and gentility of 18th century New England with all the amenities of the 20th century.*
Each guest room has private bath, telephone, comfortable four-poster or canopy bed, handsewn quilts and air conditioning. Rich colonial colours and antiques decorate every corner of the inn and the tavern is now a cosy common room where guests gather fireside to play checkers on an antique board.
In the award-winning restaurant rediscover authentic American fare such as cranberry pot roast. Nearby, pick apples, browse in antique shops, hike or simply gaze upon majestic Mount Monadnock. Local protected woodlands provide habitat for bear, moose, deer, bobcat and coyote. Explore miles of uncrowded hiking and cross-country skiing trails as well as clean lakes and ponds for skating, boating and fishing.

| | | | | | |
|---|---|---|---|---|---|
| 33 Main Street, Hancock, NH 03449 | Tel 603 525 3318 Fax 603 525 9301 Freephone in US 800 525 1789 | Owner/Innkeepers: Joe & Linda Johnston | 11 rooms Doubles $98 - $158 B&B Tax 8% s.c. 10% | Conference facilities Nearby: tennis, golf, riding, sailing, water skiing, down-hill & cross-country skiing | Children over 12 welcome. Non-smoking VS • MC Amex • Diners |

## NEW HAMPSHIRE

# NEW LONDON INN
### NEW LONDON

This classic 1792 country inn, on the Town Green, in one of the most picturesque villages in New England at the heart of the Dartmouth Lake Sunapee Region offers 29 rooms, many with sitting areas. The inn's restaurant features delicious upscale New England fare such as hardwood grilled and house-smoked appetisers and entrées.

Fireplaced, comfortably furnished, sitting rooms, dining room and library invite you to relax after a day spent browsing in unique shops. A short walk brings you to the New London Barn Playhouse - one of the oldest, best-loved summer theatres or visit Colby-Sawyer College, just across the green. Historic Claremont Opera House and Dartmouth College, both under half an hour away, offer year-round cultural activities.

| 140 Main Street<br>PO Box 8<br>New London<br>NH 03257<br>Tel 603 526 2791<br>Fax 603 526 2749 | Freephone in US<br>800 526 2791<br>Innkeepers:<br>Kimberley & Terance<br>O'Mahoney | 29 rooms<br>Doubles $85 - $150<br>B&B<br>Tax 8% | Conference facilities<br>Nearby: tennis, golf, riding, sailing, down-hill skiing, cross-country skiiing | Children over 2 welcome. | Non-smoking<br>VS • MC<br>Amex • Discover |

# NOTCHLAND INN
### HART'S LOCATION

Get away from it all, relax and rejuvenate at our comfortable 1860's granite mansion located on 400 acres in the midst of beautiful mountain vistas.

Settle into one of our seven deluxe rooms or four spacious suites, each individually appointed and all with wood-burning fireplaces and private bath. In the evening, Notchland's wonderful 5-course dinner is served in a romantic fireplaced dining room looking out to the gazebo by our pond.

We have 8,000 feet of Saco River frontage on our property and two of the area's best swimming holes. Coco our Bernese Mountain dog will greet you on arrival while Dolly, the Belgian Draft Horse pulls our sleigh in the Winter. Mork & Mindy are miniature horses with large personalities and as for our Llamas, DC & Sid - well come and meet them for yourselves.

| Rt 302,<br>Hart's Location,<br>NH 03812<br>Tel 603 374 6131<br>Fax 603 374 6168 | Freephone in US<br>800 866 6131<br>Owners/Innkeepers<br>Les Schoof & Ed Butler | 11 rooms<br>including 4 one bedroom suites<br>2 suites in renovated 1850 "schoolhouse" | Doubles $170 - $230<br>MAP<br>Suites $190 - $250<br>Tax 8 % s.c. 15% | River swimming, cross-country skiing.<br>Nearby: outdoor & indoor pools, hiking, tennis, golf, riding, sailing. | Children over 12 welcome.<br>Non-smoking<br>VS • MC • Amex<br>Diners • Discover |

**NEW HAMPSHIRE**

# OLDE ORCHARD INN
## MOULTONBOROUGH

A restored farmhouse on twelve country acres with fruit orchards, a pond and a paddle boat for guest use. In the heart of New Hampshire's Lake region, only a mile from Winnipesaukee where a host of sailing, and water sport options are open to you.

Spring is a wonderful time to visit, as from mid-May to early June our eight acre orchard of several hundred fruit trees, apples, pears, cherries and plums, come into bloom. In late July the fruit begins to ripen, continuing into early November through the stunning Fall foliage displays. In Winter, ski from the front door with five major ski areas within an hours drive.

Children are always welcome at the inn and we offer our guests a large country breakfast with home-baked goods and all the fixin's!

| RR Box 256<br>Moultonborough<br>NH 03254<br>Tel 603 476 5004<br>Fax 603 476 5149 | Freephone in US<br>800 598 5845<br>Owner/Innkeepers:<br>Jim & Mary Senner | 9 rooms including family suite<br>1 one bedroom cottage<br>Doubles $70 - $125, | Family suite $135<br>B&B<br>Cottage $80 for 2 people EP<br>Tax 8% | Small meeting facilities<br>Nearby: tennis, golf, riding, sailing, water-skiing, | down-hill skiing, cross-country skiing<br>Children welcome.<br>Non-smoking<br>VS • MC |

# SUGAR HILL INN
## FRANCONIA

A quintessential country inn. This authentic 18th century farmhouse has been impeccably restored and appointed. Each bedroom has comfortable canopy, beehive or four poster beds, private baths (many with deep soaking tubs), most offer spectacular mountain vistas and several feature romantic fireplaces.

Mornings start with a scrumptious country breakfast, afternoon refreshments of homemade sweets and tea are provided daily. The award-winning cuisine and warm hospitality are unmatched. Please join us in a most pristine setting, where unlimited outdoor activities, chamber concerts and summer theatre are a special treat. While away your afternoon sipping lemonade on a cosy porch rocker.

| Rt 117,<br>Franconia,<br>NH 03580 | Tel 603 823 5621<br>Fax 603  823 5639<br>Freephone in US<br>800 548 4748 | Innkeepers :<br>The Quinn Family<br>Jim , Barbara,Kelly & Stephen<br>16 rooms | Doubles $155 – $245<br>MAP<br>$105 - $145 B&B<br>Tax 8% s.c. 15% | Nearby:  golf, hiking, swimming, cycling, skiing, museum, antiquing, art & gift shops | Non-smoking<br>Does not meet the needs of young children |

**NEW HAMPSHIRE**

# VILLAGE HOUSE
## JACKSON

Just beyond the covered bridge lies the pretty village of Jackson and the Village House, with a tradition of hospitality going back 100 years – the charm and personality of a small B&B with many of the amenities of a larger resort. The Village House offers affordable lodging throughout the year. In Summer, enjoy our swimming pool, jacuzzi, tennis court and wrap-around porch, plus our convenient location to all area sights and attractions. In Winter, warm yourself by a roaring fire, or in our all-season outdoor jacuzzi. Cross country from our door or downhill within minutes. Year-round enjoy our delicious breakfasts. Welcome to the charm and peacefulness of the village of Jackson and one of the loveliest, most relaxing vacations of your life. The place is the Village House... the time is of your choosing... the delights are many...

| | | | | | |
|---|---|---|---|---|---|
| PO Box 359, Rt 16A, Jackson, NH 03846<br>Tel 603 383 6666<br>Fax 603 383 6464 | Freephone in US 800 972 8343<br>Owner/Innkeeper: Robin Crocker | 14 rooms, all with private bath<br>4 rooms offer kitchenettes | Doubles $65 - $130 With kitchenettes $75 - $140 B&B | Tax 8%<br>Outdoor swimming pool. Nearby: tennis, golf, horseriding, hiking | Children welcome<br>VS • MC |

## The Welcome Privilege Card
## A SELECTION OF PROMISES

**VIRGINIA**
**BAILIWICK INN,**
Fairfax, Virginia
*Stay 4 nights, get 5th night free, any night of the week.
*Stay 2 nights get 3rd night free with arrival Sun through Thu. Not valid May, Oct, Dec.
**HIGH MEADOWS VINEYARD & MOUNTAIN SUNSET INN**
Scottsville, Virginia
*Complimentary Champagne or Virginia wine on arrival or prior to dining.
*Stay 3 nights and get 4th night at 50% discount OR
*Stay 4 nights and get 5th night Free.
**HUMMINGBIRD INN**
Goshen, Virginia
*Stay 2 nights and get 3rd night at 50%. Applies Sun - Thu year-round. Every day Nov - Apr
*Complimentary refreshments on arrival

**THE OAKS**
Christiansburg, Virginia
*Complimentary pass to local health club
*Stay 4 nights get 5th night free not available during May, Sep & Oct.
*Arrival treats and something special for celebrations.
**SEVEN HILLS INN,**
Lexington, Virginia
*Complimentary arrival treat such as homemade cookies, tea and soft drinks
*Stay 4 nights get 5th night free.

**NEW ENGLAND**
**CONNECTICUT**
**INN AT NATIONAL HALL,**
Westport, Connecticut
Complimentary arrival treat - wine, fruit, cheese.

*Welcome Privilege Cards are valid for one year from date of issue. One Card entitles a family or group of up to four people travelling together to relevant benefits. The Privilege Card is available for separate purchase at a cost of £10.00/$17.00 per card. All offers are subject to availability.

152

# The Welcome Privilege Card

is an extension of the hospitality offered during your visit to North America. It is our pleasure to include a complimentary Card with every copy of Selected Hotels & Inns. If you have not purchased your copy of the book directly from our office, call, fax, email or write, telling us at what shop, in which town and when you purchased the book and we will be delighted to despatch your personal Privilege Card immediately.

The Card offers value added benefits and savings at numerous inns and hotels. For more examples of advantages available see pages 65, 152, 214 and 253. A complete list of Privilege Promises will be included with your Card but, as new promises are continually being added, it's always a good idea to call us before you leave for your trip so we can send you a fully updated list.

LITTLE INN OF BAYFIELD, Bayfield, Ontario
*Stay 2 nights on an MAP package and receive 3rd night (accommodation only) free.
RIPPLECOVE INN, North Hatley, Quebec
*Free room upgrade valid all year excluding holidays.
CHIMNEY HILL, Lambertville, New Jersey
*Stay 2 nights and receive 3rd night free. Available any season but excludes Holiday Weekends.
EVERMAY ON THE DELAWARE, Erwinna, Pennsylvania
*Stay 2 nights, get a 3rd night at a special privilege rate. Excluding Weekends and Holidays
*Special celebration recognition for a birthday, anniversary or honeymoon.
FRENCH MANOR, South Sterling, Pennsylvania
*Special seasonal arrival gift
HIGH MEADOWS VINEYARD & MOUNTAIN SUNSET INN, Scottsville, Virginia
*Complimentary champagne or Virginia wine on arrival or prior to dining.
*Stay 3 nights and get 4th night at 50% discount OR
*Stay 4 nights and get 5th night Free.

HUMMINGBIRD INN, Goshen, Virginia
*Stay 2 nights and get a 3rd night at 50%. Applies Sun - Thu year-round. Any day of the week Nov - Apr
*Complimentary refreshments on arrival.
SEVEN HILLS INN, Lexington, Virginia
*Complimentary arrival treat such as homemade cookies, tea and soft drinks
*Stay 4 nights get 5th night free.
INN AT NATIONAL HALL, Westport, Connecticut
*Complimentary arrival treat - wine, fruit, cheese.
BLUE HARBOR HOUSE, Camden, Maine
*Discount on delicious lobster dinner.

*Welcome Privilege Cards are valid for one year from date of issue. One Card entitles a family or group of up to four people travelling together to relevant benefits. The Privilege Card is available for separate purchase at a cost of £10.00/$17.00 per card. All offers are subject to availability.

# Rhode Island

1. Bed & Breakfast on the Point — 158
2. Block Island Resorts — 155
3. Cliffside Inn — 156
4. Grandview Bed & Breakfast — 158
5. Larchwood Inn — 159
6. Vanderbilt Hall — 157
7. The Villa — 159

# RHODE ISLAND

# BLOCK ISLAND RESORTS
## BLOCK ISLAND

Sail 13 miles out to sea to discover 19th Century New England at the Hotel Manisses, an elegantly restored Victorian Hotel featuring seventeen meticulously appointed rooms with private baths and phones, some rooms with jacuzzis.

Also owned and run by the Abrams family is the 1661 Inn & Guest House and the Nicholas Ball Cottage, all recently refurbished to provide further luxury accommodations with ocean views, jacuzzis and fireplaces. Hotel Manisses' dining room serves dinner nightly. Choose delicious selections from a widely varied menu. Flaming coffees, after dinner drinks & desserts are served in the upstairs parlour. Complimentary full breakfast buffet and wine and nibble hour are included in the rates.

Life on the Island is slow-paced and relaxing – beaches, harbours, gently rolling hills and flower strewn meadows as well as a quaint Victorian town. If you're looking to get away from it all, this is for you.

Spring Street,
Box 1,
Block Island,
RI 02807
•
Tel 401 466 2421/2836
Fax 401 466 2858
•
Innkeepers:
Joan & Justin Abrams,
Rita & Steve Draper
•
38 rooms
1 three bedroom cottage

Doubles $106 - $318
B&B
•
Tax 12%. s.c.
included in rate
•
Nearby: tennis,
horseriding, sailing,
hiking
•
Children welcome
•
VS • MC • Amex

## RHODE ISLAND

# CLIFFSIDE INN
### NEWPORT

This delightful Second-Empire Victorian manor house was built in 1880 by Maryland Governor Thomas Swann and later owned by noted artist Beatrice Turner whose life and times were chronicled by LIFE magazine in 1950.

The inn's distinctive interior decor features more than 100 Beatrice Turner artworks. The fifteen elegant guest rooms are furnished with antiques, luxurious designer fabrics and linens. Twelve rooms have fireplaces, eleven have whirlpool tubs and one has a steambath.

Located in a quiet residential neighbourhood, the inn is steps from the beginning of the Cliffwalk, Newport's world famous Atlantic seaside walking trail; a five minute walk to Newport's main beach and ideally located for visiting the magnificent Newport mansions. Amenities include complimentary coffee service and full gourmet breakfast in the mornings, and afternoon Victorian tea. We look forward to welcoming you and hope that you will make Cliffside Inn your home-away-from-home.

2 Seaview Avenue,
Newport,
RI 02840
•
Tel 401 847 1811
Fax 401 848 5850
Freephone in US
800 845 1811
•
Innkeeper:
Stephan Nicolas
•
15 rooms including
7 one bedroom suites.

Doubles $175 - $325
B&B
•
Tax 12 %
•
Conference facilities
Nearby: indoor pool,
tennis, golf, sailing
•
Children over 14
welcome.
•
Non-smoking
•
VS • MC • Amex
Diners • Discover

## RHODE ISLAND

# VANDERBILT HALL
## NEWPORT

Built in 1909 by Alfred Vanderbilt for his father Cornelius and donated to the town of Newport, this architecturally distinguished building has now been brought to life again as a mansion house hotel. A clever combination of luxurious furnishings, imagination, flair and humour have been deployed to recreate the warmth and atmosphere of a comfortable historic home.

The fifty rooms offer all that the visitor to Newport could wish, with some of them catering additionally and comprehensively for the special needs of business travellers either on their own or convening for a small business meeting in one of the Hall's admirably equipped Board Rooms.

A short stroll brings you down to Newport's bustling harbour front with its inimitable atmosphere and choice of excellent shops and restaurants - the original home of the America's Cup, while just a few minutes drive takes you back in time to the magnificent summer mansions on aptly named Bellevue Avenue. Breakfasts can be enjoyed in the bright airy conservatory while gourmet candlelit dinners created by the talented, award-winning chef Scott Hoyland should not be missed.

41 Mary Street,
Newport,
RI 02840
•
Tel 401 846 6200
Fax 401 846 0701
•
Freephone in US
888-VAN-HALL
•
Managing Director:
Grant Howlett
•
50 rooms
including 3 one bedroom
suites, 5 two bedroom suites

Doubles $95 - $255 EP
Suites $225 - $695
•
Tax 12% s.c. 8%
•
Indoor pool. Nearby: tennis,
horse riding, water-skiing,
golf, sailing
•
Parking $8 per day
•
Children over 12 welcome
•
Smoking in designated areas
•
VS•MC•Amex•Diners

## RHODE ISLAND

# BED & BREAKFAST ON THE POINT
## NEWPORT

This century-old Victorian style home is 1½ blocks from Narragansett Bay, just fifteen minutes walk to the centre of Newport. Take a guided tour of Newport's historic sites; the harbour or the Mansions. Other attractions are the International Tennis Hall of Fame and the Museum of Newport History.

Your hosts, local history buffs, have an excellent collection of nineteenth century photos and art work displayed on walls. The bedrooms feature King size or twin beds and are furnished with some antique furniture and colourful fabrics. A substantial continental breakfast is served in the wicker filled common room. Most important of all, New England hospitality is featured.

| 102 Third Street Newport RI 02840 | Tel 401 846 8377 Innkeeper: George C. Perry | 4 rooms including 1 two bedroom suite. (3 rooms have private bath) | Doubles $95 - $155 B&B (May-Oct) Suite $150 - $190 (Off season rates lower) Tax 12% | Nearby: tennis, golf, sailing, water skiing, Parking available free of charge. | Children over 12 welcome. Non-smoking VS • MC |

# GRANDVIEW BED & BREAKFAST
## WESTERLY

Enjoy a splendid ocean view from the stone wrap-around porch of this turn of the century hilltop home. A large comfortable living room offers a haven to read, visit with friends – new and old, or just relax on the oversized couch in front of the beautiful stone fireplace. Hearty continental breakfast is served on the large cheery sunporch. Watch Hill and Westerly Beaches are nearby.

Enjoy local theatre, shopping, antiquing or dining in one of the area's many fine restaurants. Explore the delightful fishing village of Stonington, visit Mystic Seaport and Aquarium or drive to lively Newport with its shops, restaurants and the fabulous "Summer Cottages". Foxwoods and Mohegan Sun, two new casinos, are only a short drive away.

| 212 Shore Road, Westerly, RI 02891 | Tel 401 596 6384 Freephone in US 800 447 6384 | Owner: Pat Grande | 10 rooms, 4 of which have private bath Doubles $75 – $95 | Tax 12% Nearby: golf, tennis, beaches | Non-smoking Children welcome VS • MC • Amex |

## RHODE ISLAND

# LARCHWOOD INN
## WAKEFIELD

The village of Wakefield is the perfect setting for a visit to a real, family-run country inn, which has kept pace with the twentieth century without sacrificing any of its rural beauty and traditions. The three storey Larchwood Inn, surrounded by wide expanses of landscaped grounds and located at the quiet end of the village, has also survived the necessities of modernisation, whilst carefully, preserving the charm of its 150 years of history.

Comfortable guest rooms and the choice of four different dining rooms and a cocktail lounge, enhance the warm hospitality of your welcome and offer you an ideal location for exploring all of Rhode Island. Take a ferry to lovely Block Island, tour the incredible Newport mansions, or simply enjoy the nearby sheltered beaches, boating, horseriding and cycling. Whatever your mood, the Larchwood Inn can suit it!

| 521 Main Street, Wakefield, RI 02879 | Tel 401 783 5454 Fax 401 783 1800 Freephone in US 800 275 5450 | Innkeepers: Francis & Diann Browning 20 rooms, 11 with bath en suite | Doubles $60 - $110 EP Tax 12% | Nearby: tennis, golf, horseriding, sailing | Children over 12 welcome VS • MC Amex • Diners |

# THE VILLA
## WESTERLY

Open year round, The Villa is situated at the crossroads of historic Westerly and Watch Hill, minutes from the pristine shoreline of Rhode Island and within easy reach of attractions such as the Newport Mansions and Old Mystic Village. On 1½ landscaped acres and surrounded by beautiful gardens and lawns, the inn offers both privacy and luxury in seven individual and delightfully decorated suites. Friendliness and personal care are provided by your host Jerry Maiorano.

Swim in the sparkling sapphire pool surrounded by lush green plants or relax in the outdoor Jacuzzi spa. Summers are warm and golden with cool ocean breezes and a breakfast buffet is served by the pool, in the dining area or brought to your room. In the winter enjoy the privacy and cosiness of your own fireplace or jacuzzi suite.

| 190 Shore Road, Westerly RI 02891 | Tel 401 596 1054 Fax 401 596 6268 Freephone in US 800 722 9240 | Owner: Jerry Maiorano 7 suites, 5 with separate sitting areas. | Doubles $75 - $205 B&B Tax 12% | Outdoor pool, hot tub Nearby: tennis, golf, riding, sailing, water skiing | Does not meet the needs of children VS • MC • Amex |

Make your holiday in New England an authentic one. These Original Historic Inns have been hosting weary travelers since the days of the colonial stage. You can be assured of gracious accommodation, sumptuous dining, time honored hospitality, and a little bit of history.

# You Can Still Holiday in the Colonies...

**The Old Tavern**
Grafton, Vermont

**The Hancock Inn**
Hancock, New Hampshire

**The Deerfield Inn**
Deerfield, Massachusetts

**Longfellow's Wayside Inn**
Sudbury, Massachusetts

**The Red Lion Inn**
Stockbridge, Massachusetts

**The Griswold Inn**
Essex, Connecticut

*See individual listings for inn details. Ask about special itineraries from New York & Boston!*

www.wayside.org/ohine.html

## The Original Historic Inns of New England

# Hike or Bike
## ... Inn to Inn

Slow down to enjoy a holiday which is designed to sooth both the senses and the soul. Self-guided hiking and biking vacations are tailored to suit your personal preferences...or join a small hiking group led by local naturalists.

Over twenty years of experience assure your satisfaction, whether you choose to explore the surroundings of a couple of nearby inns or decide to tour the length of Vermont in a more expanded adventure. Either way, enchanting inns, exceptional cuisine, miles of captivating countryside, and attractions that are uniquely "*New England*" will make your holiday memorable.

## Country Inns Along the Trail

RR #3 Box 3115, Brandon, VT 05733 U.S.A.

1 (802) 247-3300 / Fax: 1 (802) 247-6851

E-Mail: rciatt@sover.net

*Visit us on the Internet – http://www.inntoinn.com*

# Vermont

Newport
Craftsbury Common
Stowe
Burlington
Waterbury
Montpelier
St. Johnsbury
Middlebury
Waitsfield
Warren
Brandon
Rutland
Killington
Quechee
White River Junction
Woodstock
Plymouth
Grafton
Dorset
Manchester
Arlington
Bennington
West Dover
Brattleboro

NEW YORK
NEW HAMPSHIRE
MASSACHUSETTS

# Vermont

| | | |
|---|---|---|
| ① Ardmore Inn | 184 |
| ② Barrows House | 184 |
| ③ Basin Harbor Club | 165 |
| ④ Blueberry Hill Inn | 185 |
| ⑤ Brandon Inn | 185 |
| ⑥ The Castle | 186 |
| ⑦ Chipman Inn | 186 |
| ⑧ Churchill House Inn | 187 |
| ⑨ Cornucopia of Dorset | 166 |
| ⑩ Cortina Inn | 167 |
| ⑪ Deerhill Inn | 187 |
| ⑫ Equinox | 168 |
| ⑬ Four Columns Inn | 169 |
| ⑭ Gables Inn | 188 |
| ⑮ Golden Eagle Resort | 170 |
| ⑯ Green Mountain Inn | 188 |
| ⑰ Hamilton House | 189 |
| ⑱ Hawk Inn & Mountain Resort | 171 |
| ⑲ Inn at Essex | 172 |
| ⑳ Inn at Ormsby Hill | 173 |
| ㉑ Inn at the Brass Lantern | 189 |
| ㉒ Inn at the Round Barn Farm | 190 |
| ㉓ Inn at West View Farm | 190 |
| ㉔ Inn on the Common | 174 |
| ㉕ Jackson House Inn | 191 |
| ㉖ Landgrove Inn | 191 |
| ㉗ Lareau Farm Country Inn | 192 |
| ㉘ Maple Leaf Inn | 192 |
| ㉙ Middlebury Inn | 193 |
| ㉚ Mountain Road Resort | 175 |
| ㉛ October Country Inn | 193 |
| ㉜ Old Tavern at Grafton | 176 |
| ㉝ Pitcher Inn | 177 |
| ㉞ Quechee Bed & Breakfast | 194 |
| ㉟ Rabbit Hill Inn | 178 |
| ㊱ Red Clover Inn | 179 |
| ㊲ Shield Inn | 194 |
| ㊳ Shire Inn | 195 |
| ㊴ The Siebeness | 195 |
| ㊵ Smugglers' Notch Inn | 196 |
| ㊶ Sugar Lodge at Sugarbush | 196 |
| ㊷ Sugarbush Inn & Resort | 180 |
| ㊸ Sugartree | 197 |
| ㊹ Tucker Hill Lodge | 197 |
| ㊺ Vermont Inn | 198 |
| ㊻ Village Country Inn | 198 |
| ㊼ West Hill House | 199 |
| ㊽ West Mountain Inn | 199 |
| ㊾ Whitford House Inn | 200 |
| ㊿ Wiley Inn | 200 |
| 51 Willough Vale Inn | 201 |
| 52 Windham Hill Inn | 181 |
| 53 Woods | 201 |
| 54 Woodstock Inn & Resort | 182 |

# A Week in Vermont Lasts a Lifetime in a Photo Album.

You'll have the opportunity virtually anywhere you turn in Vermont: from cozy villages to forested mountains... from simple clapboard houses to pristine church spires... from sparkling lakes of blue to endless fields of green.

Yes, Vermont says "New England" like nowhere else. But a picture is worth a thousand words. So, pack plenty of film when you come. And leave some pages open in that album. A lot of pages.

INTERNATIONAL **(802) 828-3237** FAX **(802) 828-3233**
or write: VERMONT TOURISM & MARKETING, DEPT. 729
134 STATE STREET, MONTPELIER, VT 05602 U.S.A.
http://www.travel-vermont.com

**VERMONT**
the nature of
New England

# VERMONT

## BASIN HARBOR CLUB
### VERGENNES

Since 1886 the Beach family has welcomed travellers to Vermont's historic Champlain Valley. This seven hundred acre resort features sweeping lawns and gardens, rolling meadows and stands of ancient trees, with spectacular views of Lake Champlain. Families have vacationed here for generations. Recreational amenities include an 18 hole golf course, five tennis courts, sailing, water skiing, canoeing and swimming (lake and large pool), bicycling, nature walks and just plain loafing. Daily activities feature an active children's programme, lectures, movies, dancing and entertainment. Accommodations include seventy seven picturesque cottages with one to three bedrooms and baths, all within easy walking distance of the resort's facilities. Fine dining and the Wine Spectator's Award of Excellence round out a grand vacation.

Basin Harbor is just two hours drive from Montreal, four and a half hours from Boston and five hours from New York. Connecting flights via Burlington, VT. are available from major East Coast hubs in the U.S.

Vergennes,
VT 05491
•
Tel 802 475 2311
Fax 802 475 6545
Freephone in US
800 622 4000
•
Innkeepers, Owners:
The Beach Family
•
44 rooms
77 one, two and three
bedroom cottages

Doubles $230 - $280 AP
Cottages $260 - $300
B&B rates also available
except in July & August
•
Tax 7%. s.c. 15%
•
Outdoor swimming pool,
tennis, golf, horseriding,
sailing, water skiing,
hiking, exercise room
•
VS • MC

**VERMONT**

# CORNUCOPIA OF DORSET
## DORSET

Cornucopia, an 1880 colonial surrounded by colourful country gardens, offers the intimacy of a bed and breakfast and the service and amenities of the finest full service inn, including champagne check-in, full evening turn-down, wake-up trays of coffee or tea with fresh flowers and sumptuous, candlelit breakfasts.

Most rooms have fireplaces and all have sitting areas, with thoughtful extra touches to enhance your visit – oversized bath sheets, terry cloth bathrobes, Crabtree and Evelyn toiletries, fresh fruit, chocolates, luxurious down comforters or colourful Vermont made quilts, (depending on the season) and in-room telephones.

Visit this quintessential New England Village with its craft and antique shops, fine restaurants and live theatre, all a short stroll from the inn.

Come and be pampered at Cornucopia.
"We'd like to make our home, your home".

PO Box 307, Rt 30,
Dorset, VT 05251
•
Tel 802 867 5751
Fax 802 867 5753
Freephone in US
800 566 5751
•
Innkeepers:
Linda & Bill Ley
•
5 rooms
including 1 one-bedroom cottage suite with self-catering facility

Doubles $115 - $155 B&B
(special rates for stays of
7 nights or longer)
Cottage suite $205 - $225
•
Tax 7%
•
Nearby: swimming, tennis, golf
•
Children over
12 welcome
•
Non-smoking
•
VS • MC • Amex

**VERMONT**

# CORTINA INN
## KILLINGTON

Killington's most luxurious inn... it's the little things that make a difference.

A staff that caters to your every wish, fresh flowers, afternoon tea, delicious breakfasts, room service, and award winning food bring guests back time and time again to our AAA Three Diamond, Mobil Three Star award winning inn.

We have blended the hospitality and cosy charm of a country inn with the amenities of a resort hotel. We offer continuous transport to skiing slopes, indoor pool, sauna, fitness center, games room, sleigh rides, snowmobiling and beautifully decorated fireplaced rooms and suites.

It is all of this which goes to make Cortina a truly four-season destination.

HC 34, Box 33,
US rt 4,
Killington, VT 05751
•
Tel 802 773 3333
Fax 802 775 6948
Freephone in US
800 451 6108
•
Innkeepers:
Bob & Breda Harnish
•
97 rooms and suites

Doubles $89 - $169 B&B
Suites $169 - $269
•
Tax 7%
•
Indoor pool,
8 tennis courts, golf,
fitness center,
games room
•
Children welcome
•
VS • MC • Amex

**VERMONT**

# THE EQUINOX
## MANCHESTER

A member of Historic Hotels of America, the Equinox has recently been beautifully and painstakingly restored to its original splendour and stands on 1,100 acres of land. The hotel offers deluxe accommodations in air-conditioned rooms or deluxe townhouses with cable tv, in-room movies and a choice of mountain, village or garden views. The new Charles Orvis Inn at the Equinox comprises one and two bedroom suites. Hotel services include laundry, dry-cleaning, shoe-shine, concierge, valet parking, room service and nightly turn down.

The hotel holds the AAA Four Diamond award and offers superb sporting facilities both on site and in the surrounding areas. The newly renovated Gleneagles Golf Course has been awarded Golf Magazine's Silver Medal.

There are three restaurants at the resort, The Colonnade Room, The Marsh Tavern and the Dormy Grill offering a range of dining choices from elegant to casual.

The Equinox is a drive of about 4 hours from New York and about 3½ hours from Boston.

PO Box 46
Manchester Village,
Manchester, VT 05254

•

Tel 802 362 4700
Fax 802 362 4861
Freephone in US
800 362 4747

•

General Manager & Vice President: S.L. Bowden

•

163 rooms
10 one-bedroom suites
27 additional rooms and suites in townhouse units,
some with self-catering facilities
Doubles $169 - $299 EP
Suites $339 - $559

•

Tax 7%

•

Indoor and outdoor pools, tennis, golf, horseriding, fitness center, hiking, spa, conference facilities, British School of Falconry, Equinox Cross Country Ski Touring Centre

•

VS • MC • Amex • Diners

**VERMONT**

# FOUR COLUMNS INN
## NEWFANE

*The magic begins to work when you first see the Four Columns Inn, set in the picture book village of Newfane, it continues as you enjoy quiet comforts, escaping for a time the hectic everyday world. Individually decorated guest rooms, each with private bath, await your arrival. Whether you choose a room with a fireplace, a view of the common, or a jacuzzi for two, the result will be the same, a feeling of serene contentment.*

*Spring, Summer, Fall or Winter, our 150 acres of woodland, gardens, ponds and trails offer you a chance to whet your appetite for some of the best food in New England. Greg Parks has been our Chef for 13 years, his culinary imagination and use of Vermont's abundance of local ingredients has earned us Four Diamonds from the AAA and the Distinguished Restaurants of North America Award in 1993.*

*Come to our inn any time of the year, and enjoy innkeeping as it was when life moved at a more comfortable pace.*

West Street,
PO Box 278,
Newfane,
VT 05345
•
Tel 802 365 7713
•
Owners/Innkeepers:
Pam & Gorty Baldwin
•
12 rooms
4 one bedroom suites
•
Doubles $110 - $125 B&B
$210 - $225 MAP

Suites $140 - $195 B&B
$240 - $295 MAP
•
For the last week in September and first two weeks in October, MAP rates only
•
Tax 7%.
•
Outdoor swimming pool.
Nearby: golf, tennis, riding
•
VS • MC • Amex
Diners • Discover

**VERMONT**

# GOLDEN EAGLE RESORT
## STOWE

The Golden Eagle is one of New England's most affordable AAA Four Diamond resorts. Family owned and operated for 30 years, this 4-season resort is located ½ mile from picturesque Stowe Village, minutes from Mt. Mansfield State Park and Ski area, and a short drive from Burlington International Airport.

Nestled on 80 acres of landscaped lawns, flower gardens, mountain and pondside views, this is the perfect setting for a vacation escape. Accommodations range from spacious rooms to one and two bedroom apartments with fireplaces. Some rooms have whirlpools, all have private bath, telephones, tv, refrigerators, individual heat and air conditioning. A coffee shop and two dinner restaurants offer a variety of New England specialities.

Relax in the library by a wood-burning stove, surrounded by literature, magazines and classical music. Experience a tradition of warm hospitality and service.

The Mountain Road,
PO Box 1090, Stowe,
VT 05672

•

Tel 802 253 4811
Fax 802 253 2561
Freephone in UK
0800 969 240

•

General Manager/President:
Neil Van Dyke

•

42 rooms. 10 suites
(1 & 2 bedrooms)
2 & 3 bedroom chalets
and houses available

Doubles $89 - $159 EP
Suites/apartments
$159-$259

•

Tax 7%

•

Heated indoor & outdoor pools, fitness center, tennis, trout ponds, hiking, skiing, ice-skating. Childrens' activities & playground

VS • MC • Amex
Diners • Discover

**VERMONT**

# HAWK INN & MOUNTAIN RESORT
## PLYMOUTH

Step from the hearthside warmth of a luxurious Hawk mountain villa, surrounded by endless sunlit Green Mountain vistas in summer, silent snow-ribboned peaks in winter or the glorious fall colours of a New England autumn. Hawk's 1,200 acres invite you to experience the essence of Vermont's unspoiled natural beauty.

In the valley below, Hawk's fifty room, Four Diamond inn meanders along the banks of the Black River, flowing into the crystal clear waters of a chain of mountain lakes. Guests are pampered with cool mountain air in summer, down comforters and plush robes in winter. After a day of activities, enjoy fine dining at the River Tavern, on the terrace overlooking the river or by the warmth of the fieldstone fireplace.

In summer, hike and bike through the valley, paddle, row and sail from Hawk's mountain lake marina, fly fish for trout, enjoy the challenges of the riding stable, tennis courts, twenty meter pool or six nearby golf courses and a clay shooting preserve. Winter brings challenging downhill skiing, ice skating, fishing, cross-country skiing and snowshoeing and evening sleigh rides under the stars.

HCR 70, Box 67, Rt 100
Plymouth, VT 05056
•
Tel 802 672 3811
Fax 802 672 5067
Freephone in US
800 685 Hawk
•
Executive Vice President/General Manager: James M. Nielsen
Innkeeper: Jurgen Dinger
•
50 inn rooms. 2, 3 & 4- bedroom villas

Doubles $142 - $293 B&B,
Villas $209 - $761 EP
•
Tax 7%
•
Outdoor & indoor pools, tennis, riding, sailing, biking, skiing
Nearby: golf
•
Children welcome.
•
Non-smoking
•
VS • MC • Amex
Diners • Carte Blanche
Discover

**VERMONT**

# INN AT ESSEX
## ESSEX

The Inn at Essex is an AAA Four Diamond small country hotel on the outskirts of Burlington, the town on Lake Champlain. It is a colonial style building set on 18 acres and is ideally located between the beautiful Green Mountains of Vermont and the scenic Adirondacks of New York State.

The Inn offers 97 elegantly furnished and spacious rooms with all amenities for business or pleasure, 30 rooms have woodburning fireplaces for the colder months. Dining is an experience not to be missed at the Inn, savour the glorious food of our two restaurants, prepared by 18 chefs and 100 students of the New England Culinary Institute. Choose Butler's fine dining room with continental cuisine or the more casual Birch Tree Cafe with new American fare.

A host of museums and shops are within 30 minutes of the Inn and not to be missed is a tour round Ben & Jerry's Ice Cream Factory or the Vermont Teddy Bear Company.

70 Essex Way,
Essex,
VT 05452
•
Tel 802 878 1100
Fax 802 878 0063
Freephone in US
800 727 4295
•
General Manager:
James Lamberti
•
94 rooms
2 one bedroom,
1 two-bedroom suite

Doubles $99 - $185 EP
Suites $185 - $385
•
Tax 7%
•
Indoor pool, fitness center, outdoor heated pool conference facilities
Nearby: tennis, golf, horseriding, sailing, water skiing, Vermont's premier factory-outlet shopping
•
VS • MC • Amex • Diners

**VERMONT**

# INN AT ORMSBY HILL
## MANCHESTER CENTER

*When you visit Ormsby Hill, you will be surrounded by a spectacular setting with breathtaking views of the Battenkill Valley and the Green Mountains, a patio and porch inviting you to relax and renew, classical music in the background, a place so serene that once you pass through our antique wrought-iron gates and enter our front door, you will never want to leave.*

*Ormsby Hill is a restored manor house, circa 1764, listed on the Register of Historic Places. Enjoy our nationally-acclaimed dining, served in the magnificent Conservatory/Dining Room, featuring a full gourmet breakfast, with dinner offered on Friday and Saturday evenings.*

*Our romantic bed chambers have canopies, fireplaces, air-conditioning and luxurious bathrooms with Jacuzzis for two. Ormsby Hill is renowned for comfort, heartfelt hospitality and profound attention to detail.*

Historic Route 7A
Manchester Center
VT 05255
•
Tel 802 362 1163
Fax 802 362 5176
Freephone in US
800 670 2841
•
Innkeepers:
Ted & Chris Sprague
•
10 rooms
Doubles $110 - $210 B&B
Dinner served on Friday &
Saturday only

Tax 7%
•
Conference facilities for 20
Nearby: outdoor & indoor
pools, tennis, golf, riding,
cross-country & downhill
skiing, fly fishing, hiking,
cycling
•
Does not meet the needs
of children
•
Non-smoking
•
VS MC Amex

**VERMONT**

# INN ON THE COMMON
## CRAFTSBURY COMMON

*Perched on 15 hilltop acres with unrivalled views of the surrounding Green Mountains, the Inn is a renowned sanctuary of comfort, fabulous food, caring service and true Vermont hospitality. Enjoy one of the sixteen impeccably decorated bedrooms and suites, many with fireplaces, innovative cuisine from a talented young chef and an award winning wine cellar. For 15 consecutive years, the Inn has received the distinguished AAA Four Diamond Award.*

*Surrounded by landscaped gardens the Inn is perfectly situated in the unspoiled Northeast Kingdom. The town, Craftsbury Common, is one of Vermont's uncommon gems - historically designated, every building painted white whilst the surrounding countryside is quintessential New England. The Inn is proud to be a member of the Independent Innkeepers Association.*

Main Street,
Craftsbury Common,
VT 05827
•
Tel 802 586 9619
Fax 802 586 2249
Freephone in US
800 521 2233
•
Innkeepers/Owners:
Michael & Penny Schmitt
•
14 rooms
2 two bedroom suites

Doubles from
$220 - $270 MAP
Suites from $240 - $270
•
Tax 7%  s.c. 15%
•
Outdoor pool, tennis,
golf, biking,
canoeing, hiking,
skiing
•
VS • MC

**VERMONT**

# MOUNTAIN ROAD RESORT
## STOWE

*Stowe's newest AAA Four Diamond Award Winner! Superlative country accommodations ranging from deluxe guest rooms to luxury condo-suites, many with fireplaces and romantic jacuzzis. We offer the atmosphere of a country inn, the amenities of a distinctive resort and the savoir faire of innkeepers who have travelled the world. Afternoon refreshments are included by the pool or by the fire in the Living Room. A deluxe continental breakfast and spirits are available in the Library or from room service. Enjoy our deluxe outdoor and indoor heated pools, whirlpool spas, sauna and mini-gym. Spacious lawns, flowering gardens and tall pines frame Stowe's intimate resort in Spring, Summer and Fall, while blankets of snow sparkle in Winter.*

*Exclusive Dine Around® and Vermont Romance plans available. Among our British guests, we've welcomed the Campbells from Herts, who said "A1. A most enjoyable stay." From Dorset, the Vastenhouts commented "Excellent. Beautiful location, lovely resort." You'll love the friendly atmosphere and feel as the Eatwells from Surrey, who said "Best accommodations we have had in two weeks of travel".*

PO Box 8 (rt 108)
Stowe, VT 05672
•
Tel 802 253 4566
Fax 802 253 7397
Freephone in US
800 367 6873
Freephone in UK
0800 89 4581
•
Innkeepers:
Bill Mintzer & Jeff Knox
•
32 rooms and suites

Doubles $95 - $205
B&B
Suites $215 - $395
•
Tax 7%
•
Outdoor and indoor pools,
tennis, fitness center, spa,
French petanque.
Nearby: golf
•
Children welcome
•
VS • MC • Amex
Diners • Discover

**VERMONT**

# OLD TAVERN AT GRAFTON
## GRAFTON

Since 1801, the Old Tavern at Grafton has been the choice of the discriminating traveller. The centrepiece of beautifully restored historic Grafton village, the Old Tavern offers 66 individually appointed accommodations and seven guest cottages, all within walking distance of the main Tavern and fine dining room. Meals are offered three times daily, with breakfast included in the room rate. Cuisine embraces the traditional and seasonal qualities of Vermont fare.

Bountiful leisure activities include bicycling, tennis, golf, fishing, nature trails, spring-fed swimming pond, nordic and alpine skiing and the historic beauty of Grafton village.

Grafton is easily reached by car off exit 5 of Interstate 91. Major airlines service Hartford's Bradley International Airport. Direct flights are available to Rutland or Keene, both one hour away.

Recognized as the fifth oldest continuously operating Inn in America, the Old Tavern is a member of Historic Hotels of America.

Grafton,
VT 05146
•
Tel 802 843 2231
Fax 802 843 2245
Freephone in US
800 843 1801
•
President-Windham
Foundation: Stephan Morse
•
65 rooms
1 one bedroom suite
7 guest cottages, 5 with
fully equipped kitchens,
living rooms etc.

Doubles
$95 - $170 B&B
Cottages
$480 - $570
•
Tax 7%
•
Outdoor swimming
pond, tennis, hiking,
snow-making at
cross country
ski centre

•
VS • MC

**VERMONT**

# THE PITCHER INN
## WARREN

*The Pitcher Inn, combines the best of old and new. Destroyed by fire a few years back, the inn has been lovingly and carefully rebuilt in the footprint of the original, with each of the eight rooms in the main inn and two suites in the adjoining barn incorporating a Vermont theme in structure and furnishings.*

*This second incarnation of the Pitcher Inn has allowed for conveniences of the modern world that would have turned the original nineteenth-century guests as green as the surrounding mountains with envy. Each room has a private bath with Jacuzzi tub and is equipped with fax, computer hook-ups, hideaway television, vcr, and air-conditioning. For cold New England winters, many rooms offer cosy fireplaces and even private steam rooms. Located right opposite Warren's picturesque general store which sells everything from coffee to clothes, the Pitcher Inn invites you to step in, stay a while and enjoy some traditional Vermont hospitality.*

Main Street,
Warren,
VT 05674

•

Tel 802 496 6350
Fax 802 496 6354

•

Freephone in US 1-888 to Pitch(er)

•

Innkeepers: Heather & John Carino

•

10 rooms, including 2 one bedroom suites, 2 two bedroom suites

Doubles $165 - $300 B&B
Suites $250 - $325

•

Tax 9%

•

Nearby: indoor pool, tennis, horse riding, golf, cross-country and down-hill skiing

•

Children welcome

•

Non-smoking

•

VS•MC

**VERMONT**

# RABBIT HILL INN
## LOWER WATERFORD

A tiny, enchanting hamlet that is an Historic District, is the setting for this 1795 American classic country inn, in two Federal period buildings on 15 acres above the Connecticut River. Rated Four Diamond by the AAA and Four Star by Mobil, elegantly stylish and romantic, the Inn is renowned for exceptional personal service and caring attention to detail. It has been repeatedly designated one of America's Ten Best Inns by travel and guide writers.

The 20 bedrooms and suites, each with private bath, and many featuring canopied beds, fireplaces and two person jacuzzis, offer a sense of timelessness and pampered relaxation.

From oil lamps on porches to unusual turn-down service, discover whimsical surprises. Start your day with a delicious full country breakfast and, in the evening, relax and enjoy acclaimed gourmet dining in two stunning dining rooms, soothed by a chamber musician. We invite you to join us in our partnership with the past. Rabbit Hill is our home, and the hospitality is from our hearts.

Lower Waterford,
VT 05848
•
Tel 802 748 5168
Fax 802 748 8342
Freephone in US
800 76 BUNNY
•
Innkeepers:
John & Maureen Magee
•
16 rooms 4 suites
•
Doubles $179 - $269 MAP
Suites $229 - $269

Tax 7%. s.c. 15%
•
Book and film library, swimming pond, hiking, fishing, sledding, cross-country skiing, ice skating and snow shoeing. Nearby: cycling, mountain climbing, golf, down-hill skiing, museum, antiquing
•
Children over 12 welcome
•
VS • MC

**VERMONT**

# RED CLOVER INN
## MENDON

Down a tree lined country road in the shadow of the Green Mountains, this rambling 1840's farmhouse on thirteen acres, offers warmth, pampering by caring staff and attentive innkeepers and exceptional gourmet fare complemented by an award-winning wine list.

Guestrooms are comfortably furnished with thoughtful attention to detail and many offer whirlpools for two, gas fireplaces and decks or balconies with mesmerising mountain views. From this central location explore Vermont's picture-book villages and choose from seasonal activities - hiking, golfing, swimming, riding, viewing glorious fall foliage, down-hill and cross-country skiing or (if your energy deserts you) indulge in a horse-drawn sleigh ride.

In summer the pool and grounds are perfect for gazing at sweeping mountain views while in colder weather the inn welcomes you back to relax by a cosy fire. Dine leisurely and sumptuously from an excellent and extensive menu featuring the freshest local produce, dairy and game and enjoy the welcome that always awaits at this idyllic country inn.

7 Woodward Road,
Mendon,
VT 05701
•
Tel 802 775 2290
Fax 802 773 0594
Freephone in US
800 752 0571
•
Owners/Innkeepers: Sue &
Harris Zuckerman
•
14 rooms,
including 2 one bedroom
suites

Doubles $140 - $350 MAP
Suites $160 - $230
•
Tax 9%   s.c.15 %
•
Outdoor pool
Nearby: indoor pool, tennis,
horse riding, cross-country
and down-hill skiing, golf
•
Children over 10 welcome
•
Non-smoking
•
VS•MC•Discover

**VERMONT**

# SUGARBUSH INN & RESORT
## WARREN

Sugarbush offers the undisturbed beauty of quiet villages, steepled churches, clapboard buildings, covered bridges, sparkling rivers and a valley filled with rolling meadows and farms. Readers of Snow Country magazine rank Sugarbush among the top ten ski resorts in North America for quality and variety of accommodation. Lodging options include deluxe condominiums and homes to a full-service 46 room country inn.

Sugarbush winter activities are cross-country skiing with 300 km of groomed trails, ice skating, tobogganing, snowshoeing, horse-drawn sleigh rides, Icelandic pony rides, snowmobiling or the indoor sports centre. Summer means mountain biking and guided hikes; an 18-hole Robert Trent Jones golf course or tennis at two of the top 50 tennis resorts in the US. In addition there's canoeing, kayaking, swimming in the Mad River or soaring in a glider.

Sugarbush/Mad River Valley boasts over 40 shops and boutiques, ranging from country quaint to extremely elegant and a range of superb dining options.

RR1 Box 350
Warren, VT 05674
•
Tel 802 583 3333
Fax 802 583 3209
Freephone in US
800-53-SUGAR
•
250 rooms
including one bedroom - four bedroom fully equipped houses & apartments.
•
Doubles $104 - $230 B&B w/ski tickets in winter

Houses & Apartments
$104 - $880
•
Tax 7%
•
Outdoor & indoor pools, tennis, golf, conference facilities, down-hill, & cross-country skiing
•
Children welcome. Varied programmes available. Cost on application.
•
Non-smoking
VS • MC • Amex

**VERMONT**

# WINDHAM HILL INN
## WEST TOWNSHEND

Most Windham Hill guests journey here looking for a retreat - a quiet and natural setting in which to relax and unwind. Discover a peaceful country house with spotless rooms, an elegant-yet-approachable cuisine, "comfortable" dress code, books, puzzles and music in many forms. Experience pampering by a caring staff and innkeepers eager to share the pleasures of their Green Mountain home and the warmth of their Vermont hospitality.

In Spring, Summer and Fall, hike the inn's trails, 10 km of pine and maple forest with waterfall and swimming hole. In winter, ski 20 km of groomed cross-country trails (lessons and rental equipment available), sample down-hill skiing 25 minutes away at Mount Snow, take a toboggan ride, skate our pond or snowshoe from the back door.

We are conveniently located in central southern Vermont, a comfortable drive from country fairs, art and craft shows, picturesque villages and numerous events and attractions.

RR1 Box 44,
West Townhend,
VT 05359
•
Tel 802 874 4080
Fax 802 874 4702
Freephone in US
800 944 4080
•
Innkeepers:
Grigsby & Pat Markham
•
18 rooms
•
Doubles $210 - $285 MAP

Tax 7%. s.c. 15%
•
Outdoor pool, tennis,
cross-country skiing
Nearby: golf, riding, down-hill skiing
•
Children over 12 welcome.
•
Non-smoking
•
VS • MC • Amex
Diners • Discover

**VERMONT**

# WOODSTOCK INN & RESORT
## WOODSTOCK

The ultimate New England country inn with resort facilities, located in the heart of quintessential Woodstock, offers 144 comfortably luxurious rooms and suites, many with fireplaces. The elegant dining room serves continental and New England cuisine, while a more casual alternative is the Eagle Café for country kitchen dining.

Play the 18 hole Robert Trent Jones golf course, or enjoy the fully equipped Health & Fitness Center. Close by are the Woodstock Ski Touring Center with 60km of cross country trails plus the "Suicide Six" downhill ski area.

Stroll one of America's prettiest sidewalks, lined with unique shops, galleries and restaurants, laze by the outdoor pool amidst beautifully landscaped gardens, browse in the cosy library, enjoy complimentary tea and cookies in a delightful wicker furnished sitting room complete with grand piano, or relax in front of the huge stone hearth in the comfortable lobby. The Inn holds the AAA Four Diamond and Mobil Four Star awards, and is a member of the prestigious Small Luxury Hotels of the World.

14 The Green,
Woodstock,
VT 05091-1298

•

Tel 802 457 1100
Fax 802 457 6699
Freephone in US
800 448 7900

•

President &
General Manager:
Chet Williamson

•

146 rooms
7 one bedroom suites
3 townhouses

Doubles $149 - $265 EP
Suites $399 - $499
Tax 7%

Outoor and indoor
pools and tennis
courts, racquetball,
squash, golf,
horseriding, fitness
center, hiking, skiing,
sleigh rides.

•

VS • MC • Amex

# Shelburne Museum

## NOT SO MUCH A MUSEUM MORE A WAY OF LIFE ★★★

Founded in 1947 by Electra Havemeyer Webb, and set on 45 beautifully landscaped acres in north west Vermont, three centuries of the American way of life are reflected in an amazing collection of over 80,000 everyday and unusual objects.

A superb decoy collection; exquisite quilts, each with its own history; a 500 foot miniature circus parade; weather vanes; tools; carriages; a museum of hats; paintings and prints from folk art to impressionist; complete historic houses; blacksmith, printing and weaving shops all in full working order; a schoolhouse, a stagecoach inn, a lighthouse, a jail and a general store, not to mention the 220 foot steamboat Ticonderoga – we could continue, but why not come and see?

Open daily 10.00 - 5.00 May to October (daily guided tours of selected buildings available the rest of the year scheduled at 1.00pm) with daily demonstrations of printing, weaving and blacksmithing; an operating circus carousel and weekly talks. Free shuttle tram provides transport throughout the 37 buildings of the museum.

### Shelburne Museum

PO Box 10, Shelburne, VT 05482
Tel 802 985 3346   Fax 802 985 2331
*Located on US rt 7*
*Seven miles south of Burlington VT.*

**VERMONT**

# ARDMORE INN
## WOODSTOCK

A small, classic New England Inn, the Ardmore offers spacious, gracious accommodations together with the charm and warmth of personal service, in what has been acclaimed as one of the ten most beautiful villages in the U.S.

A talented chef will surprise and delight you with delicious and imaginative breakfast creations. Each of the guest bedrooms is individually decorated and furnished in a variety of delightful styles.

Woodstock is a quaint, historic village, offering a variety of attractions including antiquing, theatre, galleries, and some of New England's finest restaurants. Delight in Vermont's fresh air; walking or biking on back roads and mountain trails, golf, tennis, fishing and polo. In winter enjoy sleigh rides or down-hill and cross-country skiing at the many nearby outstanding Vermont ski areas.

23 Pleasant Street, Woodstock, VT 05091-0466
Tel 802 457 3887
Fax 802 457 9006

Freephone in US 800 497 9652
Innkeeper: Giorgio Ortiz

5 rooms
Doubles $85 - $165 B&B
Tax 7%

Nearby: outdoor & indoor pools, tennis, golf, riding, water skiing, down-hill & cross-country skiing

Does not meet the needs of children.

Non-smoking
VS • MC
Amex • Diners

---

# BARROWS HOUSE
## DORSET

Set on 11 flower-filled acres in a small picturebook village the Barrows House offers a unique blend of charm and country hospitality, whether you stay in one of the charming outbuildings or the main inn.

Furnished with comfort foremost in mind, there are plenty of antiques but they are the sort that beg to be used. Enjoy a hot drink in front of the fire after skiing, or a cool drink on the patio in the warmth of a summer evening, we want you to feel equally at peace and at home.

Best of all, meals in the inn's lovely plant-filled airy dining extension are an informal, delicious and unforgettable experience. A member of the Independent Innkeepers Association, and holder of the 3 Diamond and 3 Star Awards, come and experience Barrows House for yourselves - you'll be welcome!

Rt 30 Dorset, VT 0521
Tel 802 867 4455
Fax 802 867 0126

Freephone in US 800 639 1620
Innkeepers: Linda & Jim McGinnis

19 rooms
8 one-bedroom, 1 two-bedroom suite
Doubles $145 - $205 MAP

Suites $200 - $240
Tax 7%. S.c. 15%
Outdoor pool, tennis, lawn games

Nearby: golf, horseriding, fishing, sailing, small conference facility

Children welcome
VS • MC • Amex

**VERMONT**

# BLUEBERRY HILL INN
## GOSHEN

*Share with us a special way of life. Within the restored 1813 farmhouse lies another world - intimate, isolated, tranquil. Bask in the morning sun of the greenhouse, sipping coffee among the flowers; stretch out under the apple trees on the lawn; pick all the sun-ripened blueberries you can eat; stroll up Hogback Mountain for a spectacular view of the world; swim in the spring-fed pond, hike and cross-country ski, miles of trails from the front door.*

*At the end of the day soak in a hot bath before joining other guests for a convivial social hour, followed by a sumptuous four course meal served dinner-party style in the candlelit dining room.*

*We offer no radios, no televisions, no bedside telephones - just Vermont!*

| Goshen VT 05733  Tel 802 247 6735  Fax 802 247 3983 | Freephone in US 800 448 0707  Owner: Tony Clark & Shari Brown | 24 rooms  Doubles $164 - $210  MAP  Tax 7% s.c 15% | Swimming pond, sauna, gardens, hiking, cross-country skiing. | Nearby: tennis, golf, horseriding  Children welcome | Non-smoking  VS • MC |

---

# BRANDON INN
## BRANDON

*Restored 1786 family run inn, listed on the National Historic Register and set on the village green in a charming Vermont town, within an hour of many tourist attractions.*

*Visit Fort Ticonderoga, tour the Maple and Marble Museums or Ben and Jerry's Ice Cream Factory. The Inn also houses the Vermont Ski Museum.*

*Large individually decorated guest rooms, beautifully appointed and spacious public rooms, cosy tavern and secluded back acres with an outdoor pool. Award-winning cuisine.*

*We are 15 miles north of Rutland, on rts 7 and 73, a 3½ hour drive from Boston or Montreal.*

| 20 Park Street  Brandon  VT 05733 | Tel 802 247 5766  Fax 802 247 5768  Freephone in US 800 639 8685 | Innkeepers:  Louis & Sarah Pattis  35 rooms & suites | Doubles $125 - $175  MAP. B&B rates also available  Suites $155 - $195 | Tax 7% s.c. 15%  Nearby: tennis, golf, horseriding, sailing, water skiing, fitness center, skiing. | Children welcome  VS • MC • Amex |

**VERMONT**

# THE CASTLE
## PROCTORSVILLE

Follow a winding drive to a grand three storey, stone manor house, nestled amongst six beautifully landscaped acres and surrounded by rolling hills. Wonderful summer days great for hiking, biking, fishing, or plain relaxing; the spectacular glory of leaf season; or the winter season with terrific skiing and, at all times, craft and antique shopping, museums, art and a rich history.

The 1901 inn, built as a private home, and recently, lovingly restored by Dick & Erica Hart has ten wonderfully spacious guest rooms, magnificently crafted woodwork, moulded ceilings and a unique feeling of space, elegance and comfort. Rooms, in deep rich colours but full of sunshine and light, offer oriental rugs, sitting areas with couches, fireplaces and a wonderful sense of privacy.

| PO Box 547, Ludlow, VT 05153 Tel 802 226 7222 Fax 802 226 7853 | Freephone in US 800 697 7222 Owners Dick & Erica Hart | 10 one bedroom suites Doubles $95 - $195 B&B $153 - $255 MAP | Tax 7% s.c. 15% Outdoor pool, tennis, conference facilities | Nearby: golf, riding, water skiing, down-hill & cross-country skiing | Children over 12 welcome. Non-smoking VS • MC • Amex |

# CHIPMAN INN
## RIPTON

Just a few miles from the home of the poet Robert Frost is the Chipman Inn and if you take a stroll from one to the other you will find the way posted with those unforgettable poems. A stay here in this classic Vermont country inn is uncrowded, undemanding, peaceful and informal. Streams meandering over stone, scenic walks along back-country roads or swimming and canoeing at nearby Lake Dunmore provide daytime entertainment.

The inn's guest rooms are furnished comfortably, and for relaxing after your walks there is a sitting room, still with the original kitchen hearth or a sunny reading room. Hearty breakfast is on offer to start you off with a full stomach and special arrangements can be made with the innkeepers if you should want to dine in on an excellent five course meal which varies from day to day.

| Route 125, Ripton, VT 057666 | Tel 802 388 2390 Fax 802 388 2390 Freephone in US 800 890 2390 | Owners/Innkeepers: Joyce Henderson & Bill Pierce | 8 rooms all with private bath Doubles $85 - $115 B&B | Tax 9% Nearby: golf, cross-country & down-hill skiing | Smoking in designated areas VS•MC•Amex Discover |

## VERMONT

# CHURCHILL HOUSE INN
## BRANDON

This charming, century old country inn is located at the edge of the spectacular Green Mountain National Forest. Known for its excellent cuisine, rates include dinner and breakfast. Dinner around the candlelit antique oak table creates a wonderful party atmosphere. We do not hold a liquor license so bring along your favourite beverage.

The Inn offers eight individually decorated guest rooms with private baths and three common rooms where guests gather for hors d'oeuvres and congenial company. Within easy reach of Vermont attractions, we also organise self-guided inn to inn hiking, biking and skiing trips and small leader-guided hikes. In Winter you can cross-country ski from the door. Located 4 miles east of Brandon on rt 73.

| RR#3, Box 3265 Brandon, VT 05733 | Tel 802 247 3078 Fax 802 247 6851 | Innkeepers: The Jackson family 8 rooms | Doubles $150 - $180 MAP. Special packages available Tax 7% s.c. 15% | Outdoor pool and sauna, bicycle rentals, hiking, cross-country skiing, golf, fishing. | Children welcome VS • MC |

# DEERHILL INN & RESTAURANT
## WEST DOVER

The Deerhill is set amidst the stunning scenery of the Green Mountains. Linda and Michael Anelli (confirmed Anglophiles!), are fully attuned to the needs of their UK guests - tea in one of the creatively furnished sitting rooms, cocktails in the English-style "Snug" bar and lively discussions of flyfishing or gardening!

Enjoy candlelit dining, gourmet cuisine and thoughtful service in one of Vermont's most popular restaurants! Hearty breakfasts, beautifully appointed rooms, an ever-changing art gallery and attention to detail are all reasons to visit. The seasons and variety of activities make you want to stay; Winter offers Nordic and downhill skiing, Spring, golf and fishing, Summer, music and museums and the Fall the dazzling spectacle of Autumn.

| Valley View Road, Box 136, West Dover, VT 05356-0136 Tel 802 464 3100 Fax 802 464 5474 | Freephone in US 800 99 DEER 9 | Owners/Innkeeper & chef: Linda & Michael Anelli 15 rooms including 2 suites | Doubles $90 - $150 B&B. MAP rates available Suites $200 - $260 Tax 7% s.c. 15% | Outdoor pool, tennis. Nearby: golf, horseriding, hiking, biking, skiing, swimming | Children over 8 welcome VS • MC • Amex |

**VERMONT**

# GABLES INN
## STOWE

Originally an 1800s farmhouse, and converted around 1934, our family run inn offers individually and comfortably furnished rooms in traditional New England style, several offering views of spectacular Mt Mansfield and the valley. These views can also be enjoyed from our dining room, front porch and lawns, where our deservedly famous breakfast (voted best in Stowe) and garden lunch is served.

In Summer enjoy complimentary bicycles, swim in our outdoor pool, or take part in the many special events hosted by Stowe. Autumn brings unbelievable colours with the evocative scent of woodsmoke rising from chimneys. Winter offers alpine and cross country skiing, snowshoeing, sleigh rides and gloriously crisp air. Come, join us to celebrate life at its best!

| 1457 Mountain Road, Stowe, VT 05672 | Tel 802 253 7730 Fax 802 253 8989 Freephone in US 800 GABLES 1 | Owner/Innkeepers: Sol & Lyn Baumrind 19 rooms | Doubles $150 – $200 MAP. $90 B&B Tax 7% s.c. 10% Summer 15% Winter | Outdoor swimming pool. Nearby: golf, tennis, horseriding, skiing | Children welcome Non-smoking VS • MC • Amex |

# GREEN MOUNTAIN INN
## STOWE

At the Green Mountain Inn, you will be welcomed to a world of authentic country charm and modern comfort. Built in 1833 and beautifully restored for its 150th anniversary, the Inn offers seventy-two cosy rooms and luxurious suites in the main inn, annex, Clubhouse and Mill House. Each guestroom has its own warmth and character with period furnishings, quilts, stencilling and draperies of early American design - many offer canopy beds, Jacuzzis and fireplaces.

Casual, creative dining is available in the inn's two restaurants - the elegant Main Street Dining Room and lively Whip Bar & Grill. Guests enjoy complimentary afternoon refreshments in the inn's cosy living room and unlimited use of a fully-equipped health club with Jacuzzi, sauna, steamroom and outdoor pool.

A member of Historic Hotels of America and situated in the heart of 200-year-old Stowe Village, the Green Mountain Inn invites you to a world of historic architecture, speciality shops, galleries and restaurants.

| 1 Main Street, P.O. Box 60, Stowe, VT 05672 Tel 802 253 7301 Fax 802 253 5096 | Freephone in US 800 253 7302 Innkeeper: Patti Clark 72 rooms, including 5 one bedroom suites | 1 restaurant Doubles $89 - $279 EP Suites $119 - $329 Cottage $150 - $425 | Tax 9%, s.c. $2.00 per room, per night Outdoor pool (seasonal). Nearby: tennis, horse riding, | water-skiing, down-hill and cross-country skiing, indoor pool, golf, sailing Children welcome | Pets allowed Non-smoking VS•MC•Amex•Diners Discover |

**VERMONT**

# HAMILTON HOUSE
## WARREN

With just four guest rooms, Hamilton House offers a privacy that is rare. An elegant English country house to be enjoyed as if it were your very own retreat "far from the madding crowd". Set in twenty five wooded, landscaped acres, the spacious house is easy to get to but quietly remote.

Each guest room has its own distinct style such as the Garden Room, complete with king-size bed, fresh flowers and garden colours. Breakfast may be taken informally in the conservatory or in the more formal dining room with afternoon tea served on the terrace in fine weather. Dine at one of the many excellent restaurants nearby, or at Hamilton House itself where an extensive array of international dishes, from simple suppers to formal dinners, may be offered during your stay.

| Warren, VT 05674-9712 Tel 802 583 1066 Fax 802 583 1776 | Freephone in US 800 760 1066 Owners/Innkeepers: James & Joyce Plumpton | 4 rooms including 2 one bedroom suites Doubles $140 - $160 B&B | Suites $180 - $200 Tax 7% gratuities not accepted | Cross-country skiing Nearby: outdoor & indoor pools, tennis, golf, horseriding, skiing. | Does not meet the needs of children. Non-smoking VS • MC Amex • Discover |

# INN AT THE BRASS LANTERN
## STOWE

A traditional New England Bed and Breakfast Inn, located in the heart of Stowe, with views of Mt. Mansfield, Vermont's highest peak.

This is an award-winning restoration - a labour of love by the innkeeper. Guest rooms are decorated with period antiques and are individually heated and air-conditioned, some with fireplaces, others with whirlpool tubs. The Inn won a Restaurant of Distinction award in 95/96 from the Gourmet Dinners Society of North America.

The bustling village of Stowe offers endless activities; hiking, skiing, theatre, craft fairs and more and the innkeeper takes pride in helping guests find activities that will interest them most.

The Inn holds the AAA 3 Diamond rating and is about 3½ hours drive from Boston.

| 717 Maple Street, Stowe, VT 05672 | Tel 802 253 2229 Fax 802 253 7425 Freephone in US 800 729 2980 | Innkeeper: Andy Aldrich | 9 rooms Doubles $75 – $185 B&B | Tax 7% Non-smoking | Does not meet the needs of children VS • MC • Amex |

**VERMONT**

# INN AT THE ROUND BARN FARM
## WAITSFIELD

The inn that lives in your imagination; rich in history, elegant, luxurious and charming, without the least bit of pretension. Dream-like guest rooms, roaring fireplaces, relaxing steamshowers, Jacuzzi tubs and canopied beds so comfortable you'll feel like you're sleeping in a big hug! The only thing worth getting out of bed for is a scrumptious breakfast of blueberry Belgian waffles and cinnamon coffee.

In Summer, stroll our 85 acres of lush gardens, meadows, ponds and woodlands, our sculpture gardens provide a wonderful walking path that takes you on a journey through Vermont's history, complete with swans. In Winter enjoy the best views in the valley on 30 km of cross-country ski trails.

Rated AAA Three Diamond, Mobil Three Star.

| | | | | |
|---|---|---|---|---|
| RR1, Box 247, East Warren Road, Waitsfield, VT 05673 | Tel 802 496 2276 Fax 802 496 8832 | Owners/Manager: Jack & Doreen Simko, AnneMarie Defreest | 11 rooms Doubles $115 – $195 B&B ($15 added to rates 15/9 - 25/10) | Tax 7% Indoor swimming pool, hiking Non-smoking | Children over 10 welcome VS • MC • Amex |

# INN AT WEST VIEW FARM
## DORSET

The Inn at West View Farm enjoys a tradition of fine hospitality and has welcomed guests since the turn of the century. Our restored farmhouse, offers the amenities of a full service inn and excellent restaurant in a beautiful pastoral setting and has been chosen by Glamour Magazine as one of Vermont's great romantic country inns.

Our historic buildings have undergone loving restoration and await your arrival. Come and experience the tranquility of a Vermont vacation.

In summer, enjoy our wrap-around porch and the shade of the majestic maples which dot our lawns and meadow. In winter, cosy up to one of our two fireplaces, unwind in the Tavern or relax in our cheerful sunroom.

| | | | | |
|---|---|---|---|---|
| Rte 30 Dorset VT 05251 Tel 802 867 5715 Fax 802 867 0468 | Innkeepers: Dorothy & Helmut Stein | 10 rooms including 1 two bedroom suite. | Doubles $85 - $140 B&B Tax 7%. s.c. 15% | Nearby: golf, riding, sailing, water skiing, down-hill skiing, cross-country skiing | Children over 12 welcome. Non-smoking VS • MC • Amex |

**VERMONT**

# JACKSON HOUSE INN
## WOODSTOCK

The Jackson House was built in 1890 by Wales Johnson, a local sawmill owner whose aim was to create the finest examples of late Victorian architecture possible. Floors of cherry and maple complement fine antique furniture; Oriental rugs, French-cut crystal, a library of the classics, and a parlour with a welcoming fire. Fifteen bedrooms include four new one-room luxury suites with fireplaces, thermal massage tubs, and splendid views of the four acre landscaped gardens. Enjoy the shade of huge ancient trees or stroll across the arched bridge to the pond, home to the resident snow geese, ducks and trout.

Breakfast is a memorable occasion, warm fruit compote with champagne, almond-crusted French toast, ricotta pancakes, frittatas with fresh asparagus and oven-cured tomatoes. Every evening the Innkeepers host a complimentary hors d'oeuvre buffet with wine and champagne. Dinner is relaxed yet elegant. The cathedral-ceiling dining room has a striking granite open hearth fireplace and magnificent views. Chef Brendan Nolan prepares elegant new American cuisine.

| | | | | | | |
|---|---|---|---|---|---|---|
| Route 4 West, Woodstock, VT 05091 Tel 802 457 2065 Fax 802 457 9390 | Freephone in US 800 448 1890 Owner: Juan Florin Innkeeper: Jennifer Barba | 15 rooms including 6 one bedroom suites Doubles $170 - $190 B&B | Suites $240 - $260 Tax 9% Nearby: hiking, indoor pool, tennis, horse riding, golf, | sailing, swimming pond, cross-country and downhill skiing, sleigh rides, ice skating, snowshoeing | Children over 14 welcome Non-smoking VS•MC•Amex |

# LANDGROVE INN
## LANDGROVE

Three generations of the Snyder family are currently active in operating this cheerful red clapboard country inn in rural Vermont, where cows graze in undulating fields and horse-drawn carriages amble along miles of canopied roads. Comfortable guest rooms are furnished in an antique colonial style with stencilling on the walls, hard-rock maple armoires and rocking chairs.

A day at the inn begins with a hearty country breakfast and in the evening you may choose one of the fine restaurants in the area or enjoy a candlelit meal at the inn itself, finishing up with one of Kathy's delicious desserts. Whether you choose to partake of the many activities available at the inn, visit the surrounding areas or simply relax in the quiet beauty of the landscape, the Landgrove Inn provides you with the true Vermont experience!

| | | | | | |
|---|---|---|---|---|---|
| R D 1 Box 215, Landgrove/Weston Road, Landgrove, VT 05148 | Tel 802 824 6663 Fax 802 824 3055 Freephone in US 800 669 8466 | Owners: Jay & Kathy Snyder 16 rooms Doubles $85 - $120 B&B | Tax 7% Outdoor pool, tennis, cross country skiing, conference facilities fishing, horse-drawn sleigh. | Nearby: indoor pool, golf, horseriding, down-hill skiing Children welcome. | Non-smoking VS • MC Amex • Discover |

**VERMONT**

# LAREAU FARM COUNTRY INN
## WAITSFIELD

A restored 1832 Greek Revival farmhouse nestled in a picturesque meadow beside the Mad River, but within minutes of shopping and skiing. We offer views of the woods and river, together with hospitality that is "a cut above", filling our inn with guests seeking restful getaways, ski holidays, outdoor excursions and country romance in a peaceful rural setting.

Delicious aromas from the kitchen, the heart of the house, are a welcome wake-up. It is here that fancy country breakfasts and home baked goods are prepared and guests linger long over coffee with the innkeepers. Dinners can be arranged for groups or special evenings and on Fridays and Saturdays our Flatbread Kitchen produces the best pizza in New England from a wood-fired earthen oven.

| | | | | | |
|---|---|---|---|---|---|
| P.O. Box 563, Route 100<br>Waitsfield<br>VT 05673 | Tel 802 496 4949<br>Freephone in US<br>800 833 0766 | Owners:<br>Dan & Susan Easley<br>13 rooms including 1 one bedroom suite | Doubles $70 - $125<br>B&B<br>Tax 7% | Nearby: outdoor & indoor pools, tennis, golf, riding, down-hill skiing, cross-country skiing | Children welcome.<br>Non-smoking<br>VS • MC |

---

# MAPLE LEAF INN
## BARNARD

The Maple Leaf is a faithful Victorian farmhouse reproduction, nestled snugly within sixteen acres of maple and birch trees a stone's throw from historic Woodstock. As you approach the inn, trees unfold to reveal gables, dormers, wrap-around porch, gingerbread trim windows, and soaring chimneys.

Stencilling, stitchery, and handmade quilts blend with antique and reproduction furnishings, contributing to the warm, welcoming atmosphere. Most guest rooms feature king-size bed, sitting area, wood-burning fireplace, tv, vcr, phone, and whirlpool tubs.

Enjoy the bright and airy parlour and savour late afternoon refreshments by the fire. Books and artefacts collected from world travels adorn the walls and shelves in the library where comfortable chairs invite guests to read or relax.

| | | | | | |
|---|---|---|---|---|---|
| P.O. Box 273<br>Barnard<br>VT 05031 | Tel 802 234 5342<br>Freephone in US<br>800 51-MAPLE | Owner/Innkeeper:<br>Gary & Janet Robison<br>7 rooms | Doubles $100 - $160<br>B&B<br>Tax 7% | Cross-country skiing<br>Nearby: tennis, golf, riding, sailing, down-hill skiing | Does not meet the needs of children<br>Non-smoking<br>VS • MC |

**VERMONT**

# MIDDLEBURY INN
## MIDDLEBURY

The Middlebury Inn has presided over happenings since 1827, establishing a great tradition of hospitality, comfort and service. There are 76 recently redecorated rooms with each area of the inn having its own charm, combining past traditions with present day amenities.

Dining choices vary seasonally with plentiful New England fare in the Founders Room and Stewart Library. During warm weather, the wide sweeping porch is a natural for lunch or dinner. Our Tavern provides the best in liquid refreshment and the Country Peddler is a unique combination of café, gifts, New England crafts and antiques. There is never any lack of choices for "what to do today," or for that matter, tomorrow, and the day after.

Court Square,
PO Box 631
Middlebury
VT 05753
Tel 802 388 4961
Fax 802 388 4563

Freephone in US
800 842 4666
Innkeeper:
Frank Emanuel

76 rooms including 8 one bedroom suites
Doubles $80 - $200
B&B including afternoon tea

Suites $144 - $275
Tax 7%
Conference facilities
Nearby: outdoor pool, tennis, golf, riding,

sailing, down-hill skiing, cross-country skiing
Parking available free of charge.

Children welcome.
Non-smoking
VS • MC • Amex
Diners • Discover

# OCTOBER COUNTRY INN
## BRIDGEWATER

Arrive at a cozy, casual, rustic 19th century farmhouse to pots of fresh coffee, tea or lemonade, just-baked cookies, and welcoming smiles. Relish Patrick's hearty breakfast feasts and family-style evening meals - sociable and fun - with international dishes to delight you. In warmer weather enjoy gardens, apple trees, lilacs and swimming pool, or settle by the fireplace or potbellied stove to read and doze.

Guests often join the innkeepers (devout and knowledgeable theatre buffs themselves) for a delicious pre-performance picnic on the riverbank behind one of New England's best summer theatres. Actors and directors often come too! Located near Woodstock, Hanover and Weston, October Country offers plenty to do...whilst still being off the beaten track. Kick off your shoes, put up your feet - you've found the perfect place to relax.

PO Box 66
Upper Road
Bridgewater Corners
VT 05035
Tel 802 672 3412

Freephone in US
800 648 8421
Innkeeper:
Richard Sims

10 rooms, 8 with private baths
Doubles $124 - $157
MAP

Tax 7% s.c. 10%
Outdoor pool, conference facilities

Nearby: indoor pool, tennis, golf, riding, sailing, water skiing, down-hill & cross-country skiing

Children welcome.
Non-smoking
VS • MC • Amex

**VERMONT**

# QUECHEE BED & BREAKFAST
## QUECHEE

Welcome to a warm and gracious AAA 3 Diamond, Mobil 3 Star, colonial country inn set on a cliff overlooking the Ottauquechee River – a spectacular and memorable view at all times of year. Spacious guest rooms are thoughtfully furnished with comfort and privacy in mind. Enjoy a hearty country breakfast served at individual tables, or relax in the spacious living room, with striking brick and granite fireplace and stunning views. Annual, perennial and herb gardens together with locust and chestnut trees surround the inn.

A short walk through the covered bridge brings you to the waterfall and Quechee Village, famous for its glassblowing, antique shops and restaurants. This is an area rich in natural beauty, a wonderful blend of country and sophistication.

| Rt 4 and Waterman Hill, PO Box 80, Quechee, VT 05159 | Tel 802 295 1776<br>Innkeeper:<br>Susan Kaduboski | 8 rooms<br>Doubles $94 – $139<br>B&B | Tax 7% | Four season sports activities all available nearby<br>Non-smoking | Does not meet the needs of children<br>VS • MC |

# SHIELD INN
## WEST DOVER

Create some wonderful musical memories at Shield Inn and at the same time experience the serenity and beauty of Vermont's exhilarating air, whether your trip is timed for the summer months or to enjoy brilliant foliage and great winter snow.

Shield Inn is a cosy and intimate, non-smoking country inn with twelve beautiful and tastefully decorated rooms. Each room has its own motif and individual charm with private bath and colour, cable tv - some are available with romantic fireplaces and soothing two person Jacuzzi's. During ski season (December to March) a hearty dinner is served. A full breakfast is served every morning throughout the year. The Shield Inn has established a reputation for its fine music programmes. A large Steinway grand piano is an integral part of the character, charm and unique attraction of this lovely inn. Excellent chamber music and jazz concerts are presented throughout the year in an intimate living room setting.

| Rt.100, PO Box 366, West Dover, VT 05356<br>Tel 802 464 3984<br>Fax 802 464 5322 | Owners/Innkeepers:<br>Phyllis & Lou Isaacson<br>12 rooms, including 1 one bedroom suite | Doubles $70 - $170<br>B&B•MAP optional December to March<br>Suites $126 - $210<br>Tax 9% s.c.15% | Nearby: tennis, horse riding, golf, water-skiing, lake swimming, sailing, fishing, boating, biking, | hiking, down-hill and cross-country skiing, snowshoeing, snowboarding, sleigh rides, tubing | Children over 10 welcome<br>Non-smoking<br>VS•MC |

**VERMONT**

# SHIRE INN
## CHELSEA

In a quintessential New England Village, white and serene, your recently redecorated room in this Federal-style inn awaits you. Tall windows, excellent beds, hand-ironed, soft, 100% cotton, sheets, cosy down comforters and quilts, and a crackling fire. Modern private baths with the softest, plushest towels we could find. Rocking chairs. Privacy. Comfort!

Karen, innkeeper and chef, believes dining should be an event to please all senses, candlelight, and soft background romantic music add to your pleasure. After a meal which may include Dijon-mustard chicken breast or veal scallopine stuffed with wild rice and apricots, followed by homemade cheesecake or chocolate torte with raspberry sauce, sip a cup of hot coffee as you sigh with contentment.

| Main Street P.O. Box 37 Chelsea VT 05038-0037 | Tel 802 685 3031 Fax 802 685 3871 Freephone in US and Canada 800 441 6908 | Owner/Innkeeper: Jay & Karen Keller 6 rooms | Doubles $140 - $185 MAP Tax 7% s.c. 15% | Cross-country skiing Nearby: golf, riding, down-hill skiing | Children over 7 welcome. Non-smoking VS • MC |

# THE SIEBENESS
## STOWE

A warm welcome is guaranteed at our charming country inn nestled in the foothills of Mt. Mansfield. Romantic guest rooms are uniquely decorated with beautiful country antiques and homemade quilts. Two bedrooms in our country cottage have jacuzzis, gas fireplaces, refrigerators, air-conditioning, tv and beautiful views.

Relax in our outdoor hot tub, or in our comfortable fireplace lounge. Wake up to the aroma of a freshly cooked country breakfast – our food has made us famous. Enjoy the mountain views from our pool and grounds, take a bike ride, a walk, or in the winter, skate or ski to the picturesque village of Stowe with its delightful array of shops and restaurants.

| 3681 Mountain Road, Stowe, VT 05672 Tel 802 253 8942 Fax 802 253 9232 | Freephone in US 800 426 9001 Owner/Innkeepers: Sue & Nils Andersen | 10 rooms. Doubles $70 - $150 B&B | Cottage rooms $130 - $170 Tax 7% s.c. 10% | Outdoor pool. Nearby: tennis, golf, skiing. Non-smoking. | Children welcome VS • MC • Amex |

**VERMONT**

# SMUGGLERS' NOTCH INN
### JEFFERSONVILLE

Escape to the quiet side of Mount Mansfield. Smugglers' Notch Inn, built as a farmhouse in 1791 and welcoming guests since the mid-1800's, has just the right mix of old and new, to make you start relaxing the minute you walk in the door. Eleven guest rooms are decorated in simple charming country style, with fluffy towels, locally hand-made quilts and lamps and individual touches to make you feel right at home. The living room invites with comfy furniture, brick fireplace, abundant games, books, and a tv. After a day of adventure or leisure, enjoy the deck and year-round hot tub or the swimming pool in summer months. Our old-fashioned, semi-circular copper-railed bar is a comfortable location for an afternoon chat or a cocktail before or after hearty meals, which can be enjoyed in the old converted ballroom, now a casual, comfortable, candlelit restaurant.

| | | | | | |
|---|---|---|---|---|---|
| Church Street, P.O.Box 280, Jeffersonville, VT 05464 | Tel 802 644 2412 Fax 802 644 2881 Freephone in US and Canada 800 845 3101 | Owner/Innkeepers: Cynthia Barber & Jon Day 11 rooms | Doubles $60 - $125 B&B Tax 9% | Outdoor pool, hot tub Nearby: tennis, golf, fly-fishing, down-hill and cross- country skiing, hiking, biking | Children welcome Smoking in designated areas VS•MC•Amex |

# SUGAR LODGE AT SUGARBUSH
### WARREN

Located in central Vermont at Sugarbush Resort, we offer the privacy and amenities of a small hotel with the hospitality of a country inn.

Our rooms offer all home comforts with a choice of king, queen or two double beds, full private baths, colour cable television and telephone. In the evenings, relax by the fire in our living room with a cup of hot chocolate or spiced cider and home-made chocolate chip cookies!

Enjoy the snow covered Vermont countryside as the shuttle takes you to the slopes, or one of the many fine nearby restaurants or shops. In summer enjoy, all of the numerous outdoor and indoor sports facilities in the immediate area.

| | | | | | |
|---|---|---|---|---|---|
| Sugarbush Access Road Warren VT 05674 Tel 802 583 3300 Fax 802 585 1148 | Freephone in US 800 982 3465 Innkeeper David B. Jackson | 22 rooms Doubles $59 - $119 B&B Tax 7% s.c. 3% | Nearby: outdoor & indoor pool, tennis, golf, riding, sailing, conference facilities, down-hill & cross- | country skiing, hiking, canoeing, fishing Children welcome. | Childrens' programme Summer or Winter $55 daily. Non-smoking VS • MC • Amex |

**VERMONT**

# THE SUGARTREE
## WARREN

*In summer, the chalet-style Sugartree's window boxes overflow with colourful flowers and you may find a hummingbird outside your window. In winter, views are of glistening trees and the snow covered trails of the Sugarbush ski area just ¼ mile away.*

*Quilts, comforters and antiques adorn guest rooms, some of which have canopy beds and throughout the inn, needlework, Frank's handcarved Santas, whimsical and interesting pictures, books and games. Join a singalong by our 100 year old pump organ or curl up by the fire with a good book. Thoughtful extra touches make your stay more comfortable ... phones, hair dryers, a guest pantry with refrigerator, maps, attraction brochures and in winter, a free ski shuttle to the mountain. Cricket spoken here! Frank is a member of the local team and organiser for the area's annual cricket festival.*

| | | | | | | |
|---|---|---|---|---|---|---|
| RR1 Box 38<br>Sugarbush Access Road<br>Warren, VT 05674<br>Tel 802 583 3211<br>Fax 802 583 3203 | Freephone in US<br>800 666 8907<br>Innkeepers:<br>Frank & Kathy<br>Partsch | 9 rooms<br>including 1 one<br>bedroom suite.<br>Doubles $80 - $124<br>B&B | Suites $100 - $135<br>Tax 7%<br>Nearby: Outdoor pool,<br>indoor pool, tennis, | golf, riding,<br>conference facilities,<br>down-hill & cross-<br>country skiing | Children over 7<br>welcome.<br>Non-smoking<br>VS • MC • Discover |

# TUCKER HILL LODGE & RESTAURANT
## SUGARBUSH/MAD RIVER VALLEY

*Set on 14 acres of wooded hillside, with swimming pool and lovely country gardens, this inn offers homey, rustic rooms with handmade quilts, bouquets of flowers, a mountain cabin feeling and a good restaurant. Dinner can be enjoyed in the panelled and beamed dining room or the delightful greenhouse style addition. Entrees are beautiful to see and heavenly to eat, homemade desserts are spectacular – try the maple creme brulee, or perhaps go for the strawberry praline torte.*

*To work off those calories, in Summer there are tennis courts, an outdoor pool and cycling trails while in Winter there is skiing from the back door.*

| | | | | | |
|---|---|---|---|---|---|
| RD 1, Box 147,<br>Sugarbush Mad River<br>Valley, VT 05673 | Tel 802 496 3983<br>Fax 802 496 3203<br>Freephone in US<br>800 543 7841 | Owner/Innkeepers:<br>Susan &<br>Giorgio Noaro | 22 rooms, 16 of which<br>have private baths.<br>2 one bedroom suites | Doubles $70 – $90<br>B&B<br>Suites $110 – $115<br>Tax 7% | Outdoor pool,<br>tennis, hiking<br>Children welcome<br>VS • MC • Amex |

**VERMONT**

# VERMONT INN
## KILLINGTON

*Please join us at our small country inn on five acres in the Green Mountains, we offer the charm of a family-run inn with excellent New England and Continental cuisine. We are proud to have been awarded the Killington Champagne Dine-Around Award for fine dining for three consecutive years.*

*Built as a farmhouse in 1840, original wood beams are exposed in the living room, where you can listen to music, watch television or simply relax in front of a crackling fire when there is a chill in the air. Our lounge offers an intimate setting with wood stove and beautiful mountain views. Guest rooms are unique and cosy, with country charm and the inn also offers a sauna, hot tub, tennis court and swimming pool.*

| Rt 4<br>Killington<br>VT 05751<br>Tel 802 775 0708<br>Fax 802 773 2440 | Freephone in US<br>800 541 7795<br>Innkeepers:<br>Megan & Greg Smith | 18 rooms<br>Doubles $90 - $225<br>MAP<br>Tax 7%  s.c. 15% | Outdoor pool, tennis<br>Nearby: indoor pool, golf, riding, down-hill skiing, cross-country skiing | Children over 6 welcome.<br>Non-smoking | VS • MC<br>Amex • Diners |

# VILLAGE COUNTRY INN
## MANCHESTER

*Rose chintz fabrics; lace; antiques; rocking chairs on a porch bedecked with baskets of flowers; formal gardens cascading with colour; a romantic gazebo and a terrace of fountains. Choose Le Fleur suite with its King-sized bed, separate sitting room, white wicker furniture and clawfoot tub on a platform; Rose Noir with sitting area, fireplace and a two-person bathtub; or one of the Garden rooms where you can open your door and walk directly into the beautiful gardens.*

*Your stay at the inn includes full country breakfast and a delicious four-course candlelit dinner with time to enjoy a cocktail in the inviting Tavern in the Green first.*

*In historic Manchester Village with its wonderful shops and galleries there is plenty to see and do, or perhaps your preference is to just pick a rocking chair and watch the world go by.*

| PO Box 408<br>Route 7A<br>Manchester Village<br>VT 05254<br>Tel 802 362 1792<br>Fax 802 362 7238 | Freephone in US<br>800 370 0300<br>Owners:<br>Anne & Jay Degen | 33 rooms including 9 one bedroom suites, 9 deluxe suites & rooms | Doubles $150 - $185<br>MAP<br>Deluxe rooms & Suites $200 - $300<br>Tax 7% s.c. 15% | Outdoor pool<br>Nearby: golf, riding, down-hill & cross-country skiing, | Children over 12 welcome.<br>Non-smoking<br>VS • MC<br>Amex • Discovery |

**VERMONT**

# WEST HILL HOUSE B&B
## WARREN

*Our peaceful nine acre property is less than one mile from Sugarbush Ski slopes and adjacent to the (Robert Trent Jones) Sugarbush Golf Course and cross country ski centre. Lovely perennial gardens, meadows, a beaver pond and splendid views of the nearby mountains from our great front porch provide a setting for relaxation and getting away from the pressures of daily life.*

*There is much to do as you enjoy the ever changing beauty of the surroundings. The area offers fishing, canoeing, horseback, riding, soaring, hiking, biking, tennis, golf and superb cross-country and down-hill skiing. Fine restaurants, quaint villages with shops, covered bridges, antiquing, galleries, summer concerts and theatre are all nearby.*

| | | | | |
|---|---|---|---|---|
| *Breads from our woodfired bake oven are a special treat.* | West Hill Road RR1 Box 292 Warren VT 05674 Tel 802 496 7162 Fax 802 496 6443 | Freephone in US 800 898 1427 Proprietor: Dotty Kyle | 7 rooms including 1 one bedroom suite | Doubles $85 - $135 B&B Suite $105 - $135 Tax 7% |

# WEST MOUNTAIN INN
## ARLINGTON

*This view is reserved for you. Nestled on 150 mountainside acres, cradled between the Taconic and Green Mountain ranges, this full-service inn has welcomed travellers for nearly two decades. From its perch overlooking the famous Battenkill River and historic village of Arlington, guests relax in comfortable surroundings, dine on creative country cuisine and partake of a myriad of outdoor adventure opportunities.*

*Antiques and country furnishings invite you to relax and rejuvenate in a setting where nature surrounds you, whether it's the fishpond, bird sanctuary, woodland wildflower trails, or llamas and goat in residence in the pasture.*

*Candlelit dinners, hearty country breakfasts and warm and spacious common spaces - this indeed is a "special peace of Vermont" where you enter as a cherished guest and leave as one of the folks.*

| | | | | | |
|---|---|---|---|---|---|
| River Road Arlington VT 05250 | Tel 802 375 6516 Fax 802 375 6553 Innkeeper: Paula Maynard | 18 rooms including 3 one bedroom suites, 3 two bedroom suites | Doubles $145 - $199 MAP (reflects seasonally variable rates) Suites $209 - $239 Tax 7% s.c. 15% | Conference facilities, cross-country skiing Nearby: tennis, golf, riding, cross-country skiing | Children welcome. Non-smoking VS • MC • Amex Diners • Discover |

199

**VERMONT**

# WHITFORD HOUSE INN
## VERGENNES

On a knoll in the middle of rich farmland near beautiful Lake Champlain and surrounded by vegetable, flower, and herb gardens, the Whitford House Country Inn overlooks broad flowing grain fields, majestically framed by the vast green Adirondack Mountain range. Tranquillity is the hallmark of this lovely restored eighteenth century Vermont farmhouse where spectacular views are enjoyed by three comfortable bedrooms with private baths, and a self-contained guest house with bedroom, bath, and sitting room. Welcoming touches include turn-down service, individual robes, fresh produce from the inn's gardens, and lots of helpful sightseeing tips from Bruce and Barbara.
Hiking and canoeing are within a few miles and you can walk, bicycle, bird-watch and, in winter, cross-country ski from the inn's back door through acres of open fields and woods. Historic and cultural sites abound within an hour's distance.

| | | | | |
|---|---|---|---|---|
| RR1 Box 1490, Vergennes, VT 05491  Tel 802 758 2704  Fax 802 758 2089 | Freephone in US 800 746 2704  Owners: Bruce & Barbara Carson | 4 rooms including 1 cottage  Doubles $100 - $135 B&B | Cottage $150 - $175  Tax 9%  Cross-country skiing, bicycling, walking | Nearby: outdoor pool, tennis, horse riding, water-skiing, golf, sailing, down-hill skiing | Children welcome  Non-smoking  VS•MC |

# WILEY INN
## PERU

Ten miles north of Manchester, Vermont, the Wiley Inn has been welcoming guests for over fifty years. Relish a romantic break in a lovely Victorian room with canopy bed, choose one with a clawfoot tub or luxuriate in a two-person Jacuzzi in the flickering firelight.
Families are also well catered for in another area of the inn where three two bedroom suites; two small and three large rooms can adapt to accommodate different age ranges and requirements. Parents can relax while kids enjoy the lounge, equipped with toys, games and a movie library.
Outdoors, a variety of pleasures: four down-hill and six cross-country ski areas; snowmobiling; sleigh rides; ice skating and an outdoor hot tub for viewing (and singing if you wish!) 'Moonlight in Vermont'. In warmer months, mountain breezes cool you as you read or doze in the hammock; tan on the deck; swim in the pool; hike the Appalachian Long Trail; fish the Battenkill river; mountain bike; canoe or simply sit and watch the trout jump.

| | | | | |
|---|---|---|---|---|
| Route 11, PO Box 37, Peru, VT 05152  Tel 802 824 6600  Fax 802 824 4195 | Freephone in US 888 843 6600  Innkeepers: Judith & Gerald Goodman | 16 rooms including 10 one bedroom suites and 3 two bedroom suites | Doubles $85 - $185 B&B  Family Room/Suites $120 - $220 (Sleeps four)  Tax 9% s.c. 10% | Outdoor pool and Coleman Spa Hot-Tub. Nearby: horse riding, down-hill and cross-country skiing, golf, sailing | All children welcome  Visa•MC•Amex |

**VERMONT**

# WILLOUGHVALE INN ON LAKE WILLOUGHBY
## WESTMORE

In the heart of Vermont's Northeast Kingdom, lies the WilloughVale Inn on Lake Willoughby offering casual lodging and dining in an exquisite natural setting. Choose from eight unique main inn rooms with beautiful views and hand-crafted furnishings, or four cosy lakefront cottages with fireplaces, fully-equipped kitchens, private screened porches, decks and private docks. Relax on the inn's inviting wrap-around porch or gather with locals and guests in the warmth of the inn's tap room bar and main dining room to enjoy conversation, creative specialities and sweeping mountain and lake views.

Referred to as the "Lucerne of America" due to its spectacular scenery of wooded mountains and dramatic granite cliffs towering over crystal-clear waters, Lake Willoughby beckons you to enjoy swimming, fishing, boating, hiking, biking, ice fishing, snowmobiling and cross-country skiing from the inn's door. Lake Willoughby in any season will warm the heart and heighten the senses!

| | | | | | |
|---|---|---|---|---|---|
| Route 5A, RR2 Box 403, Westmore, VT 05860 Tel 802 525 4123 Fax 802 525 4514 | Freephone in US 800 594 9102 Owners: David & Simon Gameroff 8 rooms including 1 one bedroom | suite, 4 cottages Doubles $79 - $159 B&B Suites $99 - $159 Cottages $99 - $215 Tax 9% s.c. $2.00 per | room/cottage per night Water-skiing, sailing, hiking, biking, snowshoeing, canoeing. | Nearby: horse riding, golf, down-hill skiing, rock/ice climbing, (bike, canoe, snowmobile, snowshoe rentals available) | Children welcome Pets allowed Non-smoking VS•MC•Amex Diners•Discover |

# THE WOODS
## KILLINGTON

Immerse yourself in luxury at The Woods' unique condominium and cluster homes. Three miles from the base of Killington, offering unmatched comforts and unexpected amenities; full kitchens with microwave and dishwasher; oversized whirlpool tubs; colour cable tv, vcr and basic supplies for your convenience. Daily housekeeping service is provided.

A complimentary shuttle transports you to the finest skiing in the East. Ice skating, horse-drawn sleigh rides - all only minutes away. Indulge yourself in such apres ski offerings as Swedish massage, a swim in the 75 foot lap pool, or a workout in our fully equipped exercise studio. Tempt your palate at one of the best restaurants in the area - Panache, featuring unique award winning cuisine in a casual yet elegant atmosphere.

| | | | | |
|---|---|---|---|---|
| RR#1, Box 2325, Killington, VT 05751 Tel 802 422 3244 Fax 802 422 3320 | Director Guest Services: Tammy Howard Euber | 40 fully equipped one, two and three bedroom apartments & houses with jacuzzi and fireplaces. | Houses $266 - $425 EP Tax 7% | Indoor pool, tennis, conference facilities, down-hill & cross-country skiing (shuttle service to slopes) | Nearby: golf, riding, sailing, water skiing Children welcome. Non-smoking VS • MC • Amex |

# SOUTHEASTERN STATES

### FLORIDA
| | | |
|---|---|---|
| **1** | Amelia Island Plantation | 203 |
| **2** | Blue MoonHotel | 207 |
| **3** | Chalet Suzanne | 207 |
| **4** | Darst Victorian Manor | 208 |
| **5** | Elizabeth Pointe Lodge | 204 |
| **6** | Heron House | 205 |
| **7** | Hibiscus House | 208 |
| **8** | Verona House | 209 |
| **9** | Lakeside Inn | 206 |

### GEORGIA
| | | |
|---|---|---|
| **10** | 1842 Inn | 211 |
| **11** | Glen-Ella Springs | 211 |
| **12** | Little St. Simons Island | 210 |

### NORTH CAROLINA
| | | |
|---|---|---|
| **13** | First Colony Inn | 212 |
| **14** | Lords Proprietors' Inn | 214 |
| **15** | Swag Country Inn | 213 |

### SOUTH CAROLINA
| | | |
|---|---|---|
| **16** | Ashley Inn | 217 |
| **17** | Cannonboro Inn | 217 |
| **18** | Fulton Lane Inn | 215 |
| **19** | Planters inn | 216 |
| **20** | Red Horse Inn | 218 |

## FLORIDA

# AMELIA ISLAND PLANTATION
### FERNANDINA BEACH

In deliberate and perfect harmony with nature... nestled between the beautiful marshes and estuaries of the Intracoastal Waterway and the Atlantic, the resort is an integral part of the island's ecosystem. Sandpipers forage the cool wet sand, the fragrance of bursting blossoms permeates the dense forests of ancient oaks. Spaciousness, privacy and peace are all pervading.

There are twenty three world-class tennis courts, health & fitness center, sportfishing, seven miles of nature walks, cycle paths and jogging trails and no less than 25 sparkling swimming pools. Choose a hotel room, a sumptuous penthouse suite or a fully equipped villa - most accommodations offer spectacular views of the ocean or maritime forests.

Choose the Amelia Inn Restaurant for oceanside dining or the Beach Club Sports Bar for more casual fare. At Amelia Island Plantation the natural beauty is breathtaking, the service warm and friendly and the pleasures endless.

PO Box 3000
Fernandina Beach
Fl 32034-3000
•
Tel 904 261 6161
Fax 904 277 5945
Freephone in US
800 874 6878
Cellet Travel Service Inc.
01564 79 4999
•
Resort Manager:
Jeff Johnson
•
462 rooms

including 130 one bedroom, 127 two bedroom & 78 three bedroom suites, & villas.
•
Doubles: $125 - $219 EP
Suites, & villas $146 - $530
•
Tax 9%
•
Outdoor & indoor pools, cycling, tennis, golf, conference facilities
Childrens' programmes
•
VS • MC • Amex

## FLORIDA

# ELIZABETH POINTE LODGE
### AMELIA ISLAND

Rated amongst the 12 Best Waterfront Inns in America, focusing on individualised attention and located on the barrier island of Amelia with long stretches of often deserted beach, porches surround the main floor of this 1890s "Nantucket shingle". An abundance of rockers, sunshine and lemonade invite you to relax, whilst a full complimentary breakfast is served in a sunny room overlooking the ocean.

Although each of the guest rooms is different, making room hunting down the winding halls a pastime, they have in common fresh flowers, cable tv with movie channels, and oversized soaking tubs. Light lunch, dessert and room service are available all day. Complimentary wine and hors d'oeuvres are available at 6.00 p.m.

Sailing, fishing charters, tennis, golf, and horseback riding are nearby. Touring bikes, beach equipment and airport pickup are always available. Special tours, outings, and charters can be arranged to suit your adventure. The historic seaport of Fernandina is a short bike ride away for dining and shopping.

98 So. Fletcher Ave
Amelia Island
Florida 32034

•

Tel 904 277 4851
Fax 904 277 6500
Freephone in US
800 772 3359

•

Owner:
David J. Caples

•

25 rooms
including 1 one bedroom suite, 1 two bedroom suite

Doubles  $100 - $195
B&B

•

Tax  8%

•

Conference facilities

•

Children welcome.

•

Non-smoking

•

VS • MC
Amex

**FLORIDA**

# HERON HOUSE
## KEY WEST

*In the heart of historic Key West, meticulously designed by gifted artists and craftsmen for the discerning traveller, a genuine sense of caring pervades every aspect of this very unique private retreat.*

Don't expect a standard hotel room here, our style has been inspired by the informality of the Florida Keys' natural environment. With generous private decks and balconies, your private room merges with luxuriant tropical gardens. Interior and exterior spaces blend and flow together with ample use of natural materials such as teak, oak and cedar. A unique trademark is our handgrown rare orchids and we even have our own vintage champagne ready to put on ice.

The beach is just four blocks from the inn whilst for epicurean delights, entertainment, boutique shopping or a gallery, Duval Street is only one block away. Heron House is casual elegance presented in a warm relaxing atmosphere of luxury without pretence. Here you will always have the freedom to be yourself.

512 Simonton Street
Key West
FL 33040
•
Tel 305 294 9227
Fax 305 294 5692
Freephone in US
800 294 1644
•
Owner/General Manager:
Fred Geibelt
•
23 rooms
including 8 one bedroom suites.

Doubles & Suites
$99 - $249 B&B
•
Tax 11.5 %.
•
Outdoor pool
Nearby: tennis, golf, sailing, water skiing
•
Does not meet the needs of children
•
VS • MC
Amex • Diners

**FLORIDA**

# LAKESIDE INN
## MOUNT DORA

Listed on the National Register of Historic Places, this vintage Victorian Inn has been a favourite destination for vacationers and diners alike for over one hundred years. Set on the shores of Lake Dora, surrounded by lush landscape of parks and trees, the inn is a charming centre piece in this quaint Florida town, reminiscent of a southern plantation with the ambience of a gentler era.

Guest rooms are exquisitely decorated offering a romantic atmosphere that includes such special touches as soft cotton robes, early morning coffee, continental breakfast and room service. Sunday Brunch on the huge front porch at the Inn is also an experience not to be missed. With its elegant Victorian decor and delectable American Regional cuisine, the Inn's Beauclaire Dining Room has won several awards and commendations whilst the Tremain's Lounge welcomes you to cosy fireside gatherings, friendly conversations and easy listening live entertainment. Enjoy the Lakeside experience, where, what once was.....still is!

100 N. Alexander St
Mount Dora
FL 32757
•
Tel 352 383 4101
Fax 352 735 2642
Freephone in US
800 556 2089
•
General Manager:
Tom Fultz
•
88 rooms
including 18 one
bedroom suites

Doubles $80 - $140 B&B
Suites $100 - $155
•
Tax 9%
•
Outdoor pool, tennis,
sailing, conference facilities
Nearby: golf, riding, water
skiing
•
Children welcome.
•
VS • MC • Amex
Diners • Discover

**FLORIDA**

# BLUE MOON HOTEL
## MIAMI BEACH

A touch of Monte Carlo on South Beach. Works of art, splashing fountains, stained glass and a charming garden courtyard. The Blue Moon is ideally situated in the heart of the Art Deco District just steps away from the world famous beaches, bistros, boutiques and unique atmosphere of Ocean Drive and within walking distance of the Miami Beach Convention Centre, Jackie Gleason Theatre, and art galleries and attractions of Lincoln Road Mall.

Luxurious, intimate and quaint with a Mediterranean flavour, sleeping accommodations feature fresh flowers and bottled water upon arrival, coffee makers and cd players, safes for valuables and minibars, voicemail and two telephone lines, soft cotton bathrobes and complimentary beach towels, nightly turndown service, air-conditioning, and cable tv.

944 Collins Avenue, Miami Beach, FL 33139
Tel 305 673 2262
Fax 305 534 5379

Freephone in US 800 724 1623
Owner: Merv Griffin
General Manager: Walter Chapman

21 rooms including 17 one bedroom suites, 1 two bedroom suite
40 cottages and suites with kitchens

Doubles $139 - $205 EP
Suites & Cottages $225 - $265
Tax 12.5%

Nearby: golf, ocean beaches, tennis, night-life, shopping, restaurants

Children welcome
Smoking in designated areas
VS•MC•Amex•Diners

---

# CHALET SUZANNE COUNTRY INN
## LAKE WALES

A 70-acre compound, nestled among orange groves, half an hour and a world away from Disney. From the moment guests walk through the wrought iron gates and see the unique towers, turrets and gables of Chalet Suzanne, they know they are in for a most unusual experience.

Guest rooms are individually decorated, fresh flowers are everywhere. Antiques, collectibles and potted greenery combine with oriental rugs and subtle colours to create a warm and cosy environment. Toiletries, hair-dryers, a decanter of sherry, fresh fruit and cable tv are a few of the in-room amenities.

Rated as one of the best restaurants in the US, five dining rooms overlook the lake. More than gourmet meals, more than comfort in a storybook setting, the Chalet Suzanne is rare balm for curing the ills of a busy world.

3800 Chalet Suzanne Drive
Lake Wales, FL 33853

Tel 941 676 6011
Fax 941 676 1814
Freephone in US 800 433 6011

Owner/Innkeepers Vita & Carl Hinshaw

30 rooms
Doubles: $135 - $195 B&B
Tax 10 %.

Outdoor pool, tennis courts, golf course, horseriding, sailing, water skiing, conference facilities, private airfield.

Children welcome.
VS • MC • Amex
Diners • Discover

**FLORIDA**

# DARST VICTORIAN MANOR
## MOUNT DORA

Come to relax, shop or enjoy the sunset in our AAA Four Diamond Victorian inn overlooking beautiful Lake Dora and transport yourselves back to a time when every day was a peaceful one. Wake to freshly brewed coffee and a full gourmet breakfast each morning, later in the day relax and relish complimentary afternoon tea and desserts. In the evening, choose from the many acclaimed restaurants within easy walking distance.

Room choices include our Queen Victoria three room, lake-view, turret suite, Judi's Room, featuring a 1920s French Deco bed with canopy and a bay window sitting area or The Priscilla with dramatic black and rose colouring. After a relaxing bath or soothing shower, wrap yourself in a velour robe, as fresh flowers fill your room with fragrance, or work on a jigsaw puzzle in the homey atmosphere of the parlour.

| 495 Old Highway 441, Mount Dora FL 32757 | Tel 352 383 4050 Fax 352 383 7625 Owner/Innkeeper: Jim & Nanci Darst | 6 rooms including 2 one bedroom suites. | Doubles $125 - $200 B&B Suites $180 - $200 Tax 9%. | Outdoor pool open from early '97 Nearby: tennis, golf, riding, sailing, water skiing, | Children over 12 welcome. Non-smoking VS • MC • Amex |

---

# HIBISCUS HOUSE
## WEST PALM BEACH

Rated one of the ten best B&Bs in Florida and located in the historic district next to the Intracoastal Waterway. Hibiscus House provides easy access to the ocean and to the town of Palm Beach with its fabulous homes, excellent shopping and delightful restaurants.

Relax by our secluded heated pool and sip complimentary cocktails, enjoy the comfort of your room with air conditioning, paddle fans, tv and phones or step through French doors onto your private terrace to take in the beauty of the lush foliage.

A full two course breakfast is served each morning in the tropical gardens surrounding the pool or in the inn's formal dining room. We invite you to spend some time with us and enjoy tropical elegance at its best.

| 501 30th Street, West Palm Beach FL 33407 Tel 561 863 5633 Fax 561 863 5633 | Freephone in US 800 203 4927 Owner: Raleigh Hill | 7 rooms including 1 one bedroom suite. 1 two bedroom suite. | 1 cottage with 2 bedrooms, 2 bathrooms & kitchen Doubles $65 - $125 B&B | Suites & cottage $120 - $160 Tax 10%. Outdoor pool, tennis, sailing | Children over 12 welcome. Non-smoking VS • MC Amex • Diners |

## FLORIDA

# VERONA HOUSE
## BROOKSVILLE

Verona House is a 1925 Sears and Roebuck catalogue house in historic downtown which, unlike most of Florida, boasts hills and picturesque oak-tree lined streets. This small town of 7,500 people offers a quiet get-away from the fast pace of city life and your hosts, Bob & Jan Boyd extend true southern hospitality, sharing with you the historical background of the area.

Four guest rooms are decorated in cherished pieces. Smoking is permitted on the porch but not indoors. Enjoy Jan's fresh baked casserole and delicious fruits for breakfast. Canoeing, horseback riding, golf and tennis are all nearby with major attractions such as Disneyworld, SeaWorld and Busch Gardens only an hour away.

| 201 So. Main Street Brooksville FL 34601 Tel 352 796 4001 | Freephone in US 800 355 6317 Owners: Bob & Jan Boyd | 4 rooms. 2 rooms with private bath 1 cottage | Doubles $45 - $80 B&B Cottage $90 - $100 Tax 8%. | Hot tub Nearby: tennis, golf, riding | Does not meet the needs of children. Non-smoking VS • MC • Amex |

## COMPLIMENTARY BOOKING SERVICE

Don't forget we offer an advisory and booking service and you can make all your reservations with just one phone call to us. The service is completely free and prices are not loaded in any way.

Call for a chat on
## 01895 622233

## GEORGIA

# LITTLE ST. SIMONS ISLAND
### ST. SIMONS ISLAND

*Your own private island awaits! A privately-owned 10,000 acre barrier island along the Georgia coast - paradise for nature lovers and outdoor enthusiasts, offering a wide variety of activities from its pristine beaches to ancient maritime forests and tidal creeks. The beauty of the landscape is punctuated by opportunities to observe the area's wildlife in this natural setting.*

*Accessible only by boat and accommodating just 24 overnight guests, gracious accommodations are set amongst the legendary moss-draped live oaks and shimmering marshes.*

*Culinary staff use nature's abundant regional offerings to create delicious cuisine home-style and brimming with flavours from the sea. Breakfast, lunch and dinner are served family-style in the main dining room or picnics are gladly prepared. During June to September, childrens' programmes available.*

P.O. Box 21078,
St. Simons Island,
GA 31522
•
Tel 912 638 7472
Fax 912 634 1811
•
Resident Managers;
Debbie & Kevin McIntyre
•
12 rooms
2 four bedroom houses
•
Doubles $290 - $515 AP
Four bedroom houses
$1360 - $1860

Exclusive use of the island
$3150 - $4550
•
Tax 7% s.c. 15%
•
Outdoor pool, riding, naturalist programmes, birding, boating, canoeing, angling, cycling, hiking, conference facilities
•
Children over 6 welcome
Oct to May. All ages
June - Sept
•
Non-smoking
•
VS • MC

## GEORGIA

# 1842 INN
## MACON

Listed on the National Register of Historic Places, the 1842 Inns Greek Revival, antebellum building, houses twenty-one guest rooms; sitting rooms and library; overlooks a quaint courtyard and garden and has a real southern "Gone with Wind" atmosphere.

Breakfast is brought to your bedroom each morning together with a morning newspaper while fresh flowers and evening turndown service are just two of the thoughtful little touches that make your stay special at this Four Diamond award winning inn. Some bedrooms have four-poster beds, working fireplaces and whirlpool tubs; the inn is within easy walking distance of local restaurants and nearby museum houses.

| | | | | | |
|---|---|---|---|---|---|
| 353 College Street, Macon, GA 31201 | Tel 912 741 1842￼Fax 912 741 1842￼Freephone in US￼800 336 1842 | Owner/Innkeeper: Phillip Jenkins￼21 one bedroom suites | Doubles $115 - $185￼B&B￼Tax 12% | Nearby: Outdoor and indoor pools, tennis, horse riding, golf, access to private country club | Children welcome￼Non-smoking￼VS•MC•Amex |

# GLEN-ELLA SPRINGS INN
## TURNERVILLE

Down a gravel road at the edge of the Chatahoochee National Forest, just 90 miles north of Atlanta, lies one of the area's hidden surprises. Listed on the National Register, this 100-year old inn, the holder of several awards for restoration, is situated on 18 acres with swimming pool, lovely gardens, meadows and mountain streams.

Barrie and Bobby Aycock, their family and staff make every effort to welcome each guest and assist them in exploring the beautiful mountain areas of Northeast Georgia. Excellent hiking and whitewater rafting are nearby, while charming villages with fine folk art, antiques and craft shops provide more passive activities.

A bountiful breakfast is provided, with the inn's reputation for exceptional food attracting dinner guests from Atlanta and surrounding areas.

| | | | | | |
|---|---|---|---|---|---|
| 1789 Bear Gap Road, Turnerville GA 30523￼Tel 706 754 7295￼Fax 706 754 1560 | Owners:￼Barrie & Bobby Aycock | 16 rooms including 2 one bedroom suites. | Doubles $100 - $160￼B&B￼Tax 11% | Outdoor pool, conference facilities, 18 acres of meadows, gardens, mountain stream | Nearby: tennis, golf, riding, water skiing￼Children over 6 welcome.￼VS • MC • Amex |

211

## NORTH CAROLINA

# FIRST COLONY INN
### NAGS HEAD

*Glorious beaches, refreshing ocean breezes, the uniquely calm and peaceful atmosphere of the Outer Banks and true southern hospitality at the historic First Colony Inn. Choose to lounge by the pool, follow the boardwalk to the gazebo on the ocean dune, visit numerous area attractions or simply relax in a rocking chair on the wrap-around verandah.*

*In 1988 your hosts, the Lawrence family, with their own roots deep in the area, took this "Grand Old Lady" ravaged by time and the encroaching Atlantic and, overcoming a myriad of obstacles, had the building cut into three sections and moved south. They then proceeded to return the inn to its former glory, scrupulously maintaining its character and history, whilst unobtrusively adding every modern convenience and comfort - heated towel rails, tv, phones, refrigerators, and in some rooms - kitchenettes, sitting rooms and private screened porches. This labour of love is now an internationally recognised, AAA Four Diamond Award winner and welcomes new generations to the old fashioned pleasures of the Outer Banks.*

6720 S. Virginia Dare Trail,
Nags Head,
NC 27959

•

Tel 919 441 2343
Fax 919 441 9234
Freephone in US
800 368 9290

•

General Manager:
Camille Lawrence

•

26 rooms
including 6 one bedroom suites.
Plus 5 two or three bedroom cottages.

Doubles Summer
$100 - $250 B&B,
Cottages $450 - $800 EP
(weekly Sat-Sat)

•

Tax 10%
Outdoor pool, beaches.
Nearby: indoor pool, tennis, golf, riding, sailing, water skiing, diving, windsurfing, hang gliding, fishing

•

Children welcome.
Non-smoking

•

VS • MC
Amex • Discover

## NORTH CAROLINA

# SWAG COUNTRY INN
### WAYNESVILLE

*Made of hand-hewn logs and set on 250 acres, Swag Country Inn has its own private entrance to the 500,000 acre Great Smoky Mountains National Park. A consistent winner of the Mobil Four Star award, the inn offers a unique combination of handsewn quilts, antler chandeliers, rustic furniture, luxurious amenities and the great outdoors.*

*Each of the guest accommodations is different, some in log cabins, some featuring woodstoves, private porches and cathedral ceilings with thoughtful extras such as refrigerators, coffeemakers with grinders and terry cloth robes. Wake to a symphony of bird song and the sight of a Smoky Mountain sky at dawn, explore pristine waterfalls and stop for a delicious picnic lunch on a mountaintop. Spring invites romantics and nature enthusiasts to enjoy the wildflowers and birds that are beginning to migrate home. Summer is enchanting with lazy days by mountain streams and cool evening breezes. Fall is ablaze with colour, roaring fires and steamy saunas. Dining is sensational at the inn and the warmth of good conversation is part of every meal.*

*Join us, discover the beauty and simplicity of nature in ideal surroundings.*

Route 2, Box 280-A
Waynesville, NC 28786
•
Tel 704 926 0430
Fax 704 926 2036
Freephone in US
800 789 7672
•
President/Innkeeper:
Deener Matthews
•
17 rooms
including 2 one bedroom
suites, 1 two bedroom suite.
3 cabins including 1 two
bedroom cabin

Doubles & Suites $190 -
$350 AP (rates are highest
at weekends)
Cabins $295 - $440
•
Tax 9%   s.c. 15%
•
Outdoor pool, conference
facilities, racquet ball,
hiking
•
Children over 7 welcome.
•
Non-smoking
•
VS • MC • Discover

**NORTH CAROLINA**

# THE LORDS PROPRIETORS' INN
## EDENTON

*Jane and Arch Edwards, hosts at the Lords Proprietors' sum up their attitude to innkeeping - "It's our desire to provide personal and at the same time, professional hospitality. We hope that each of our guests will feel welcomed and appreciated without feeling smothered". This view permeates the three beautifully restored homes on two acres of grounds in Edenton's Historic District and is evidenced by thoughtful touches such as guest kitchens stocked with homemade cookies, tea, coffee and soft drinks.*
*Guest rooms are large and meticulously decorated with antiques and fine reproductions. Cable tv, vcr and phones are also provided in each room. A hearty breakfast is served each day and on Tuesday through to Saturday fine dining is available, which might include such delights as Chef Kevin Yokley's striped bass with pistachio vinaigrette and one of his signature chocolate desserts. Just one block from the inn is the Visitors' Center which offers wonderful guided walking tours of the Historic District several times each day.*

| | | | | | |
|---|---|---|---|---|---|
| 300 North Broad Street Edenton, NC 27932 | Tel 919 482 3641 Fax 919 482 2432 Hosts: Arch & Jane Edwards | 20 rooms Doubles $185 - $235 MAP | Tax 8% Nearby: tennis, canoeing, biking | Parking available no charge Children welcome. | Smoking in parlour No credit cards accepted. |

# The Welcome Privilege Card
# A SELECTION OF PROMISES

**MAINE**
**BLUE HARBOR HOUSE,**
Camden, Maine
*Discount on delicious lobster dinner until 15th November '98
**KENNEBUNKPORT INN**
Kennebunkport, Maine
*Stay 2 nights, receive 3rd night free. Available Nov 1st through May 1st excluding Columbus Day weekend in Mid-October.

**MASSACHUSETTS**
**CAPTAIN'S HOUSE INN OF CHATHAM**
Chatham, Massachusetts
*Discounted Whale-watch trip tickets
*Complimentary split of Champagne for birthdays, honeymoons or anniversaries
*Specially decorated cake for special celebrations

**DAN'L WEBSTER INN.**
Sandwich, Massachusetts
*Two nights with Continental breakfast
Nov 15 '98 - Mar 25 '99 $129
Mar 28 '99 - May 20 '99 $149
**SALEM INN,**
Salem, Massachusetts
*Two complimentary tickets to museum of your choice
**CAPTAIN NICKERSON INN**
South Dennis, Massachusetts
*Stay 1 night and get 2nd night at half price. Available Sun - Thu beginning of March - 15th May and Oct16th - Dec 21st.

*Welcome Privilege Cards are valid for one year from date of issue. One Card entitles a family or group of up to four people travelling together to relevant benefits. The Privilege Card is available for separate purchase at a cost of £10.00/$17.00 per card. All offers are subject to availability.

# SOUTH CAROLINA

# FULTON LANE INN
## CHARLESTON

*This romantic retreat is situated on a quiet pedestrian lane in the heart of Charleston's Historic District. The spirit of an antebellum Charleston summer home is beautifully recaptured - light filtering softly through louvered shades, fine woods, natural textures and soft pastels invite you to indulge in the simple pleasures of a more gracious time.*

*Spacious rooms and suites offer a full compliment of services including continental breakfast delivered on a silver tray, morning newspaper, wine and sherry in the lobby each evening and nightly turndown service with chocolates. Many rooms feature fireplaces, canopied beds, large whirlpool baths and cathedral ceilings. Across from Saks Fifth Avenue, the inn is within walking distance of Charleston's finest restaurants, antique shops and boutiques.*

*Other inns of Charleston include Kings Courtyard Inn, John Rutledge House Inn, Victoria House Inn and, opening early 1998, The Wentworth Mansion. Each different in architecture and style, but sharing a common link of gracious hospitality.*

202 King Street Charleston
South Carolina SC 29401
•
Tel 803 720 2600
Fax 803 720 2940
Freephone in US
800 720 2688
•
Innkeeper: Randall Felkel
•
27 rooms
including 5 one bedroom suites
•
Doubles $105 - $210 B&B
Suites $180 - $255

Tax 12%
•
Conference facilities
Nearby: indoor pool, tennis, golf, sailing
•
Parking $5.00 per day.
•
Children over 12 welcome.
•
Non-smoking
•
VS • MC • Amex
Diners • Discover

**SOUTH CAROLINA**

# PLANTERS INN
## CHARLESTON

The heart and soul of historic Charleston, located at the entrance to the bustling City Market, the Planters Inn combines the care and charisma of an old world inn with the ambience and amenities of a full service hotel.

Elegant guest rooms and lavish suites are the most spacious in the city, boasting high ceilings, oversized marble baths and four poster Charleston Rice Beds. Each room is individually appointed some featuring working fireplaces and hardwood floors.

Included in your rates are breakfast delivered to your door and an afternoon wine and cheese reception. After an excellent meal at the Planters Café, fast becoming one of the most acclaimed restaurants in the city, retire to the comfort of your room to find your bed turned down with a chocolate and the following day's weather forecast.

Charleston's legends are only just beyond our lobby!

112 North Market Street
Charleston, SC 29401
•
Tel 803 722 2345
Fax 803 577 2125
Freephone in US
800 845 7082
•
General Manager:
Larry Spelts
•
41 rooms including
5 one-bedroom suites
•
Doubles $100 - $165
B&B

Tax 10%
•
Parking available
•
Conference facilities
•
Nearby: swimming,
golf, horseriding
•
Children welcome
•
31 rooms are
non-smoking
•
VS • MC • Amex • Diners

**SOUTH CAROLINA**

# ASHLEY INN
## CHARLESTON

This architectural treasure is tastefully furnished with antique four poster, pencil post and canopied rice beds. Private baths, air conditioning and cable tv add to your comfort. Warm hospitality and professional service are unmatched, let us assist with personal tours, restaurants and hints on all "must sees".

Sleep in until the aroma of fresh brewed coffee and sizzling bacon lures you to breakfast overlooking a beautiful Charleston garden. Guests rave over creations such as savoury sausage soufflé with fluffy zucchini and crunchy (yes crunchy!) french toast with hazelnut peach syrup.

To enhance your taste of gracious living, Southern style, enjoy afternoon tea, sumptuous home baked goods and evening sherry. Complimentary touring bikes offer the best way to see the city, hassle free!

201 Ashley Avenue,
Charleston, SC 29403
Tel 803 723 1848
Fax 803 768 1230

Owners:
Bud & Sally Allen

6 rooms including
1 one-bedroom suite
Doubles $69 - $115
B&B

Tax 10%
Parking available
no charge

Smoking only
on porches
Children over
10 welcome

VS • MC
Amex • Discover

# CANNONBORO INN
## CHARLESTON

With the true taste of southern hospitality, this c.1853 historic home skilfully combines old and new, offering six beautifully decorated bedrooms with antique and canopied beds but not forgetting air-conditioning and colour tvs. Known as Charleston's Gourmet Breakfast Place, the Cannonboro Inn is a place to be pampered.

Relish your delicious start to the day whilst relaxing in the columned piazza overlooking a low country garden and fountain. After breakfast you can tour nearby historic sites on complimentary bicycles, on foot or by horse-drawn carriage and enjoy beautiful Charleston, a city that will charm you with its slower more gracious pace.

At days end return to afternoon tea, sherry and sumptuous homebaked goods. This is what Charleston is all about – we look forward to seeing you.

184 Ashley Avenue,
Charleston,
SC 29403

Tel 803 723 8572
Fax 803 768 1230

Owners:
Bud & Sally Allen

6 rooms
Doubles $69 - $115
B&B
Tax 10%

Parking available
no charge
Smoking only
on porches

Children over
10 welcome
VS • MC
Amex • Discover

## SOUTH CAROLINA

# RED HORSE INN
## LANDRUM

The Red Horse Inn is situated on 190 acres in the midst of an area known for its equestrian opportunities. Sweeping mountain views, pastoral vistas and endless sky surround five charming, romantically secluded Victorian cottages. Each cottage is delightfully furnished and decorated and offers kitchen, bedroom, bath, living room with fireplace, colour tv and air conditioning. Three cottages have Jacuzzi's and an extra sleeping loft and are therefore an ideal option for those travelling with family. For recreation the area boasts two championship golf courses, hiking, fishing, bird hunting, sporting clay courses, antiquing and beagling. Nine of the finest South Carolina State Parks are within a short drive. Innkeepers Mary and Roger Wolters spare no effort to ensure that your visit to The Red Horse turns out exactly as you hope it will.

| 310 North Campbell Road, Landrum, SC 29356 | Tel 864 895 4968 Fax 864 895 4968 | Owners: Mary & Roger Wolters 5 rooms | Cottages $85 B&B Tax 8% | Nearby: outdoor pool, tennis, horse riding, golf, hiking, fishing, fox hunting, bird hunting, beagling | Children welcome Non-smoking VS•MC |

## THE BEST INSPECTORS ARE OUR GUESTS!

Your feedback is the basis on which our business is built.

Were your expectations met?
Was the welcome warm?
Did you feel you received good value for the money you spent?

It is vital to maintain the excellent standard of U.S. Welcome's Selected Hotels and Inns and your input is of great value to us. If you have a moment, please write, call, fax or email and let us know what you think of the hotels and inns in which you stayed.

U.S. Welcome Limited
FREEPOST (HA 4595) Northwood, England, HA6 3BR
Tel (0)1895 622233  Fax (0)1895 622244
mail@uswelcome.com   www.uswelcome.com
Freephone in the U.S. 888 INN VISIT

**FREE** 960-PAGE TRAVELLER'S HANDBOOK WHEN YOU JOIN

# WEXAS

Est. 1970

## Discount scheduled airfares worldwide

WEXAS International, the UK's Premier Travel Club, offers a range of membership publications and tailor-made travel services, including scheduled flights from a choice of UK airports to hundreds of destinations worldwide at special members-only fares. Business and leisure travellers alike can enjoy all the benefits and money-saving advantages of belonging to a large reputable travel organisation from just £43.93 a year (1998 subscription).

## JOIN NOW

by calling the
WEXAS Membership Services Department on

# 0171-589 3315

INVESTOR IN PEOPLE  ABTA V2128 91989  IATA ACCREDITED AGENT  ATOL 2873

**WEXAS International**
45-49 Brompton Road, Knightsbridge, London SW3 1DE
Tel: 0171-589 3315   Fax: 0171-589 8418   email: mship@wexas.com

# SOUTHWESTERN STATES

## COLORADO
- **3** Hearthstone Inn — 222
- **4** Hotel Jerome — 222
- **5** Queen Anne Bed & Breakfast — 223

## ARIZONA
- **1** Casa Sedona — 221
- **2** Merv Griffin's Wickenburg Inn — 221

# ARIZONA

## CASA SEDONA
### SEDONA

Sedona's newest Four Diamond award-winning bed and breakfast inn is a southwestern style property, set on an acre of secluded land blessed with spectacular Red Rock views. Located in West Sedona, each of the inns sizeable sixteen guest rooms is individually and beautifully decorated with cosy fireplaces, luxurious baths with large Jacuzzi tubs and plush bath robes in which to wrap yourself. At the end of the day, relax and stargaze from the outdoor hot tub. Delicious, traditional southwestern style breakfasts are the speciality here, often served out of doors under the shade of the Juniper trees where the rising sun throws light on to Chimney Rock in the near distance. John and Nancy are only too delighted to share their love of Sedona with their guests from around the world. With typical thoughtfulness, special hiking and driving maps (including a day trip to the Grand Canyon) are provided to help guests get the very best out of their time at Casa Sedona.

| | | | | |
|---|---|---|---|---|
| 55 Hozoni Drive, Sedona, AZ 86336 | Tel 520 282 2938 Fax 520 282 2259 Freephone in US 800 525 3756 | Owners/Innkeepers: John & Nancy True 16 rooms $120 - $210 B&B | Tax 12.05% Nearby: outdoor and indoor pools, tennis, horse riding, golf | Children over 10 welcome | Non-smoking VS•MC |

## MERV GRIFFIN'S WICKENBURG INN AND DUDE RANCH
### WICKENBURG

Where the pavement ends and the adventure begins - the ultimate ranch experience with warm hospitality and authentic western charm. Explore miles of rugged high Sonoran Desert on horseback with cowboys as your guides. There are trail rides for all levels, and you can sharpen your riding skills with lessons. Try your hand at herding steers on a real cattle drive, and enjoy weekly rodeos, hay-rides and cowboy cookouts under the stars.
When you've finished a days riding, take in a game of tennis, check out the nature museum, stop by the arts and crafts studio, or simply relax around the pool. Tuck into three deliciously hearty meals daily and then as night draws in, retire to the comfort of your own adobe casita nestled in the hillside, complete with a wood-burning fireplace. Here, every day springs to life with unlimited possibilities for true western adventure and the experiences of a lifetime.

| | | | | |
|---|---|---|---|---|
| 34801 North Highway 89, Wickenburg, AZ 85390 | Tel 520 684 7811 Fax 520 684 2981 Freephone in US 800 942 5362 | Manager: James Bradley 63 rooms including 31 one bedroom suites, 11 two bedroom suites | Doubles $185 - $395 AP Suites $420 - $730 Tax 6.5% s.c. 16% | Outdoor pool, tennis, horse riding, cattle drives, guest rodeos Nearby: golf | Children welcome Smoking in designated areas VS•MC•Amex•Diners |

## COLORADO

# HEARTHSTONE INN
## COLORADO SPRINGS

The Hearthstone Inn is celebrating its twentieth year of caring for guests. In the heart of Colorado Springs you are welcomed to a beautiful 1885 Victorian mansion, converted into a charming and comfortable twenty-three guest room inn. With a meeting room that holds forty and a dining room seating forty-eight, the Hearthstone can cater for larger groups, but its friendly staff, comfortable and impeccably clean rooms, attention to detail and the warmth of its atmosphere, foster that personal touch that brings guests back again and again. The Hearthstone is non-smoking and in true country inn style there are no televisions or in-room telephones to intrude on your thoughts, although naturally, the innkeepers are always happy to take messages so that you are not out of touch. The parlour and sitting room have cosy wood burning fireplaces, as do three of the guest rooms and a full breakfast, featuring such specialities as caramel French toast served with mouth-watering fresh Colorado peaches and cream, can be enjoyed each morning.

506 North Cascade,
Colorado Springs,
CO 80903
Tel 719 473 4413
Fax 719 473 1322

Freephone in US
800 521 1305
Owner: Dot Williams

23 rooms
including 3 one
bedroom suites
Doubles $90 - $140
B&B

Suites $150 - $170
Tax 8.1%
Nearby: (walking distance) tennis,

jogging, museums,
shops & restaurants
Short drive to horse riding, golf, indoor pool

Children welcome
Non-smoking
VS•MC•Amex

---

# HOTEL JEROME
## ASPEN

Renowned for its tradition of quiet elegance, hospitality and unobtrusive pampering, the Hotel Jerome offers all the amenities and services expected of a luxury hotel. Built in 1889, and restored to its original Victorian splendour, the Jerome features ninety-three spacious guest rooms and suites, each richly appointed with original period antiques. Just three miles from Aspen Airport and in the heart of downtown Aspen, the Jerome is just steps away from Aspen's world-famous boutiques, restaurants and nightlife.
Two on-site restaurants and two bars provide a range of dining choices. Enjoy a delicious breakfast or lunch in Jacob's Corner, dinner creations in the Century Room or relax into the overstuffed chairs of Jerome's Library for an after dinner drink. Be sure not to miss the J-Bar, Aspen's favourite watering hole since the silver mining days of the 1880's.

330 E. Main Street,
Aspen,
CO 81611
Tel 970 920 1000
Fax 970 925 2784

Freephone in US
800 331 7213
General Manager:
Anthony Di Lucia

93 rooms
including 16 one
bedroom suites

Doubles $160 - $805
EP
Suites $395 - $2000
Tax 8.2%

Outdoor pool
Nearby: golf, tennis,
horse riding, down-
hill and cross-country
skiing

Children welcome
VS•MC
Amex•Diners

222

## COLORADO

# QUEEN ANNE BED & BREAKFAST INN
## DENVER

*Experience Victorian elegance, relaxed ambience and Denver history in the first and largest of the bed and breakfast inns, downtown in this seeing-doing city which is also the gateway to Colorado and the Rocky Mountains. Facing a quiet park, the inn's two side-by-side Victorians offer fourteen rooms and suites and border downtown on the East Side, making it an easy walk to museums, restaurants, shops and business centres.*

*The inn's downtown location and comfortable atmosphere welcome business travellers and holidaymakers from every state and twenty-two nations. Each evening the King family host a reception for their guests, serving fine Colorado wine and each morning a hot breakfast (in bed if desired) is available for two hours. Specialities of the house include crustless quiche, blueberry strudel and American scones. The inn has been awarded various honors and has been named one of the best ten bed and breakfasts in the nation and also one of the most romantic.*

2147-51 Tremont Place,
Denver,
CO 80205

Tel 303-296-6666
Fax 303-296-2151
Freephone in US
800-432-4667

Owners/Innkeepers:
The King Family
14 rooms
including 4 one bedroom suites

Doubles $75 - $145 B&B
Suites $135 - $175
Tax 11.8 %

Nearby: tennis, horse riding, cross-country & down-hill skiing, indoor pool, jogging

Children over 12 welcome
Non-smoking
VS•MC•Amex•Diners
Discover•Eurocard

# THE BEST INSPECTORS ARE OUR GUESTS!

**Your feedback is the basis on which our business is built.**

**Were your expectations met?
Was the welcome warm?
Did you feel you received good value for the money you spent?**

It is vital to maintain the excellent standard of U.S. Welcome's Selected Hotels and Inns and your input is of great value to us. If you have a moment, please write, call, fax or email and let us know what you think of the hotels and inns in which you stayed.

U.S. Welcome Limited
FREEPOST (HA 4595) Northwood, England, HA6 3BR
Tel (0)1895 622233   Fax (0)1895 622244
mail@uswelcome.com    www.uswelcome.com
Freephone in the U.S. 888 INN VISIT

# WEST COAST

### CALIFORNIA
1. Beazley House — 225
2. Blackthorne Inn — 229
3. Carter House Victorians — 229
4. Casa Cody — 230
5. Goose & Turrets — 230
6. Joshua Grindle Inn — 231
7. La Playa Hotel — 226
8. Martine Inn — 227
9. Ollalieberry — 231
10. Seal Beach Garden Inn — 228
11. Willows Historic Inn — 232

### OREGON
12. Campbell House, A City Inn — 233
13. Hood River Hotel — 233

### WASHINGTON
14. Haus Rohrbach Pension — 234
15. Sun Mountain Lodge — 234
16. Turtleback Farm — 235
17. Willcox House Country Inn — 235

# CALIFORNIA

## BEAZLEY HOUSE
### NAPA

Napa's first bed & breakfast inn sits, surrounded by lush lawns and gardens, in a quiet neighbourhood of century-old Victorian houses, but is just a short stroll from the old town area with its delightful restored shopping area and gourmet restaurants. Located at the south end of the Napa Valley, the inn is a perfect base for exploring both the surrounding vineyards and is an easy hour's drive north of San Francisco.

This 1902 landmark mansion has six lovely rooms with a meticulous reproduction of the mansion's original carriage house nestled in the gardens behind the main building. Here each of five spacious rooms has a fireplace and the modern day luxury of a private, two-person spa. The innkeepers are happy to offer dining suggestions and reservations with personalised guidance to the local wineries and can arrange for gliding, cycling or a trip to Calistoga's famous mud baths. At Beazley House they declare their aim is to ensure that your needs are more than met, they're anticipated!

1910 First St,
Napa,
CA 94559

•

Tel 707 257 1649
Fax 707 257 1518
Freephone in US
800 559 1649

•

Owners/Innkeepers: Jim & Carol Beazley

•

11 rooms

Doubles $115 - $160 B&B
Suites $200 - $225

•

Tax 12%

•

Nearby: outdoor pool, tennis, horse riding, water-skiing, golf, wine-tasting

•

Children welcome

•

Non-smoking

•

VS•MC•Amex

## CALIFORNIA

# LA PLAYA HOTEL
### CARMEL-BY-THE-SEA

La Playa Hotel and Cottages-by-the-Sea are located in the delightful village of Carmel-by-the-Sea. With its proximity to the Pacific Ocean, its impeccably landscaped grounds, an intimate lobby and professional staff, it comes as no surprise that La Playa has been recognised as the Grande Dame of Carmel.

Each of La Playa's seventy-five comfortable rooms offers views of the ocean, the colourful gardens or charming Carmel itself. La Playa's best kept secret is its five cottages. Nestled among sprawling oaks, Monterey pines and cypress, the cottages are just a half-block from the hotel. Amenities such as a heated outdoor swimming pool, free parking, twice daily maid service, concierge, room service and five function rooms for meetings and receptions, make La Playa and its Cottages-by-the-Sea the only full-service hotel in Carmel.

The Terrace Grill Restaurant features innovative California cuisine. Here guests may enjoy breakfast, lunch and dinner either indoors or alfresco on a beautiful heated open-air terrace overlooking award-winning gardens.

Camino Real and 8th,
Carmel,
CA 93921
•
Tel 408 624 6476
Fax 408 624 7966
Freephone in US
800 582 8900
•
General Manager:
Tom Glidden
•
80 rooms
including 3 one bedroom suites, 1 two bedroom suite

Doubles $125 - $275 EP
Suites & Cottages $230 - $495
•
Tax 10.5%
•
Outdoor pool
Nearby: tennis, horse riding, golf, sailing
•
Children welcome
•
Smoking in designated areas
•
VS•MC•Amex•Diners

**CALIFORNIA**

# MARTINE INN
## PACIFIC GROVE

*Imagine a stunning, mediterranean style mansion, set high on the cliffs of Pacific Grove, overlooking beautiful Monterey Bay. Imagine it restored to its former glory so that guests experience turn of the century ambience provided by carefully researched and selected furnishings such as the mahogany bedroom suite that was exhibited in the 1893 Chicago Worlds Fair or an 1860 Chippendale Revival four poster bed.*

*Added to this, your hosts Marion & Don (who, incidentally, were married in the delightful walled courtyard of the inn) have made a collection of Victorian and Old Sheffield silver which is in daily use and, for vintage car aficionados, there are Don's meticulously preserved, locally raced, MGs.*

*Warm touches - a fresh rose, fruit basket, huge bath sheets and chocolate on your pillow at night all add to your welcome. The inn is ideally located within four blocks of the Monterey Bay Aquarium and five minutes from 17-Mile Drive and other famous attractions.*

255 Oceanview Boulevard,
Pacific Grove,
CA 93950
•
Tel 408 373 3388
Fax 408 373 3896
Freephone in US
800 852 5588
•
Owner/Innkeeper:
Don Martine
•
19 rooms
•
Doubles $135 - $240 B&B
Suites $290

Tax 10%
•
Billiards, spa,
vintage auto display
Nearby: Outdoor and indoor pools, tennis, horse riding, water skiing, golf, sailing
•
Children over 16 welcome
•
Smoking in designated areas
•
VS•MC•Amex•Diners Discover

**CALIFORNIA**

# SEAL BEACH GARDEN INN
## SEAL BEACH

An elegant, historic inn in a charming urban seaside village, just one block from the Pacific, the Seal Beach sits amidst lush flowers and greenery. The combination of the exquisitely detailed and colourful gardens; library; tea room; outdoor pool, and delightful guest rooms, provide a welcome that soothes the soul and enchants the eye.

Each of the inn's suites and rooms are individually decorated with comfortably handsome furnishings some with kitchens and sitting areas. The beach, pier, marina, shops, theatres, restaurants and parks are within walking distance. Nearby freeways give quick and easy access to major Southern California attractions, such as Disneyland, Knott's Berry Farm, Universal Studios and The Queen Mary.

At this delightful inn, a sincerely caring staff looks forward to serving visitors in the old world traditions of warmth and hospitality.

212 5th St,
Seal Beach,
CA 90740
•
Tel 562 493-2416
Fax 562 799 0483
Freephone in US
1-800 Hideaway
•
Owner/Innkeeper:
Marjorie Schmaehl
•
23 Rooms
including 14 one bedroom suites, 1 two bedroom suite
Doubles $125- $225 B&B
Suites & Cottages $155 - $295

Tax 9%
•
Outdoor pool
Nearby: tennis, water-skiing, indoor pool, golf, sailing, jetskiing, surfing, parasailing, biking
•
Does not meet the needs of children
•
Non-smoking
•
VS•MC•Amex•Diners• JCB Discover

## CALIFORNIA

# BLACKTHORNE INN
## INVERNESS

Nestled among the treetops in the heart of the beautiful Point Reyes Wilderness, the Blackthorne is the embodiment of romantic seclusion. This unique inn was built in the 1970's and combines many historical materials, such as windows by Julia Morgan and beams from San Francisco piers, with the spectacular design of a luxury treehouse.

The multiple levels of this magical inn are interconnected with a spiral staircase with five guest rooms leading off, culminating at the very top in the Eagle's Nest. This octagonal, glass-enclosed tower room affords a once in a lifetime experience with its view of treetops and sky and the illusion that you are sleeping among the stars. Awaken to the sunlight of a brand new morning and the pleasures of an imaginative and substantial buffet breakfast.

After a day on the magnificent hiking trails and beaches of the Point Reyes Seashore, return to the Blackthorne's large and cosy stone hearth or step into the hot tub set on the upper deck among the treetops.

| 266 Vallego Avenue, P.O. Box 712, Inverness, CA 94937 | Tel 415 663 8621 Fax 415 663 8635 Owners: Susan & Bill Wigert | 5 one bedroom suites Suites $175 - $225 B&B | Tax 10% Hot Tub Nearby: Horse riding, golf | Children over 14 welcome | Non-smoking VS•MC•Amex |

# CARTER HOUSE VICTORIANS
## EUREKA

Three different inns, each with its own character, form the Carter House Victorians - The Original Carter House, the Hotel Carter and the newly renovated Bell Cottage. Located on the northern border of Eureka's historic Old Town area, they offer a true taste of the West retaining their historic ambience but cleverly combining this with warm hospitality and modern comforts.

Between them, the three different properties offer every option, whether you are looking for a family holiday, a romantic retreat or, as a business traveller, working facilities in a unique setting. Many of the rooms have sitting areas, glorious marina views and, in the Carter House Country Inn and the Bell Cottage, kitchens thoughtfully stocked for guest use. At the end of a day, enjoy a superb meal at the award winning Restaurant 301 at the Hotel Carter - where herbs, and vegetables from the hotel's own gardens are matched with delicacies such as Humboldt Bay oysters or fresh salmon straight from the Pacific.

| 301 L. Street, Eureka, CA 95501 Tel 707 444 8062 Fax 707 444 8067 | Freephone in US 800 404 1390 Owners: Mark J. Carter, Christi Carter 31 rooms | including 11 one bedroom suites Doubles $125 - $250 B&B Suites $195 - $295 | Cottage (sleeps 6) $205 Tax 9% Nearby: tennis, horse riding, water-skiing, | indoor pool, golf, sailing, kayaking, hiking, surfing Children over 6 welcome at Carter House | Non-smoking VS•MC•Amex•Diners Discover |

**CALIFORNIA**

# CASA CODY, COUNTRY INN
## PALM SPRINGS

Historic and romantic, this hideaway dates back to the early nineteen hundreds when Palm Springs was still a tiny Indian settlement. Founded by Harriet Cody, whose architect husband was a cousin of the legendary Buffalo Bill Cody, the inn nestles against the spectacular San Jacinto mountains at the heart of Palm Springs Village. Built around several brilliantly hued citrus and bougainvillaea-filled courtyards, the early California hacienda style buildings have been beautifully restored. Interiors have Santa Fe inspired decor and feature tiled floors, pine furnishings, dhurri rugs and original art work. Two heated pools offer year-round swimming or you can relax in the secluded tree-shaded whirlpool spa.

Peaceful though it is, the inn stands only blocks away from the Desert Museum, Heritage Centre, boutiques, galleries, restaurants and sidewalk cafes, whilst hiking trails and tennis courts are close by. Riding and golf are minutes away by car as are the Moorten Botanical Garden and the Palm Springs Aerial Tramway.

175 S. Cahuilla Road, Palm Springs, CA 92262
Tel 760 320 9346
Fax 760 325 8610

Freephone in US 800 231 2639
Owners: Frank Tysen/ Therese Hayes

23 rooms including 8 one bedroom suites, 2 two bedroom suites
Doubles $49 - $129

B&B
Suites & Cottages $89 - $199
Tax 10%

Outdoor pools
Nearby: tennis, horse riding, golf
Children welcome

Smoking in designated areas
VS•MC•Amex•Diners Discovery

---

# GOOSE & TURRETS
## MONTARA

The Goose & Turrets Bed & Breakfast built in 1908, enjoyed a varied history as a post office, grocery store and music studio. Nowadays it is an historic, earth friendly inn catering to readers, nature lovers, and enthusiastic eaters and well known for its delightful, if idiosyncratic mascot geese.

On foggy days the warmth of fireplaces and down comforters welcome you home, as does tasty afternoon tea. Generous four-course breakfasts send you satisfied to undertake some serious sightseeing, armed with helpful tips from the innkeepers, both of whom are keen pilots and naturalists.

Nearby attractions include an elephant seal rookery and Montara beach and Mountain for walking and hiking. More sedentary folk may prefer historic Half Moon Bay with its art galleries, book stores and excellent restaurants. Located just twenty minutes from San Francisco airport and ten minutes walk from beaches, this is a convenient headquarters for visiting Santa Cruz and its mountain wineries, Monterey and its aquarium, Sausalito or spectacular Muir Woods.

835 George St, Box 937, Montara, CA 94037-0937

Tel 650 728 5345
Fax 650 728 0141
Owners/Innkeepers: Raymond & Emily M. Hoche-Mong

5 rooms
Doubles $85 - $115
B&B
Tax 10%

Nearby: horse riding, golf, sailing, surf-casting and charter boat fishing, kayaking,

bird watching, nature trails, bicycling
Children welcome

Non-smoking
VS•MC•Amex•Diners Discover

## CALIFORNIA

# JOSHUA GRINDLE INN
## MENDOCINO

Built on two beautifully landscaped acres in historic Mendocino, this elegant inn is modelled on the crisp white clapboard homes of the Northern Maine coastline, where Joshua Grindle was raised in the mid 1800's.

Quiet and romantic, the inn overlooks the National Register Historic District of Mendocino village and the Pacific Ocean and offers a choice of rooms with features such as four poster beds, wood-burning fireplaces, deep-soak or whirlpool tubs, comfortable sitting areas and views of the ocean. Chat with fellow guests over gourmet breakfasts served on an 1830's New England harvest table and enjoy evening sherry or tea with fresh baked goodies in the parlour. Park your car and forget about it during your stay, while you explore the village and rugged ocean headlands on foot or stroll to an intimate and creative dinner nearby at several of California's finest restaurants. In the words of Jim and Arlene Moorehead - relax, refresh and rejuvenate!

| | | | | |
|---|---|---|---|---|
| P.O.Box 647, 44800 Little Lake Road, Mendocino, CA 95460 | Tel 707-937-4143 Freephone in US 800-Grindle (474-6353) | Owners: Jim & Arlene Moorehead 10 rooms | Doubles $95 - $185 B&B Guest House $200 (2 people) - $250 (4 people) | Tax 10% Nearby: Tennis, golf, canoeing, kayaking, hiking | Does not meet the needs of children Non-smoking VS•MC |

# OLALLIEBERRY INN
## CAMBRIA

The Olallieberry's nine guest rooms have beautiful wall coverings, carefully chosen fabrics and antiques. Fireplaces feature in six rooms while the Creekside Suite can comfortably sleep up to four people.

Peter and Carol Ann have always had a passion for cooking and to them, the preparation and serving of good food is as important as the cleanliness of the inn, the warmth of their welcome and the comfort of their rooms. In fact, Peter has just completed his first cookery book. Complimentary hors d'oeuvres and local wines are served in the afternoon and you'll be tempted by Baked Brie in puff pastry with toasted almonds; smoked salmon and cream cheese pate; fresh salsa and platters of fresh vegetables. Mornings bring gourmet breakfasts including freshly squeezed juices, stuffed French toast, poached apple crepes or eggs baked in a hash brown potato crust - enough to keep you smiling all day.

Located in Historic East Village and within walking distance of shops, galleries and restaurants, Hearst Castle is seven miles north and Central Coast wineries about thirty minutes away.

| | | | | |
|---|---|---|---|---|
| 2476 Main Street, Cambria, CA 93428 Tel 805 927 3222 Fax 805 927 0202 | Freephone in US 888 927 3222 Owners: Peter & Carol Ann Irsfeld | 9 rooms, (all baths are private - 6 en-suite, 3 outside room) including 1 one bedroom suite | Doubles $90 - $175 B&B Suite $175 Tax 9% | Nearby: tennis, horse riding, indoor pool, golf Does not meet the needs of children | Smoking in designated areas VS•MC |

## CALIFORNIA

# WILLOWS HISTORIC PALM SPRINGS INN
### PALM SPRINGS

A Mediterranean villa with a history of celebrity visitors - the honeymoon choice of Clark Gable and Carole Lombard and a favourite retreat of Albert Einstein - the Willows has been sympathetically restored to its former glory. It offers a luxurious and intimate option in Palm Springs.

Eight rooms feature carefully chosen antique furniture, sumptuous linens and individually designed bathrooms. Each room has its own character and different options for you to enjoy - stone fireplaces, cathedral ceilings, two-person bath tubs, beautiful garden patios with mountain, garden or waterfall views and some rooms have private entrances to make your retreat more complete. Delicious breakfasts, afternoon wine tasting, evening appetisers and fine music all add to your enjoyment of this exceptional small inn.

| 412 West Tahquitz Canyon, Palm Springs, CA 92262 | Tel 760 320 0771 Fax 760 320 0780 President: Tracy Conrad | 8 rooms Doubles $250 - $500 B&B Tax 10% | Outdoor pool Nearby: tennis, horse riding, water-skiing, cross-country skiing, golf, hiking | Children over 16 welcome Non-smoking | VS•MC•Amex•Diners Discover Carte Blanche |

## COMPLIMENTARY BOOKING SERVICE

Don't forget we offer an advisory and booking service and you can make all your reservations with just one phone call to us. The service is completely free and prices are not loaded in any way.

Call for a chat on

# 01895 622233

# OREGON

## CAMPBELL HOUSE, A CITY INN
### EUGENE

Originally built in 1892 for the daughter of a successful gold miner and set on an acre of landscaped grounds, the Campbell House is a delightful alternative to larger city hotels. From here it is just over an hour to the coast, an hour to the mountains and the wine-growing area and only half an hour to scenic lakes or, for the more adventurous, whitewater rafting. Conveniently located within walking distance of a wide variety of restaurants, the Hult Center for the Performing Arts and the University of Oregon, the inn offers every comfort. Each of its rooms features tv and vcr, and some have the additional benefits of fireplaces, four poster beds, private entrances and wonderful views of the city and eastern foothills. Breakfast is served each morning in the dining room and includes delicious fresh-baked delicacies.

252 Pearl Street, Eugene, OR 97401

Tel 541 343 1119
Fax 541 343 2258
Freephone in US
800 264 2519

Owner: Myra Plant
18 rooms
including 2 one bedroom suites

Doubles $85 - $275 B&B
Suites $149 - $350
Tax 9.5%

Nearby: tennis, fishing, whitewater rafting
Children welcome

Non-smoking
Parking available free of charge
VS•MC•Amex Discover

## HOOD RIVER HOTEL
### HOOD RIVER

Listed on the National Historic Register, the Hood River Hotel sits in the centre of the quaint little historic town of Hood River which in turn is nestled in the scenic Columbia River Gorge. Each room is individually decorated in Victorian-style featuring brass beds, canopies and sleigh beds. Choose one of the smaller courtyard rooms, a river view room or a suite featuring full kitchen.
After the day's excursions, relax by the wood burning fire in the lobby/lounge or enjoy a wonderful meal in adjoining Pasquale's Ristorante which serves fine Italian and Northwest cuisine featuring seafood, wild game and more. Our 2,400 square foot banquet facility and wine cellar is the perfect setting for a special function or meeting.
Enjoy soaking in our Jacuzzi, sauna and exercise facility. Other nearby activities include shopping, theatres and galleries, windsurfing, skiing, hiking and many more outdoor activities.

102 Oak Avenue, Hood River, OR 97031
Tel 541 386 1900
Fax 541 386 6060

Freephone in US
800 386 1859
Owners: Jacquie & Pasquale Barone

41 rooms including 9 one bedroom suites
Doubles $49 - $99 EP
Suites $75 - $145

Tax 8%
Jacuzzi, sauna, exercise facility
Nearby: tennis, horse riding, water-skiing, down-hill and cross-country skiing, indoor pool, golf, sailing
On street parking

Children welcome
Smoking in designated areas
VS•MC•Amex•Diners Discover

# WASHINGTON

## HAUS ROHRBACH PENSION
### LEAVENWORTH

Haus Rohrbach, tucked in an alpine valley of the majestic North Cascade Mountains, is reminiscent of an alpine chalet - bedecked with flower-filled boxes, surrounded by lawns, gardens and meadow - it invites you to put aside your cares. Warm sunny summers, crisp colourful autumns, snowy winters and soft green springs punctuated with wildflowers provide an ever-changing panorama.

Guest rooms and suites are appointed with fine linens, down quilts, fluffy pillows, bouquets of fresh flowers and private balconies. Three luxury suites are extra indulgent with whirlpool tubs for two, stone fireplaces and decks with spectacular views. Larkspur and Snowberry also have a kitchen bar plus a spacious bathroom with double shower heads and radiant heated floors to keep your feet happy even on cold winter mornings. Whenever you stay, whatever you like to do, a spirit of true hospitality makes your visit memorable.

| | | | | | |
|---|---|---|---|---|---|
| 12882 Ranger Rd, Leavenworth, WA 98826  Tel 509 548 7024  Fax 509 548 5038 | Freephone in US 800 548 4477  Owners/Innkeepers: Kathryn & Robert Harrild | 10 rooms including 3 one bedroom suites, 2 two bedroom suites  Doubles $75 - $95 B&B | Suites $125 - $160  Tax 8%  Outdoor pool, hot tub, cross-country skiing. | Nearby: tennis, horse riding, golf, sailing, down-hill skiing | Children welcome  Non-smoking  VS•MC•Amex•Diners Discover |

## SUN MOUNTAIN LODGE
### WINTHROP

With an unsurpassed setting in Washington's North Cascades, high above Methow valley and with 3,000 acres of streams, woodland and meadows, Sun Mountain Lodge is well named! The views defy description and from almost every single room of the lodge there is a different panorama whether it's the magnificent mountains, the valley or the quiet waters of Lake Patterson. Guest rooms have some excellent original art work by local artists and hand-carved furnishings, some have lava rock fireplaces, or you may prefer a cabin by the lake with its own kitchenette. Summer brings excellent whitewater rafting - or for the more leisurely inclined, scenic rafting - boating, hiking or biking. While in Winter skiers come for the wonderful slopes and trails, ice-skating and of course wonderful sleigh rides. All equipment and facilities are available at very reasonable rates. At the end of a day's activities there is superb dining on offer in the dining room. Sun Mountain offers a wonderful experience year-round.

| | | | | | |
|---|---|---|---|---|---|
| P.O. Box 1000, Patterson Lake Road, Winthrop, WA 98862  Tel 509 996 2211  Fax 509 996 3133 | Freephone in US 800 572 0493  General Manager: Brian Charlton  102 rooms including 6 one bedroom suites, 13 | Cottages (4-6 people)  Doubles $110 - $240 EP  Suites $185 - $275  Cottages $105 - $280  Tax 7.6% | Two outdoor pools, three hot tubs, four tennis courts, horse riding, sailing, cross-country skiing. Nearby: golf, | mountain biking, hiking, canoeing, fishing, down-hill skiing, sleigh rides, skating. Childrens' programme available July and August. | Children welcome.  Smoking in some guest rooms only  VS•MC•Amex•Diners |

**WASHINGTON**

# TURTLEBACK FARM
## EASTSOUND

On the western side of beautiful Orcas Island, with its wide valleys bordered by deep forests, punctuated with shimmering ponds and lakes, sits Turtleback Farm. Here beyond the perimeter of fir trees, in late Spring, open fields produce hay for the resident sheep.

The century old farmhouse was restored some years ago and offers seven bedrooms decorated with a tasteful blend of fine antiques and contemporary furniture. The living room boasts a Rumford fireplace, comfortable seating and a corner game table. In the morning, crisp linens, silver and fine bone china grace the tables in the sunny dining room or on the expansive deck overlooking the valley. A gourmet, farm-fresh breakfast is served daily, including fresh fruits, juices, award-winning granola and a tasty main course. New in 1997 was the Orchard House set amidst apple and pear trees. Here, four spacious king-bedded rooms offer sitting/dining areas with gas stoves, refrigerators, full baths and private decks. The Fletchers share with guests the tranquillity of lush countryside and a peaceful haven after memorable days of exploring the many highlights of this island.

Route 1, P.O.Box 650, Eastsound, WA 98245

Tel 360 376 4914
Fax 360 376 5329
Freephone in US
800 376 4914

Owners/Innkeepers: William & Susan C. Fletcher
11 rooms

Doubles $80 - $210 B&B
Tax 7.7%
Nearby: tennis, horse riding, golf,

bird-watching, sailing, sea kayaking, fishing, hiking, lake swimming, fine dining

Children over 8 welcome
Non-smoking
VS•MC•Amex Discover

# WILLCOX HOUSE COUNTRY INN
## SEABECK

With spectacular views of Hood Canal and the Olympic mountains, this waterfront country house inn is wonderfully located in a forest setting just under two hours west of Seattle and only one and half hours from Seattle/Tacoma airport. The historic 1930's mansion estate offers park-like grounds, fish ponds, private pier, rowboat, and an oyster laden saltwater beach. Comfortable period pieces and antiques enhance guest rooms, the great room, billiard room, pub, library, theatre and dining room. Included in your rate is afternoon wine and cheese, and a hearty, full breakfast served at private tables in the dining room with its delightful view. Country Inns Magazine has named this "One of the top twelve inns in North America" and it has been called at various times "A jewel within an emerald forest", "One of the most private and romantic getaways in the Pacific Northwest" and "The epitome of old fashioned luxury".

2390 Tekiu Road NW, Seabeck, WA 98380

Tel 360 830 4492
Fax 360 830 0506
Freephone in US 800 725 9477

Owners: Cecilia & Phillip Hughes
5 rooms

Doubles $119 - $189 B&B
Tax 7.6%

Nearby: golf, rowing
Children over 15 welcome

Non-smoking
VS•MC•Discover

## U.S. WELCOME

is proud to be associated with

## HISTORIC HOTELS of AMERICA

Historic Hotels of America is a programme of the National Trust for Historic Preservation in the United States. To be selected for this prestigious programme, a hotel or inn must be at least 50 years old, listed or eligible for the National Register of Historic Places or recognised as having historic significance. The HHA has identified 127 hotels across the United States that have faithfully maintained historic integrity, architecture and ambience.

U.S. Welcome fully supports the mission of the National Trust for Historic Preservation and will be donating 3% of all commissions earned on bookings with HHA hotels back to the Trust.

As well as the properties appearing on the facing page, the following U.S. Welcome Selected Hotels and Inns are also members of Historic Hotels of America:

1842 Inn GA
Balsams NH
Basin Habor Club VT
Chatham Bars Inn MA
Green Mountain Inn VT
Historic Inns of Annapolis MD
Hotel Jerome CO.
In at Montchanin Village DE
Kent Manor Inn MD

La Playa Hotel CA.
Lakeside Inn FL
Lords Proprietor's Inn NC
Middlebury Inn VT
Old Tavern at Grafton VT
Red Lion Inn MA
Sagamore NY
The Equinox VT

## HISTORIC HOTELS OF AMERICA

### CALIFORNIA
### HOTEL LA ROSE
#### SANTA ROSA

*Ideal base for touring the Wine Country, this beautiful hotel offers numerous luxurious and thoughtful extra touches and is located in Historic Railroad Square.*

308 Wilson Street,
Santa Rosa,
CA 95401
Tel 707 579 3200
Fax 707 579 3247

Freephone in US
800 527 6738
Owner: Claus Neumann
49 rooms

including 11 one bedroom suites
Doubles & Suites
$ 109- $184
Tax 9%

Wine tasting available
Nearby: tennis, horse riding and golf

Smoking in designated areas.
VS•MC•Amex•Diners Discover

---

### GEORGIA
### JEKYLL ISLAND CLUB HOTEL
#### JEKYLL ISLAND

*The grand tradition begun a century ago, continues to this day, offering a combination of natural beauty, elegant architecture and private amenities.*

371 Riverview Drive,
Jekyll Island,
GA 31527
Tel 912 635 2600
Fax 912 635 2828

Freephone in US
800 535 9547
General Manager:
Kevin Runner
134 rooms including 20

one bedroom suites
Doubles $89 - $169 EP
Suites $129 - $259
Tax 11%

Outdoor pool, tennis
Nearby: horse riding, golf, sailing, croquet, historic tours, cycling, offshore fishing

Children welcome
Smoking in designated areas
VS•MC•Amex•Diners Discover•Carte Blanche

---

### NEW MEXICO
### HOTEL ST. FRANCIS
#### SANTA FE

*Just one block from the plaza, historic Hotel St. Francis provides excellent service with old-fashioned attention to detail. We have individually decorated rooms with Afternoon Tea served daily in the lobby.*

210 Don Gaspar Avenue,
Santa Fe,
NM 87501
Tel 505 983 5700
Fax 505 989 7690

Freephone in US
800 529 5700
Managing Director:
Debra Allmann
83 rooms

including 1 one bedroom suite, 1 two bedroom suite
Doubles $78 - $188 EP
Suites $178 - $353

Tax 10.25%
Nearby: horse riding, cross country skiing, golf, fishing

Children welcome
Smoking in designated areas
VS•MC•Amex•Diners Discover

---

### SOUTH CAROLINA
### JOHN RUTLEDGE HOUSE INN
#### CHARLESTON

*Experience gracious southern hospitality in this elegant home built in 1763 by a signer of the U.S. Constitution. Located in the heart of the historic district.*

116 Broad Street,
Charleston,
SC 29401
Tel 803 723 7999
Fax 803 720 2615

Freephone in US
800 476 9741
Innkeeper: Linda Bishop
19 rooms

including 3 one bedroom suites
Doubles $155 - $245
B&B
Suites $260 - $325

Tax 12%
Nearby: tennis, water-skiing, indoor pool, golf, sailing
Children welcome

Smoking in designated areas
VS•MC•Amex•Diners Discover

# A TASTE OF THE REST

# A TASTE OF THE REST

On the following pages are just an additional taste of the wonderful choices that await when your travels take you further afield in North America.

# TASTERS

## ARKANSAS

### EMPRESS OF LITTLE ROCK
Little Rock

Wonderfully ornate mansion featuring a 64 square foot glass skylight above a stunning walnut and chestnut staircase and a 3½ storey corner tower.

Tel 501 374 7966
Fax 501 375 4537
Innkeeper:
Sharon Welch-Blair

5 rooms, 2 mini-suites,
$85 - $125  B&B
Children over 10 welcome.
VS MC Amex

## ARIZONA

### SOUTHWEST INN AT SEDONA
Sedona

Luxurious AAA 4 Diamond award winner,. Large beautiful rooms, southwest decor. Fireplaces, private decks, magnificent red rock views. 2 hours, Grand Canyon, 2 hours north of Phoenix

Tel 520 282 3344
Fax 520 282 0267
Owners:
Joel & Sheila Gilgoff

28 suites.
$115 - $195  B&B
Children welcome.
VS MC Discover

## BRITISH COLUMBIA

### LABURNUM COTTAGE
North Vancouver

The warmest hostess in the Northwest - Delphine welcomes you to beautifully appointed rooms set in half an acre of gardens, surrounded by forest yet only 15 minutes from downtown Vancouver.

Tel / Fax 604 988 4877
Owner:
Delphine Masterton

4 rooms, 2 cottages,
$100 - $150 B&B
Children welcome.
VS MC

## CALIFORNIA

### CAMELLIA INN
Healdsburg

In the heart of the beautiful Sonoma wine country, near the Russian River. Spacious rooms with antiques, inlaid hardwood floors, specially chosen beds with heaped pillows.

Tel 707 433 8182
Fax 707 433 8130
Owners/Innkeepers:
Ray, Del and Lucy Lewand

9 rooms,
Doubles $70 - $135  B&B
Children  welcome.
VS MC Amex

## CALIFORNIA

### CAMPBELL RANCH INN
Geyserville

35 acre ranch in the heart of the Sonoma County wine country. Rolling vineyards; an abundance of flowers; the warm welcome of an inn with the extra facilities of a professional tennis court and large swimming pool.

Tel 707 857 3476
Fax 707 857 3239
Owner/Innkeeper:
Mary Jane & Jerry Campbell

5 rooms, 1 two bedroom cottage,  $100 - $165  B&B
Children welcome.
VS MC Amex

## CALIFORNIA

### CHESHIRE CAT INN
Santa Barbara

Beautiful flower and fountain-filled patios and gardens, elegant suites & rooms in a southern Californian village by the sea.

Tel 805 569 1610
Fax 805 682 1876
Manger/Owner:
Christine Dunstan

14 rooms, suites, cottages
$100 - $270 B&B
Children welcome.
VS MC Amex

239

# TASTERS

## CALIFORNIA

### THE INN AT UNION SQUARE
San Francisco

In the heart of San Francisco an elegant small hotel, carefully and individually furnished, as far from a chain hotel as it is possible to be. Complimentary breakfasts, afternoon tea and evening wine.

Tel 415 397 3510
Fax 415 989 0529
General Manager:
Brooks Bayly

30 rooms & suites,
$130 - $300 B&B
VS MC Amex Diners Discover

## CALIFORNIA

### TWO ANGELS INN
La Quinta

After the style of a French chateau, this new inn, built to encompass every comfort is magnificently framed by the imposing Santa Rosa Mountains on one side and tranquil Lake La Quinta on the other.

Tel 619 564 7332
Owner/Innkeeper:
Hap & Holly Harris

11 rooms
Doubles $185 - $350 B&B
Children over 16 welcome.
VS MC Amex

## COLORADO

### ABRIENDO INN
Pueblo

Delightful choice of thoughtfully decorated and furnished rooms all with tv and phone in this conveniently situated, Foursquare architecturally styled inn in the centre of historic Pueblo.

Tel 719 544 2703
Fax 719 542 6544
Owner/Innkeeper:
Kerrelyn Trent

10 rooms,
$58 - $110 B&B
Children over 7 welcome.
VS MC Amex Diners

## COLORADO

### ALPINE INN
Telluride

A short walk to the ski slopes, no queues and the best view in North America. Visit in Summer to hike, horseride and taste the serenity that wildflowers, aspen trees and a truly welcoming inn can provide.

Tel 970 728 6282
Fax 970 728 3424
Owner: Denise Weaver
8 rooms, $70 - $135 B&B

2 cottages, sleep 4 - 6
$110 - $500 EP
Children over 10 welcome.
VS MC

## COLORADO

### CASTLE MARNE
Denver

An imposing historic mansion close to all of Denver's tourist attractions. Charming Victorian ambience, stained glass windows, games room, English garden and a full gourmet breakfast and afternoon tea.

Tel 303 331 0621
Fax 303 331 0623
Owners:
Diane & Jim Peiker

9 rooms & suites
$85 - $200 B&B
Children over 10 welcome.
VS MC Amex Diners

## COLORADO

### WOODLAND INN
Woodland Park

Cosy country inn in the foothills of majestic Pikes Peak. Surrounded by 12 private acres of aspens and firs but just minutes from Colorado Springs. Relax in the parlour and watch elk come to feed in winter and hummingbirds in summer.

Tel 719 687 8209
Fax 719 687 3112
Owners/Innkeepers:
Frank & Nancy O'Neil

7 rooms,
$50 - $80 B&B
Children welcome.
VS MC Amex

# TASTERS

## HAWAII

### CHALET KILAUEA-THE INN AT VOLCANO
Volcano

A mile from the Hawaii Volcano National Park. Experience the comfort of a B&B or the freedom of your own vacation home. Whichever you choose, taste true Hawaiian hospitality.

Tel 808 967 7786
Fax 808 967 8660
Innkeepers:
Brian & Lisha Crawford

5 rooms, 3 suites,
5 vacation homes,
$135 - $295 B&B & EP
Children welcome.
VS MC Amex Diners

## HAWAII

### SHIPMAN HOUSE INN
Hilo

National Historic Register, Old Island Family, Orchids, Lily Ponds, Wide Verandahs, Fragrant Breezes, Waterfalls, Guest Cottage, Fresh Flowers. Add to this, a warm welcome from your hostess Barbara-Ann, and you have a perfect stay.

Tel 808 934 8002
Owner: Barbara-Ann
Andersen

3 rooms, $130 B&B
Children over 15 welcome.
VS MC

## MONTANA

### BEAR CREEK LODGE
Victor

Nestled on 74 scenic acres in southwest Montana, this inn offers a truly unique experience and the opportunity to enjoy such activities as horseriding, hiking, fly fishing, rafting and white water rafting.

Tel 406 642 3750
Fax 406 642 6847
Owners:
Roland & Elizabeth Turney

8 rooms, $250 AP
off season $150 B&B
Children welcome by
prior arrangement.
VS MC Amex

## OREGON

### CHANNEL HOUSE
Depoe Bay

Perched on the rugged Oregon coastline with spectacular water views, watch migrating whales from the whirlpool on your own private deck, enjoy delicious breakfast amidst brass ships fittings and nautical antiques in the first floor serving room.

Tel 541 765 2140
Fax 541 765 2191
Owner/Innkeeper:
Vicki Mix & Carl Finseth

14 rooms & suites,
$135 - $200 B&B
Does not meet the needs
of children
Discover, Novus

## OREGON

### COLUMBIA GORGE HOTEL
Oregon

On the banks of the Columbia River which divides Oregon and Washington, stands the spectacular Columbia Gorge Hotel - one of the last of the truly romantic grand hotels. Enjoy fine dining, cosy rooms and a rose on your pillow at evening's end.

Tel 541 386 5566
Fax 541 387 5414
Owners:
Boyd & Hallo Graves

42 rooms,
$150 - $275 B&B
Children over 12 welcome.
VS MC Amex Diners

## TENNESSEE

### PEACOCK HILL COUNTRY INN
College Grove

Luxury country inn on a working cattle and horse farm. Rocking chairs on a front porch, black-eyed Susans and purple cone flowers nodding over brick walkways and only a short drive to Nashville and the Grand Old Opry.

Tel 615 368 7727
Fax 615 368 7933
Owners:
Walter & Anita Ogilvie

5 rooms, 1 log cabin
$95 - $125 B&B
Children welcome.
VS MC

# TASTERS

## TEXAS

### BROWN PELICAN INN
South Padre Island

Let gentle Gulf breezes caress you while the sun settles behind the Laguna Madre's sparkling blue waters on South Padre Island. Relax and be refreshed at the Brown Pelican Inn - a unique island experience.

Tel 210 761 2722
Fax 210 761 1273
Innkeeper:
Vicky Conway

8 rooms,
$70 - $115 B&B
Children over 12 welcome.
VS MC

## TEXAS

### MARIPOSA RANCH
Brenham

Working ranch with horse, cattle and emus and a caring hospitable welcome from Charles and Johnna with many thoughtful little touches to enhance your stay.

Tel / Fax 409 836 4737
Owners:
Charles & Johnna
Chamberlain

9 rooms & suites
$75 - $140 B&B
Children welcome.
VS MC

## TEXAS

### ROSEVINE INN
Tyler

A warm welcome at this Texan B&B inn with its white picket fence and cosy cheerful guest rooms. Helpful local knowledge willingly supplied by the Powells.

Tel 903 592 2221
Fax 903 593 9500
Owner/Innkeeper:
Bert & Rebecca Powell

7 rooms & suites,
$75 - $150 B&B
Children over 2 welcome.
VS MC Amex Diners

## WASHINGTON

### SHELBURNE INN
Seaview

A 10 minute walk from an unspoilt 28 mile stretch of Pacific Coast and a true American classic the Shelburne has offered warm hospitality, wonderful food and comfortable shelter for over a century.

Tel 360 642 2442
Fax 360 642 8904
Owners:
Laurie Anderson & David
Campiche

15 rooms & suites,
$99 - $165 B&B
Children welcome.
VS MC Amex

## WISCONSIN

### MANSION HILL INN
Madison

Round-arched windows, ornate cornices. A spiral staircase leading to a panoramic city view, 24 hour valet service, breakfast in bed, an elegant option for a 4 Diamond stay in Madison.

Tel 608 255 3999
Fax 608 255 2217
Director of Hotel Operations:
Janna Wojtal

11 suites, $100 - $270 B&B
Children over 12 welcome.
Non-smoking
VS MC Amex

# The Best of British Style

Recognised as the leading collection of privately owned hotels in Britain.

## Pride of Britain

Is as much a part of Britain as her heritage.

Your stay at a Pride of Britain hotel will be a time to remember, as each is a home reflecting the individuality and sometimes eccentricity of its owners.

No matter where you may be travelling in Britain you will never be far from the warmth and welcome of a Pride of Britain hotel.

For your FREE copy of our Pocket Directory in the USA, call
ABERCROMBIE & KENT INT INC
Tel: 708 954 2944

or for RESERVATIONS
**TOLL FREE 1-800 98 PRIDE**

In the UK call
PRIDE OF BRITAIN (HOTLINE)
01264 736604

# Ireland's Blue Book

A unique Association listing Ireland's most gracious Country Houses and gourmet Restaurants set amidst the quiet beauty of rural Ireland.

These properties are all owner managed and are renowned worldwide for all their high standards of traditional hospitality, elegant accommodation and superb cuisine.

IRELAND'S BLUE BOOK

Ask for the 'Blue Book'
at your
U.S. Welcome Hotel or Inn
or contact
Ireland's Blue Book,
Ardbraccan Glebe, Navan,
Co. Meath, Ireland.
Tel: 00-353-46-23416
Fax: 00-353-46-23292

# The Portfolio Collection

## Fine South African Country Houses and Private Game Reserves

The Country Places Collection in South Africa is one of a series of fine guides for the discerning traveller. Offering a selection of hand-picked Country Houses, Hotels and Private Game Reserves

### *Information and Reservations*
### The Portfolio Collection
Johannesburg, South Africa Tel +27 11 880 3414
Fax +27 11 788 4802
P O Box 52350, Saxonwold, 2132 Johannesburg
South Africa

# E-Mail & Web Sites

| | E-MAIL | WEB SITE |
|---|---|---|
| 1842 Inn | 1842Inn@worldnet.att.net | |
| Adair | adair@connriver.net | www.adairinn.com |
| Addison Choate | | www.cape-ann.com/addison-choate |
| Alpine Inn | johnw@alpineinn.com | http://www.sni.net/telluride |
| Andrews Lodging | 74232.116@compuserve.com | |
| Auberge des Gallant | gallant@roder.gc.ca | www.gallant.gc.ca |
| Ardmore Inn | ArdmoreInn@aol.com | http://www.ArdmoreInn.com |
| Auberge Des Sablons | sablons@cite.net | |
| Balsams | Thebalsams@aol.com | www.thebalsams.com |
| Barley Sheaf Farm, | barleysheaf@netreach.net | |
| Barrows House Inn | barhouse@vermontel.com | |
| Basin Harbor Club | res@bh-on-lc | http://www.bh-on-lc.com |
| Beazley House | jbeaz@ix.netcom.com | www.napavalley.com/beazley |
| Black Point Inn | bpi@nlis.com | |
| Blackthorne Inn | susan@blackthorneinn.com | www.blackthorneinn.com |
| Blue Harbor House | balidog@midcoast.com | http://www.travelassist.com/reg/me105s.html |
| Blue Moon | blmoon@bellsouth.net | |
| Blueberry Hill Inn | clarktg@vbi.champlain.edu | |
| Boston Harbor Hotel | sales@bhh.com | |
| Boulders | | http://www.distinctiveinns.com/bldrs/index.html |
| Briars | briars@ils.net | http://www.ils.net/briars |
| Brown Pelican Inn | Vicky0515@aol.com | |
| Buttonwood Inn | button_w@moose.ncia.net | |
| Cambridge House | innach@aol.com | |
| Camellia Inn | DLewand@aol.com | |
| Campbell House, A City Inn | campbellhouse@campbellhouse.com | www.campbellhouse.com |
| Captain Lord Mansion | captain@biddeford.com | |
| Captain's House Inn | capthous@capecod.net | http://www.distinctiveinns.com/cphse/index.html |
| Carnegie House | carnhouse@aol.com | |
| Carter House Victorians | carter52@carterhouse.com | www.carterhouse.com/carter52 |
| Casa Sedona | casa@sedona.net | www.arizonaguide.com/casasedona |
| Castle Marne | themarne@ix.netcom.com | |
| Chalet Kilauea | bchawaii@aol.com | |
| Chalet Suzanne | chaletsuz@aol.com | |
| Channel House | CFinseth@newportnet.com | |
| Chatham Bars Inn | resrvcbi@chathambarsinn.com | |
| Cheshire Cat Inn | cheshire@cheshirecat.com | |
| Chester House | chesthse@rma.edu | |
| Chesterfield Inn | chtinn@sover.net | http://www.distinctiveinns.com/chstr/index.html |
| Churchill House Inn | rciatt@sover.net | http://www.pbpub.com/inntoinn/ |
| Cliffside Inn | cliff@wsii.com | http://www.distinctiveinns.com/clfsd/index.html |
| Colby Hill Inn | infousw@colbyhillinn.com | http://www.colbyhillinn.com |
| Colonial Capital | ccbb@widomaker.com | http://www.ccbb.com |
| Colonnade | | http://www.colonnadehotel.com |
| Columbia Gorge Hotel | cghotel@gorge.net | http://www.gorge.net/lodging/cghotel/ |
| Copperfield Inn | copperfield@netheaven.com | http://www.mediausa.com/ny/cprfldin |
| Corner House | cornerhs@nantucket.net | http://www.cornerhousenantucket.com |
| Cornucopia of Dorset | cornucop@vermontel.com | http://www.cornucopiaofdorset.com |
| Cortina Inn | cortinal@aol.com | http://www.genghis.com/cortinainn.htm |
| Craftsman Inn | craftman@dreamscape.com | |

# E-Mail & Web Sites

| | | |
|---|---|---|
| Dan'l Webster Inn | | http://media3.com/dan'lwebsterinn/ |
| Deerfield Inn | drfldinn@shaysnet.com | http://www.distinctiveinns.com/drfld/index.html |
| Ellis River House | 76073.1435@compuserve.com | |
| Forest, A Country Inn | wguppy@aol.com | |
| Glen-Ella Springs | glenella@cyberhighway.com | |
| Golden Eagle Resort | stoweagle@aol.com | http://www.stoweinfo.com/saa/golden_eagle |
| Goose & Turrets | rhmgt@montara.com | www.montara.com/goose.html |
| Gorges Grant Hotel | gorgesgrant@ogunquit.com | |
| Grafton Inn | | www.sunsol.com/graftoninn/ |
| Green Mountain Inn | grnmtinn@aol.com | www.greenmountaininn.com |
| Greenville Inn | gvlinn@moosehead.net | |
| Hamilton House | | http://www.madriver.com/lodging/hamilton.html |
| Hancock Inn | innkeeper@hancockin.mv.com | |
| Haus Rohrbach Pension | | www.hausrohrbach.com |
| Hawk Inn & Mountain Resort | hawkvermont@vermontel.com | |
| Hearthstone Inn | hearthstone@worldnet.att.net | www.hearthstoneinn.com |
| Heritage Plantation of Sandwich | museumcc@aol.com | |
| Heron House | heronkw@aol.com | http://www.fla-keys.com/heronhouse |
| High Meadows Vineyard | peterhmi@aol.com | www.highmeadows.com |
| Hood River Hotel | HRHotel@gorge.net | www.HoodRiverHotel |
| Hotel Jerome | hjerome@aol.com | www.aspen.com/jerome |
| Hotel La Rose | concierge@hotellarose.com | www.hotellarose.com |
| Hotel St. Francis | hstf@1x.netcom.com | |
| Hummingbird Inn | hmgeird@cfw.com | |
| Inn at Essex | innessex@together.net | |
| Inn at Montchanin Village | montchan@gie.net | www.montchanin.com |
| Inn at Perry Cabin | perrycbn@friend.ly.net | http://www.perrycabin.com |
| Inn at Stockbridge | innkeeper@stockbridge.com | http://www.stockridge.com |
| Inn at the Brass Lantern | brasslntrn@aol.com | |
| Inn at Thorn Hill | thornhill@ncia.net | http://www.distinctiveinns.com/thhll/index.html |
| Inn at Union Square | inn@unionsquare.com | |
| Inn at West View Farm | westview@vermontel.com | http://www.vtweb.com/innatwestviewfarm |
| Jackson House Inn | innkeeper@jacksonhouse.com | www.jacksonhouse.com |
| Jared Coffin House | jchouse@nantucket.net | http://www.nantucket.net/lodging/jchouse |
| Jekyll Island Club | | www.jekyllclub.com |
| John Carver Inn | | http://media3.com/JohnCarverInn/ |
| John Rutledge House | | www.charminginns.com |
| Joshua Grindle Inn | info@joshgrin.com | www.joshgrin.com |
| Keswick Hall | keswick@keswick.com | http://www.keswick.com/keswick.html |
| Lakeside Inn | lakeside@iag.net | |
| Landgrove Inn | vtinn@sover.net | |
| La Playa Hotel | | www.monterey.infohut.com/laplayahotel |
| Lareau Farm Country Inn | Lareau@madriver.com | |
| Liberty Hill Inn | libertyh@capecod.net | www.cruising-america.com/libertyhillinn |
| Little Inn of Bayfield | littleinn@odyssey.on.ca. | http://www.odyssey.on.ca/littleinn |
| Little St. Simons Island | 102063.467@compuserve.com | http://www.pactel.com.au/lssi |
| Llewellyn Lodge | lll@rockbridge.net | |
| Longfellow's Wayside Inn | innkeeper@wayside.org | http://www.wayside.org |
| Lords Proprietors' Inn | reserv@lordspropedenton.com | www.lordspropedenton.com |
| Maine Stay Inn | mainstay@midcoast.com | http://www.distinctiveinns.com/mnsty/index.html |
| Maine Stay Inn & Cottages | copeland4@cybertours.com | |
| The Manor on Golden Pond | | http://www.distinctiveinns.com/mngld/index.html |

# E-Mail & Web Sites

| | | |
|---|---|---|
| Mansion Inn | mansion@PIL.NETu | |
| Merv Griffin's Wickenburg Inn | wickinn@primenet.com | www.merv.com |
| Middlebury Inn | midinnvt@sover.net | http://www.middleburyinn.com/vt |
| Mira Monte Inn & Suites | mburns@acadia.net | |
| Newcastle Inn | newcastinn@aol.com | http://www.distinctiveinns.com/ncstle/index.html |
| Notchland Inn | notchland@aol.com | |
| The Oaks | | http://www.innbook.com |
| Old Tavern at Grafton | tavern@sover.net | |
| Olde Orchard Inn | inkeep1@aol.com | |
| Ollalieberry Inn | olallieinn@thegrid.net | www.olallieberry.com |
| Pitcher Inn | pitcher@madriver.com | www.pitcherinn.com |
| Private Pleasure | contesa@enols.com | |
| Queen Anne Bed & Breakfast | queenanne@worldnet.att.net | www.bedandbreakfastinns.org/queenanne |
| Rabbit Hill Inn | rabbit.hill.Inn@connrivernet | http://www.distinctiveinns.com/rbthl/index.html |
| Red Clover Inn | redclovr@vermontel.com | http://redcloverinn.com |
| Red Horse Inn | | www.bbonline.com/sc/redhorse/ |
| Resorts Ontario | escapes@resorts-ontario.com | http://www.resorts-ontario.com. |
| Ripplecove Inn | ripcove@multi-medias.ca | |
| Rose Inn | roseinn@clarityconnect.com | |
| Salem Inn | saleminn@earthlink.net | |
| Shield Inn | shieldinn@aol.com | www/sover.net/~dvalnews/shieldinn.html |
| Shelburne Inn | shelinn@aone.com | |
| Shelburne Museum | | http://www.shelburnemuseum.com |
| Shipman House | bighouse@bigisland.com | |
| Shire Inn | shireinn@sover.net | |
| Siebeness Inn | siebenes@together.net | |
| Smuggler's Notch Inn | smuginn@pwshift.com | www.pbpub.com/smugglers/smuginn.htm |
| Southwest Inn at Sedona | info@swinn.com | |
| Stage Neck Inn | stageneck@aol.com | http://www.stageneck.com |
| Steeles Tavern Manor | hoernlei@milo.cfw.com | |
| Sugar Hill Inn | | http://www.musar.com/ traveler/sgnhlinn.html |
| Sugarloaf | info@sugarloaf.com | |
| Sugartree | sugartree@madriver.com | http://www.madriver.com/lodging/sugartree |
| Sun Mountain Lodge | smtnsale@methow.com | www.travel-in-wa.com/ADS/sunmtn.html |
| Thorncroft Inn | kgb@tidc.net | |
| Tucker Hill Lodge | tuckhill@madriver.com | |
| Two Angels Inn | deuxanges@aol.com | |
| Vermont Inn | vtinn@aol.com | http://www.vermontinn.com |
| Village Country Inn | vcinn@sover.net | http://www.distinctiveinns.com/cntry/index.html |
| West Hill House | westhill@madriver.com | |
| West Mountain Inn | info@westmountaininn.com | |
| Whitford House Inn | whitford@together.net | www.virtualcitiescom/ons/vt/b/vtb3703.ht |
| Wildflower Inn | wldflr@aol.com | |
| Wiley Inn | wileyinn@sover.net | www.wileyinn.com |
| Willcox House Country Inn | | www.willcoxhouse.com |
| Willoughvale Inn on Lake Willoughby | grnminn@aol.com | www.willoughvale.com |
| Willows Historic Palm Springs Inn | innkeeper@thewillowspalmsprings.co | www.thewillowspalmsprings.com |
| Windham Hill Inn | windham@sover.net | http://www.windhamhill.com |
| Woods | skivt@sover.net | |

248

# Index

|  | PAGE NOS. |  |  |
|---|---|---|---|
| 1842 Inn | 211 | Boxwood Inn | 41 |
| Abriendo Inn | 240 | Bradford Inn | 122 |
| Adair | 145 | Brandon Inn | 185 |
| Addison Choate Inn | 122 | Briars | 12 |
| Alpine Inn | 240 | Brigadoon | 74 |
| Amelia Island Plantation | 203 | Brown Pelican | 242 |
| Andrews Lodging | 90 | Buttonwood Inn | 146 |
| Antrim 1844 | 23 | Campbell House, A City Inn | 233 |
| Ardmore Inn | 184 | Cambridge House | 123 |
| Ashley Inn | 217 | Camellia Inn | 239 |
| Auberge des Gallant | 19 | Campbell Ranch Inn | 239 |
| Auberge des Sablons | 15 | Cannonboro Inn | 217 |
| Auberge Handfield | 16 | Captain Daniel Stone Inn | 82 |
| Auberge Saint-Antoine | 17 | Captain Lindsey House Inn | 92 |
| Bagley House | 90 | Captain Lord Mansion | 83 |
| Bailiwick Inn | 47 | Captain Nickerson Inn | 124 |
| Baladerry Inn | 40 | Captain's House Inn of Chatham | 104 |
| Balsams | 145 | Carnegie House | 41 |
| Bar Harbor Hotel-Bluenose Inn | 79 | Carter House Victorians | 229 |
| Barley Sheaf Farm | 40 | Casa Cody | 230 |
| Barrows House | 184 | Casa Sedona | 221 |
| Basin Harbor Club | 165 | Castle | 186 |
| Bayview Hotel | 80 | Castle Marne | 240 |
| Bear Creek Lodge | 241 | Chalet Kilauea | 241 |
| Beazley House | 225 | Chalet Suzanne | 207 |
| Bed & Breakfast on the Point | 158 | Channel House | 241 |
| Bee & Thistle Inn | 69 | Charles Hotel | 105 |
| Berkeley Hotel | 48 | Chatham Bars Inn | 106 |
| Bernards Inn | 29 | Cheshire Cat Inn | 239 |
| Bird & Bottle | 37 | Chester House | 56 |
| Black Point Inn | 81 | Chesterfield Inn | 137 |
| Blackthorne Inn | 229 | Chestnut Inn on Oquaga Lake | 37 |
| Blantyre | 102 | Chimney Hill Farm | 30 |
| Block Island Resorts | 155 | Chipman Inn | 186 |
| Blue Harbor House | 91 | Churchill House Inn | 187 |
| Blue Hill Inn | 91 | Cliffside Inn | 156 |
| Blue Moon Hotel | 207 | Clifton - The Country Inn | 56 |
| Blueberry Hill Inn | 185 | Colby Hill Inn | 146 |
| Boar's Head Inn | 49 | Colonial Capital | 57 |
| Boston Harbor Hotel | 103 | Colonnade Hotel | 107 |
| Boulders | 70 | Columbia Gorge Hotel | 241 |
|  |  | Copperfield Inn | 31 |

# Index

| | | | |
|---|---|---|---|
| Corner House Inn | 123 | Harraseeket Inn | 85 |
| Cornucopia of Dorset | 166 | Haus Rohrbach Pension | 234 |
| Cortina Inn | 167 | Hawk Inn & Mountain Resort | 171 |
| Country Inn | 66 | Hawthorne Inn | 125 |
| Craftsman Inn | 32 | Hearthstone Inn | 222 |
| Dan'l Webster Inn | 108 | Henry Clay Inn | 58 |
| Darst Victorian Manor | 208 | Heron House | 205 |
| Deerfield Inn | 109 | Hibiscus House | 208 |
| Deerhill Inn | 187 | High Meadows | 50 |
| Dexter's Inn & Tennis Club | 147 | Hillbrook Inn | 67 |
| Dockside Guest Quarters | 92 | Historic Inns of Annapolis | 26 |
| Elizabeth Pointe Lodge | 204 | Historic Smithton Inn | 43 |
| Ellis River House | 147 | Homestay | 58 |
| Embassy Inn | 64 | Homestead Inn (Greenwich) | 71 |
| Empress of Little Rock | 239 | Homestead Inn (New Milford) | 75 |
| Equinox | 168 | Hood River Hotel | 233 |
| Evermay on the Delaware | 42 | Hotel Jerome | 222 |
| First Colony Inn | 212 | Hotel La Rose | 237 |
| Forest, A Country Inn | 148 | Hotel St. Francis | 237 |
| Four Columns Inn | 169 | Hummingbird Inn | 59 |
| Foxglove | 148 | Inn at Essex | 172 |
| Franconia Inn | 149 | Inn at Gristmill Square | 59 |
| Frederick House | 57 | Inn at Millrace Pond | 30 |
| French Manor | 42 | Inn at Montchanin Village | 22 |
| Fulton Lane Inn | 215 | Inn at Narrow Passage | 60 |
| Gables | 188 | Inn at National Hall | 72 |
| Geneva-on-the-Lake | 33 | Inn at Ormsby Hill | 173 |
| George Washington University Inn | 63 | Inn at Perry Cabin | 25 |
| Glen-Ella Springs | 211 | Inn at Stockbridge | 125 |
| Golden Eagle Resort | 170 | Inn at the Brass Lantern | 189 |
| Goose & Turrets | 230 | Inn at the Round Barn Farm | 190 |
| Gorges Grant Hotel | 84 | Inn at Thorn Hill | 139 |
| Grafton Inn | 124 | Inn at Union Square | 240 |
| Grandview Bed & Breakfast | 158 | Inn at West View Farm | 190 |
| Green Mountain Inn | 188 | Inn By The Sea | 86 |
| Greenville Inn | 93 | Inn of Exeter | 140 |
| Griswold Inn | 74 | Inn on the Common | 174 |
| Halsey House | 38 | Inns at Doneckers | 43 |
| Hamilton House | 189 | Inns at Mill Falls & Bay Point | 138 |
| Hancock Inn | 149 | Isaiah Hall | 126 |
| Harbor Court Hotel | 24 | Isaiah Jones Homestead | 126 |
| Harbor Light Inn | 110 | Jackson House Inn | 191 |

# Index

| | | | |
|---|---|---|---|
| Jared Coffin House | 111 | Morrison House | 53 |
| Jekyll Island Club | 237 | Mostly Hall | 130 |
| John Carver Inn | 127 | Mountain Road Resort | 175 |
| John Rutledge House | 237 | Mr. Mole | 27 |
| Joshua Grindle Inn | 231 | New London Inn | 150 |
| Kennebunkport Inn | 93 | Newcastle Inn | 96 |
| Kent Manor Inn | 26 | Normandy Inn | 64 |
| Keswick Hall | 51 | Norwich Inn & Spa | 73 |
| King's Cottage | 44 | Notchland Inn | 150 |
| L'Auberge Provencale | 52 | Oaks | 61 |
| La Playa Hotel | 226 | Ocean Edge Resort & Golf Club | 113 |
| Laburnum Cottage | 239 | Ocean Gate | 97 |
| Lakeside Inn | 206 | Ocean Point Inn | 97 |
| Landgrove Inn | 191 | October Country Inn | 193 |
| Larchwood Inn | 159 | Old Mystic Inn | 76 |
| Lareau Farm Country Inn | 192 | Old Tavern at Grafton | 176 |
| Lawnmeer Inn | 94 | Olde Orchard Inn | 151 |
| Lenox Hotel | 112 | Ollalieberry Inn | 231 |
| Liberty Hill Inn | 127 | Onset Pointe Inn | 130 |
| Lighthouse Inn | 128 | Peacock Hill | 241 |
| Little Inn of Bayfield | 13 | Pheasant Hill | 131 |
| Little St. Simon's Island | 210 | Pineapple Hill | 45 |
| Llewellyn Lodge | 60 | Pitcher Inn | 177 |
| Lodge at Moosehead Lake | 94 | Planters Inn | 216 |
| Longfellow's Wayside Inn | 128 | Pleasant Bay Village Resort | 131 |
| Lords Proprietors' Inn | 214 | Private Pleasure | 27 |
| Maine Stay Inn | 95 | Publick House Historic Inn | 114 |
| Maine Stay Inn & Cottages | 95 | Quechee Bed & Breakfast | 194 |
| Manhattan East Suite Hotels | 34 | Queen Anne Inn (Colorado) | 223 |
| Manor House | 75 | Queen Anne Inn (Mass) | 132 |
| Manor on Golden Pond | 141 | Rabbit Hill Inn | 178 |
| Mansion Hill Inn | 242 | Red Clover Inn | 179 |
| Mansion Inn | 44 | Red Horse Inn | 218 |
| Maple Leaf Inn | 192 | Red Lion Inn | 116 |
| Mariposa Ranch | 242 | Ripplecove Inn | 18 |
| Marlborough | 129 | Riverwind Inn | 76 |
| Martine Inn | 227 | Rocky Shores Inn & Cottages | 132 |
| Mary Prentiss | 129 | Rose Inn | 38 |
| Merv Griffin's Wickenburg Inn | 221 | Rosevine Inn | 242 |
| Middlebury Inn | 193 | Roycroft Inn | 35 |
| Millcroft Inn | 14 | Sagamore on Lake George | 36 |
| Mira Monte Inn | 96 | Salem Inn | 117 |

# Index

| | | | |
|---|---|---|---|
| Seal Beach Garden Inn | 228 | Wedgewood Inn | 134 |
| Sedgwick Inn | 39 | Wedgwood Inn of New Hope | 46 |
| Settlers Inn | 45 | West Hill House | 199 |
| Seven Hills Inn | 61 | West Mountain Inn | 199 |
| Sharon Inn | 133 | Whalewalk Inn | 119 |
| Shelburne Inn | 242 | White Hart Inn | 77 |
| Shield Inn | 194 | Whitford House Inn | 200 |
| Shipman House | 241 | Wildflower Inn | 135 |
| Shire Inn | 195 | Wiley Inn | 200 |
| Siebeness | 195 | Willcox House Country Inn | 235 |
| Sise Inn | 142 | WilloughVale Inn | 201 |
| Smugglers' Notch Inn | 196 | Willows Historic Inn | 232 |
| Snowvillage Inn | 143 | Windham Hill Inn | 181 |
| Southwest Inn at Sedona | 239 | Windsor Inn | 65 |
| Spruce Point Inn | 87 | Woodland Inn | 240 |
| Stage Neck Inn | 88 | Woods | 201 |
| Staunton Hill Country Inn | 54 | Woodstock Inn & Resort | 182 |
| Steeles Tavern Manor | 62 | Yankee Clipper Inn | 120 |
| Sterling Inn | 46 | York Harbor Inn | 98 |
| Sugar Hill Inn | 151 | | |
| Sugar Lodge at Sugarbush | 196 | | |
| Sugarbush Inn & Resort | 180 | | |
| Sugarloaf | 89 | | |
| Sugartree | 197 | | |
| Sun Mountain Lodge | 234 | | |
| Swag Country Inn | 213 | | |
| Thorncroft Inn | 118 | **INDEX OF ADVERTISERS** | |
| Tides Inn | 55 | | |
| Trillium House | 62 | Country Inns Along The Trail | 161 |
| Tucker Hill Lodge | 197 | Distinctive Inns of New England | 99 |
| Turtleback Farm | 235 | Heritage Plantation of Sandwich | 135 |
| Two Angels Inn | 240 | Historic Hotels of America | 236 |
| Vanderbilt Hall | 157 | Ireland's Blue Book | 244 |
| Vermont Inn | 198 | Old Sturbridge Village | 115 |
| Verona House | 209 | Original Historic Inns | 160 |
| Villa | 159 | Plimouth Plantation | 121 |
| Village Country Inn | 198 | Portfolio Collection | 245 |
| Village Green Inn | 133 | Pride of Britain | 243 |
| Village House | 152 | Resorts Ontario | 11 |
| Wades Point Inn on the Bay | 28 | Shelburne Museum | 183 |
| Waterville Estates Resort | 144 | Vermont State | 164 |
| Weathervane Inn | 134 | Wexas | 219 |

# The Welcome Privilege Card
## A SELECTION OF PROMISES

CAPTAIN'S HOUSE INN OF CHATHAM, Chatham, Massachusetts
*Discounted Whale-watch trip tickets
*Complimentary split of Champagne for birthdays, honeymoons or anniversaries
*Specially decorated cake for other special celebrations

SALEM INN, Salem, Massachusetts
*Two complimentary tickets to a local museum of choice

CAPTAIN NICKERSON INN, South Dennis, Massachusetts
*Stay 1 night and get 2nd night at half price. Available Sun - Thu from beginning of Mar - 15th May and Oct 16th - Dec 21st.

INN AT STOCKBRIDGE, Stockbridge, Massachusetts
*Stay 2 nights get 3rd night free From Jan to May 15th excluding Holidays

SNOWVILLAGE INN, Snowville, New Hampshire
*Stay 3 nights and have 4th night free (B&B)
*Free XL ski lesson OR snowshoe rental - trails start at the inn.

ELLIS RIVER HOUSE, Jackson, New Hampshire
*Complimentary champagne for honeymoon or anniversary couple staying any 2 nights year-round.

OLDE ORCHARD INN, Moultonborough, New Hampshire
*From 1st Nov to 31st May, guests are invited to stay 2 nights and receive 3rd night free.

CLIFFSIDE INN, Newport, Rhode Island
15% off entire stay Sun through Thu. Not available Jul, Aug and Holidays.

CORTINA INN, Killington, Vermont
*Complementary fruit and cheese platter on arrival
*Or, complimentary mountainbike rental in Summer
*Complimentary sleigh ride in Winter.

GOLDEN EAGLE RESORT, Stowe, Vermont
*Welcome arrival gift.

INN AT ORMSBY HILL, Manchester, Vermont
*For stays of 3 or more nights in a fireplace or Jacuzzi room a $50 gift certificate is presented, honoured by one of two local fine dining establishments. The certificate may be redeemed Sun -Thur. Not available during Fall Foliage and Holiday periods.

OLD TAVERN AT GRAFTON, Grafton, Vermont
*$180 per night deluxe package for 2, includes accommodation; full breakfast and dinner; Grafton Village Cheese sampler; complimentary cross-country ski passes (winter) or bicycles (summer).
Sun - Thur. On Fri &- Sat rate is $220 per night. Available May 1- Sep 1 & Nov 1 - Dec 23. From Sep 1 - Oct 31 available at $220.

DEERHILL INN, West Dover, Vermont
*10% off dinner for two
*Complimentary arrival gift

INN AT THE BRASS LANTERN, Stowe, Vermont
*Discount vouchers for area restaurants, shops, attractions and activities
*Health Club privileges (some limitations during peak and Holiday periods, enquire when booking).

LANDGROVE INN, Landgrove, Vermont
*Complimentary bottle of wine. Choose to enjoy in your room or served at dinner.

SHIRE INN, Chelsea,
*3 nights lodging (B&B) for the price of 2, available year-round except public Holidays and Fall foliage Sep 15 - Oct 20.

*Welcome Privilege Cards are valid for one year from date of issue. One Card entitles a family or group of up to four people travelling together to relevant benefits. The Privilege Card is available for separate purchase at a cost of £10.00/$17.00 per card. All offers are subject to availability.

# The Welcome Privilege Card

is an extension of the hospitality offered during your visit to North America. It is our pleasure to include a complimentary Card with every copy of Selected Hotels & Inns. If you have not purchased your copy of the book directly from our office, call, fax, email or write, telling us at what shop, in which town and when you purchased the book and we will be delighted to despatch your personal Privilege Card immediately.

The Card offers value added benefits and savings at numerous inns and hotels. For more examples of advantages available see pages 65, 152, 214 and 253. A complete list of Privilege Promises will be included with your Card but, as new promises are continually being added, it's always a good idea to call us before you leave for your trip so we can send you a fully updated list.

LITTLE INN OF BAYFIELD, Bayfield, Ontario
*Stay 2 nights on an MAP package and receive 3rd night (accommodation only) free.
RIPPLECOVE INN, North Hatley, Quebec
*Free room upgrade valid all year excluding holidays.
CHIMNEY HILL, Lambertville, New Jersey
*Stay 2 nights and receive 3rd night free. Available any season but excludes Holiday Weekends.
EVERMAY ON THE DELAWARE, Erwinna, Pennsylvania
*Stay 2 nights, get a 3rd night at a special privilege rate. Excluding Weekends and Holidays
*Special celebration recognition for a birthday, anniversary or honeymoon.
FRENCH MANOR, South Sterling, Pennsylvania
*Special seasonal arrival gift
HIGH MEADOWS VINEYARD & MOUNTAIN SUNSET INN, Scottsville, Virginia
*Complimentary champagne or Virginia wine on arrival or prior to dining.
*Stay 3 nights and get 4th night at 50% discount OR
*Stay 4 nights and get 5th night Free.

HUMMINGBIRD INN, Goshen, Virginia
*Stay 2 nights and get a 3rd night at 50%. Applies Sun - Thu year-round. Any day of the week Nov - Apr
*Complimentary refreshments on arrival.
SEVEN HILLS INN, Lexington, Virginia
*Complimentary arrival treat such as home-made cookies, tea and soft drinks
*Stay 4 nights get 5th night free.
INN AT NATIONAL HALL, Westport, Connecticut
*Complimentary arrival treat - wine, fruit, cheese.
BLUE HARBOR HOUSE, Camden, Maine
*Discount on delicious lobster dinner.

*Welcome Privilege Cards are valid for one year from date of issue. One Card entitles a family or group of up to four people travelling together to relevant benefits. The Privilege Card is available for separate purchase at a cost of £10.00/$17.00 per card. All offers are subject to availability.